Certified Cloud Security Professional (CCSP)

Technology Workbook

---

www.ipspecialist.net

Document Control

Proposal Name	:	Certified Cloud Security Professional
Document Version	:	Version 1
Document Release Date	:	15th May, 2019
Reference	:	Technology Workbook

Feedback:

If you have any comments regarding the quality of this book, or otherwise alter it to better suit your needs, you can contact us through email at info@ipspecialist.net

Please make sure to include the book's title and ISBN in your message

About IPSpecialist

IPSPECIALIST LTD. IS COMMITTED TO EXCELLENCE AND DEDICATED TO YOUR SUCCESS.

Our philosophy is to treat our customers like family. We want you to succeed, and we are willing to do everything possible to help you make it happen. We have the proof to back up our claims. We strive to accelerate billions of careers with great courses, accessibility, and affordability. We believe that continuous learning and knowledge evolution are the most important things to keep re-skilling and up-skilling the world.

Planning and creating a specific goal is where IPSpecialist helps. We can create a career track that suits your visions as well as develop the competencies you need to become a professional Network Engineer. We can also assist you with the execution and evaluation of your proficiency level, based on the career track you choose, as they are customized to fit your specific goals.

We help you STAND OUT from the crowd through our detailed IP training content packages.

Course Features:

❖ Self-Paced learning
  • Learn at your own pace and in your own time
❖ Covers Complete Exam Blueprint
  • Prep-up for the exam with confidence
❖ Case Study Based Learning
  • Relate the content with real life scenarios
❖ Subscriptions that suits you
  • Get more and pay less with IPS subscriptions
❖ Career Advisory Services
  • Let the industry experts plan your career journey
❖ Virtual Labs to test your skills
  • With IPS vRacks, you can evaluate your exam preparations
❖ Practice Questions
  • Practice questions to measure your preparation standards
❖ On Request Digital Certification
  • On request digital certification from IPSpecialist LTD

About the Authors:

This book has been compiled with the help of multiple professional engineers. These engineers specialize in different fields e.g. Networking, Security, Cloud, Big Data, IoT etc. Each engineer develops content in his/her own specialized field that is compiled to form a comprehensive certification guide.

About the Technical Reviewers:

Nouman Ahmed Khan

AWS-Architect, CCDE, CCIEX5 (R&S, SP, Security, DC, Wireless), CISSP, CISA, CISM, Nouman Ahmed Khan is a Solution Architect working with a major telecommunication provider in Qatar. He works with enterprises, mega-projects, and service providers to help them select the best-fit technology solutions. He also works as a consultant to understand customer business processes and helps select an appropriate technology strategy to support business goals. He has more than 14 years of experience working in Pakistan/Middle-East & UK. He holds a Bachelor of Engineering Degree from NED University, Pakistan, and M.Sc. in Computer Networks from the UK.

Abubakar Saeed

Abubakar Saeed has more than twenty-five years of experience, managing, consulting, designing, and implementing large-scale technology projects, extensive experience heading ISP operations, solutions integration, heading Product Development, Pre-sales, and Solution Design. Emphasizing on adhering to Project timelines and delivering as per customer expectations, he always leads the project in the right direction with his innovative ideas and excellent management skills.

Muhammad Yousuf

Muhammad Yousuf is a professional technical content writer. He is Certified Ethical Hacker (CEHv10) and Cisco Certified Network Associate (CCNA) in Routing and Switching. He holds a bachelor's degree in Telecommunication, Engineering from Sir Syed University of Engineering and Technology. He has both technical knowledge and industry sounding information, which he uses perfectly in his career.

Farah Qadir

Farah Qadir is a professional technical content writer, holding bachelor's degree in Telecommunication Engineering from Sir Syed University of Engineering and Technology. With strong educational background, she possesses exceptional researching and writing skills that has led her to impart knowledge through her professional career.

Muhammad Khawar

Muhammad Khawar is a professional technical content writer. He holds a bachelor's degree in Computer Science from Virtual University of Pakistan. He was working as an IT Executive in a reputable organization. He has completed training of CCNA Routing and Switching, .NET and Web designing. He as both technical knowledge and industry sounding information.

Free Resources:

With each workbook bought from Amazon, IPSpecialist offers free resources to our valuable customers.

Once you buy this book you will have to contact us at support@ipspecialist.net or tweet @ipspecialistnet to get this limited time offer without any extra charges.

Free Resources Include:

Exam Practice Questions in Quiz Simulation: IP Specialists' Practice Questions have been developed keeping in mind the certification exam perspective. The collection of these questions from our technology workbooks is prepared keeping the exam blueprint in mind, covering not only important but necessary topics as well. It is an ideal document to practice and revise your certification.

Career Report: This report is a step by step guide for a novice who wants to develop his/her career in the field of computer networks. It answers the following queries:

- Current scenarios and future prospects.
- Is this industry moving towards saturation or are new opportunities knocking at the door?
- What will the monetary benefits be?
- Why to get certified?
- How to plan and when will I complete the certifications if I start today?

- Is there any career track that I can follow to accomplish specialization level?

Furthermore, this guide provides a comprehensive career path towards being a specialist in the field of networking and also highlights the tracks needed to obtain certification.

IPS Personalized Technical Support for Customers: Good customer service means helping customers efficiently, in a friendly manner. It is essential to be able to handle issues for customers and do your best to ensure they are satisfied. Providing good service is one of the most important things that can set our business apart from the others of its kind.

Great customer service will result in attracting more customers and attain maximum customer retention.

IPS is offering personalized TECH support to its customers to provide better value for money. If you have any queries related to technology and labs you can simply ask our technical team for assistance via Live Chat or Email.

Become an Author & Earn with Us

If you are interested in becoming an author and start earning passive income, IPSpecialist offers "Earn with us" program. We all consume, develop and create content during our learning process, certification exam preparations, and during searching, developing and refining our professional careers. That content, notes, guides, worksheets and flip cards among other material is normally for our own reference without any defined structure or special considerations required for formal publishing.

IPSpecialist can help you craft this 'draft' content into a fine product with the help of our global team of experts. We sell your content via different channels as:

1. Amazon – Kindle
2. eBay
3. LuLu
4. Kobo
5. Google Books
6. Udemy and many 3rd party publishers and resellers

Our Products

Technology Workbooks

IPSpecialist Technology workbooks are the ideal guides to developing the hands-on skills necessary to pass the exam. Our workbook covers official exam blueprint and explains the technology with real life case study based labs. The content covered in each workbook consists of individually focused technology topics presented in an easy-to-follow, goal-oriented, step-by-step approach. Every scenario features detailed breakdowns and thorough verifications to help you completely understand the task and associated technology.

We extensively used mind maps in our workbooks to visually explain the technology. Our workbooks have become a widely used tool to learn and remember the information effectively.

vRacks

Our highly scalable and innovative virtualized lab platforms let you practice the IP Specialist Technology Workbook at your own time and your own place as per your convenience.

Quick Reference Sheets

Our quick reference sheets are a concise bundling of condensed notes of the complete exam blueprint. It is an ideal and handy document to help you remember the most important technology concepts related to the certification exam.

Practice Questions

IP Specialists' Practice Questions are dedicatedly designed from a certification exam perspective. The collection of these questions from our technology workbooks are prepared keeping the exam blueprint in mind covering not only important but necessary topics as well. It's an ideal document to practice and revise your certification.

Content at a glance

Table of Contents

About this Workbook

This workbook covers all the information you need to pass the (ICS)² - Certified Cloud Security Professional (CCSP) exam. The workbook is designed to take a practical approach of learning with real life examples and case studies.

- ➢ Covers complete CCSP blueprint
- ➢ Summarized content
- ➢ Practice Questions

- ➢ 100% pass guarantee
- ➢ Mind maps

CCSP Certifications

The (ICS)² - Certified Cloud Security Professional (CCSP) certification evaluates the applicant's knowledge of cloud security. It is administered by the International Information System Security Certification Consortium. (ISC)², and was developed in partnership with the Cloud Security Alliance (CSA).

The CCSP is designed as the certification for mid-level security professionals who want to demonstrate their proficiency in the field of cloud security.

How does CCSP certifications help?

CCSP certification helps you boost your career in the following ways:

1. The CCSP positions you as an authority figure on cloud security. It's a quick way to communicate your knowledge and earn trust from your clients or senior leadership.
2. The CCSP can enhance your working knowledge of cloud security and keep you current on evolving technologies.
3. You can use your knowledge across a variety of different cloud platforms. This not only makes you more marketable, it ensures you are better equipped to protect sensitive data in a global environment.
4. The CCSP created new opportunities from being able to move into more strategic roles, to being able to add new consulting services to your business.

About the CCSP Exam

- ➢ **Exam Number:** (ICS)² Certified Cloud Security Professional(CCSP)
- ➢ **Associated Certifications:** CCSP
- ➢ **Duration:** 240 minutes (125 questions)
- ➢ **Exam Registration:** Pearson VUE

The Certified Cloud Security Professional is a 240-minutes, 125 questions assessment that is associated with the CCSP certification. This exam tests a candidate's knowledge and skills related to design, manage and secure data, applications and infrastructure in the cloud using best practices, policies and procedure established by the cybersecurity experts at (ISC)².

The following topics are general guidelines for the content likely to be included on the exam

➤ Architectural Concepts & Design Requirements	19%
➤ Cloud Data Security	20%
➤ Cloud Platform & Infrastructure Security	19%
➤ Cloud Application Security	15%
➤ Operations	15%
➤ Legal & Compliance	12%

How to become CCSP?

Step 1: Pre-requisites

1. Candidates must have a minimum of five years cumulative, paid, full-time work experience in information technology.
2. Three years must be in information security, and one year must be in one or more of the six domains of the CCSP Common Body of Knowledge (CBK).
3. Earning (ISC)² CISSP credential can be substituted for the entire CCSP experience requirement.

Step2: Prepare for the CCSP Exam

Exam preparation can be accomplished through self-study with textbooks, practice exams, and on-site classroom programs. This workbook provides you all the information and knowledge to help you pass the CCSP Exam. Your study will be divided into two distinct parts:

➤ Understanding the technologies as per exam blueprint

➤ Implementing and practicing the technologies

IPSpecialist provides full support to the candidates in order for them to pass the exam.

Step 3: Register for the exam

Certification exams are offered at locations throughout the world. To register for an exam, contact the authorized test delivery partner of CCSP, contact *Pearson VUE*, who will administer the exam in a secure, proctored environment.

Prior to registration, decide which exam to take, note the exam name and number.

How much does an exam cost?

Computer-based certification exam prices (written exam) depend on scope and exam length.

Step 4: Getting the Results

After you complete an exam at an authorized testing centre, you'll get immediate, online notification of your pass or fail status, a printed examination score report that indicates your pass or fail status, and your exam results by section.

Congratulations! You are now CCSP Certified.

Chapter 01: Architectural Concepts & Design Requirements

Technology Brief

Cloud computing is a new operational model and set of technologies for managing shared pools of computing resources. Cloud computing is the practice of using a network of remote servers hosted on the internet to store, manage and process data efficiently rather than using primitive means like on-premises servers or personal computer. It is an on-demand service of computing resources through a cloud services platform with the covenience of pay-as-you-go pricing. It is a powerful source for an organization to grow their business in terms of time saving, improved cost efficiency and extended scalability. Cloud computing provides a lot of advantages to the users and makes their work much easier. Some of its advantages are:

- **Variable Pricing:**

Variable pricing is another eminent feature of cloud computing which means to pay-as-you-go. It is more convenient and cost-efficient to pay only for the resources you avail rather than deploying and maintaining costly on-premises data centers. Cloud computing providers such as Amazon, Google and Azure build their own data centers and provide services in lower prices.

- **Estimation and Scalability:**

Access as much or as little resources you need instead of buying too much or too fewer resources by guessing your needs. Scale up and down as required with no long-term contracts.

Auto-scalability allows you to scale-up or down your computation resources automatically with respect to the defined threshold level. Monitoring services help you to monitor your running instances.

- **Increased Speed and Agility:**

New IT resources are readily available on Cloud so their functionality can be tuned according to the demand. The result is a dramatic increase in agility for the organizations.

- **Free from Maintenance Expense:**

Cloud computing also cuts short the added expenses of running and maintaining data centers. No more requirements of installing hardwares, power supplies, AC and other tools as the entire data center is on cloud, which is managed by cloud service providers.

- **Low Latency:**

Cloud service latency is one the most critical factor in availing cloud services. Higher latency in data exchanges from cloud across the internet results into higher cost for users. The cloud datacenters are deployed in different regions of the world to minimize the latency which results in efficient service delivery to the hosts with lower latency rate.

- **Trade capital expense for variable expense:**

On-demand services and Pay-as-you-go features bills only for the availed services which results into less expensive resources on cloud.

Cloud Computing Concepts

About ISO/IEC 17788

ISO/IEC 17788 gives an overview of cloud computing along with other various terms and definitions. It is a terminology foundation for cloud computing standards. It is applicable to a wide range of associations (e.g., commercial enterprise, non-profit organizations government agencies).

Cloud Computing Terminologies

Confidentiality: It focuses on protecting information from any unauthorized disclosure. We want to make sure that our secret and sensitive data is secure. Confidentiality means that only authorized personnel can work with and see our infrastructure's digital resources. It also implies that unauthorized persons should not have any access to the data. There are two types of data in general: data in motion as it moves across the network and data at rest, when data is in any media storage (such as servers, local hard drives, cloud). For data in motion, we need to ensure data encryption before sending it over the network. Another option we can use along with encryption is to use a separate network for sensitive data. For data at rest, we can apply encryption on storage media drives so that no one can read it in case of theft.

Integrity: Ensuring that authorized information is not subject to unauthorized modification or impersonation. We do not want our data to be accessible or manipulated by unauthorized persons. Data integrity ensures that only authorized parties can access or

modify data. The integrity of a message is preserved by signing the entire message. If any content of the message is changed, it will not get the same signature. Integrity is signing and verifying the message obtained by using Hash Functions.

Availability: Availability applies to services and data. If authorized personnel is unable to access data due to general network failure or Denial-of-Service (DoS) attack, then it is considered as a sevier problem from a business point of view. Apparently because it may result in loss of revenues and reputation. An organization may lose recording of some important results. Availability ensures access to services at anytime, anywhere for legitimate users and running processes.

Interoperability: Interoperability is the property that allows for the unrestricted sharing of resources between different systems. Interoperability is the ability of two or more components or systems (typically manufactured by different vendors) to exchange information and to use the information that has been exchanged.

Party: A legal person or natural person, whether or not incorporated, or a group of either.

Service Level Agreement(SLA): Service Level Agreement (SLA) defines a working relationship between parties for a service contract. It is generally applicable to businesses than to consumers and involves one or more end user parties and a service provider. SLA documents the services standards helping the service provider to meet the obligated terms. SLA also helps to manage and meet the customer's expectation.

Cloud Computing Roles

Cloud Service Customer

An individual or organization that utilizes or subscribes to cloud-based services or resources.

Cloud Service Provider

A Cloud Service Provider (CSP) offers cloud-based platform, application, infrastructure, or storage services. The CSP will possess the data centre, owns and deals with the resources (hardware or software), employs the staff, monitors service provision and security, and gives administrative assistance to the customer. The popular cloud service providers are Amazon Web Services, Microsoft's Azure, Google and Rackspace.

Cloud Service Partner

Any party which is associated or assistant to, activities of either the Cloud Service Provider or the Cloud Service Customer.

Key Cloud Computing Characteristics

On-demand Self-Service

Cloud Service Customer can customize their requirement of computing resources, such as no of instances, storage or other computational resourcesas required without requiring the involvement of an IT staff.

Broad Network Access

Broad network access implies that all resources are accessible across the globe. You can have both console & remote access to all of your network and services without physically accessing the data center. In rare cases, where physical access is requried such as power failure or broken network links, support staff of cloud service provider will take care of running hardwares..

Multi-Tenancy

Shared resources are served to multiple customers using a multi-tenant model, where various physical and virtual resources progressively assigned and reassigned according to the costumer's request. Data of multiple tenants are completely isolated from each other.

Rapid Elasticity and Scalability

Traditionally, systems are needed to be designed in a way that makes them capable of growing and expanding over time with no drop in performance. Cloud based architectures can be manually up or down-scale (on-demand scalling) or setup for auto-scalling to expand or shrink the resources to keep them highly available with optimum cost as per traffic.

Resource Pooling

Resource pooling feature allows the cloud service providers to manage a large pool of physical and virtual resources like storage, CPUs, memory, network bandwidth, and much more in order to serve customers or end-users. These resources can be allocated dynamically (assignment and re-assignment of resources) from the resource pool as per customer's demand using multi-tenant model.

Measured Service

Measured service is another feature to deliver metered services to the end-users where usually monitoring, controlled services, reporting, and billing is required.

Building Block Technologies

Virtualization

Virtualization is a technique of deploying multiple machines on a single on-premises or remote hardware. Physical hardware hosting a dedicated machine for a service can also be migrated on a powerful hardware running multiple virtual machines on it in either isolated or shared environment. Virtualizing on cloud offers much more scalability and ease of management comparatively to an on-premises virtualization.

The fundamental concept of virtualization is to deal with the burden of workload by transforming the traditional computing into modern; making it more scalable, efficient and economical. Virtualization can be classified into:

- Hardware-level virtualization
- Operating system virtualization
- Server virtualization.

Innovation of virtualization technology is an antidote to the need of having multiple hardware's, cost and energy saving, quick management of computing and networking.

Cloud computing depends on the concepts of virtualization. In cloud computing, computational resource like space/memory and processors are allotted to the users which requires a host (either an operating system or the hypervisor).

The virtualization model is consist of cloud users, service providers, virtualized models and its host softwares. Virtualization model makes it conceivable to run numerous operating systems and different applications on the same server at the same time.

Advantages of Virtualization Technology

The advantages of virtualization technology are:

- Ease of deployment, networking and management.
- It helps to make cloud computing more efficient and eco-friendly
- It is one of the cost-saving, hardware-reducing and energy-saving technique
- Isolation
- Resource sharing
- Aggregation of resources
- Dynamical resources

Storage

In Cloud, data is stored on remote storage servers. Cloud storage is a critical part of cloud computing as all the data accessed by the applications is stored there. All applications including databases, data warehouses, big data analytics, Internet of Things (IoTs), and

backup and archive depends heavily on some form of data storage architecture. Different cloud service providers offer variety of low-cost cloud storage services with high durability and availability. It offers object, file, and blocks storage choices to support application and archival requirements as well as disaster recovery use cases.

Networking

Cloud networking introduces an easy way to deploy, operate, and manage a network. It offers advance networking capabilities with highly secure environment. To imply an additional layer of security, Cloud service porviders also offer the third-party security services at very low cost. You can isolate your cloud infrastructure to make it private, connect it to internet for making available for public or design a hybrid architecture.

Unlike traditional hardware–based legacy solutions, Cloud networking mechanizes exceptionally complex tasks and make them extraordinarily easy. It enables enterprises to deploy locations in minutes and operate distributed networks with services provided by the means of a cloud infrastructure, while providing phenomenal levels of centralized control and network visibility. Cloud services are typically subscription-based and therefore decrease any upfront capital costs.

Public cloud networking and Private cloud networking are two distinctive services. Public cloud networking makes networking applications accessible to IT users over the internet with little to no deployment required inside the company's IT infrastructure.

Private cloud networking services allude to an exclusive computing networking architecture that give hosted services to the set number of users behind a firewall. Such as a company's internal IT department utilizing a private cloud infrastructure, basically hosts applications inside their own private network and gives them to their own IT users.

Databases

Cloud database conveys ventures a scalable, reliable database solution. Customers have Service Level Agreement(s) for their cloud environment, with the capacity to burst both execution levels and infrastructure as needed, to oblige the varying requests that are set on their database environment. Cloud database is deployed across a non-virtualized environment, giving the databases access to the full limit of the fundamental hardware. Cloud database provides a clear differentiation from other database solutions available in the market. Following are some features of cloud based databases:

- Agility
- Availability
- Scalability

Advantages of Cloud Database:

Some of the advantages of cloud database are:

- No software licensing
- On-demand Oracle and MS SQL server solution
- No hardware provisioning
- Portal-based self-service database solution
- Cost effective estimated 20% to 75% lower cost.

Cloud Reference Architecture

Cloud Service Categories

SaaS (Software as a Service)

- A software model which gives accessibility to the customer to use the provider's application running on a Cloud infrastructure
- The applications are available for different client devices such as PCs, laptops and smart phones
- SaaS is a complete service that is managed and hosted by the service provider.
- The customer does not manage or control the application parameters such as network, servers, operating systems, storage
- For example, Google Apps, Caspio, Nivio, Microsoft Office 365

PaaS (Platform as a Service)

- A category of cloud services which offers a platform to the cloud customers. These platforms are capable to run, deploy and manage the applications without building a complex infrastructure typically required for application development
- Platforms as a service remove the need for organizations to manage the underlying infrastructure (usually hardware and operating systems)
- The customer has control over the applications
- For example, Windows Azure, Salesforce Heroku, AWS Elastic Beanstalk, Engine Yard

IaaS (Infrastructure as a Service)

- A category of cloud services which gives ability to the customer to provision processing, storage, networks, and other fundamental computing resources
- The customer is able to deploy and run subjective software, which can incorporate operating systems and networking, hardware, and data storage space
- The customer does not manage or control the fundamental cloud infrastructure but has control over operating systems, storage, and network

- For example, Amazon EC2, Windows Azure, Rackspace, Google Compute Engine

Infrastructure as a Service (IaaS)	Provide basic building blocks for cloud IT by offering access to networking features, computers, and data storage space.
Platform as a Service (PaaS)	Manages its own underlying infrastructure, usually hardware and operating systems, and provides application development platform.
Software as a Service (SaaS)	Offers a complete product as a web service that is run and maintained by the service provider along with the management of the underlying infrastructure.

Figure 1-1: Cloud Service Categories

NaaS (Network as a Service)

- Network as a service (NaaS) is another model for delivering virtual enterprise-wide area network services
- It requires configuration of network devices such as routers, firewalls, Software-defined WAN endpoints and other related component
- NaaS can incorporate flexible and expanded Virtual Private Network (VPN), bandwidth on interest, custom routing, multicast protocols, security firewall, instrustions detection and prevention, Wide Area Network (WAN), content monitoring and filtering, and antivirus

DSaaS (Data Storage as a Service)

- Storage service allows the user to pay for the measure of data storage space
- Storage service rents the data storage space to customers
- Storage as a service promotes a convenient way to manage backup and secondary storage option
- SaaS provider typically are agreed to rent storage space on a cost-per-gigabyte-stored and cost-per-data-transfer basis
- Common examples of Storage as a service are Amazon S3, Google, Bigtable etc

Cloud Deployment Models

Public Cloud

A Public Cloud is one of the most vital model, in which service providers create resources, such as storage and application, available to the overall public over the internet or web applications/web services. Perhaps public cloud services are free or offered on a "pay-as-you-go" pricing.

In Public Cloud hardware, application and bandwidth costs are secured by the service provider so it is simple and economical set-up to the user. Google AppEngine, Windows Azure Services Platform, Amazon Elastic Compute Cloud (EC2) are example of public clouds.

Private Cloud

Private cloud offers complete control over the architecture than using a Public cloud Private cloud may be exists off premises and can be managed by a third party Private cloud is useful for companies own privacy policies however, from in advanced capital cost, it is not that much gainfull "still it cost money to buy, build and manage". Amazon's Elastic Compute Cloud (EC2) or Simple Storage Service (S3) is example of Private Cloud.

Hybrid Cloud

A Hybrid Cloud is the combination of Public and Private cloud where the infrastructure partially hosted inside the organization and remotely in a Public cloud. For example, an association may use Amazon Simple Storage Service (Amazon S3) as Public cloud service to records their data but at the same time continue in-house storage for instant access operational customer data. Hybrid storage clouds are frequently important for record keeping and backup function. It is a decent methodology for a business to exploit the cost effectiveness and scalability.

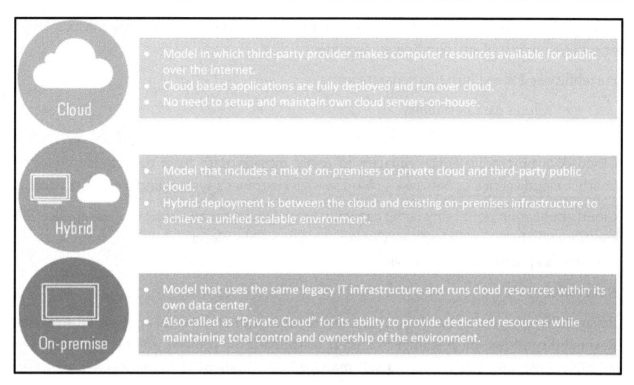

Figure 1-2: Cloud Deployment Models

Community Cloud

A Community Cloud can be perceived where various associations have comparable necessities andare willing to share infrastructure in order to take in the advantages of cloud computing. Costs are typically higher than a Public cloud . Google's "Gov Cloud" is a good example of community cloud.

Cloud Cross-Cutting Aspects

Interoperability

Application interoperability is the capability between the application segments to communicate with the other applications and processes. An application segment may be a total monolithic application or a piece of a distributed application.

Interoperability is required among various segments as well as between identical parts running in various clouds. For example, In a Hybrid cloud solution, an application part may be deployed in a Private cloud, with arrangement for a copy to be run in a Public cloud to handle traffic peaks.

Portability

The concept of portability in cloud environment is the ability to shift your data or application to another environment with no or minimal disruptions. This migration may in between cloud service providers or in between deployment models. A portable part can

be moved easily and reused regardless of the provider, operating system, platform, storage or other elements of surrounding environment.

Portability is defined into two separate areas

- Cloud data portability
- Cloud application portability

Cloud data portability is the capacity to easily transfer data from one cloud service to another cloud service or between a cloud service customer's system and a cloud service.

Cloud application portability is the capacity to easily transfer an application or application components from one cloud service to a comparable cloud service or from a cloud customer's system to a cloud service.

Reversibility

Reversibility is a process for cloud customers to recover their data and application artefacts. Reversibility allows the customer to modify or rollback the projects and deployments. For example, customer can rollback a self-managed environment to a cloud-based or third-party managed settings.

Security

In an on-premises environment, security implementation, auditing and monitoring is a periodic process which is usually either managed by the administrator or managed with co-operation of third-party. In cloud environment, plenty of advance automated security services, advance monitoring tools and governance features allows you to continuously monitor your infrastructure. It also allows you to enforce control policies intended to adhere as per regulatory compliance rules, protect information, data applications and infrastructures and controlled management of identity and access.

Security in cloud is much like security in traditional IT on-premises data centers, only without the costs of maintaining facilities and hardware. This includes protecting critical information from theft, data leakage, integrity, and deletion. In the cloud scenario, the service provider handles management of physical servers or storage devices while the customer uses software-based security tools to monitor and protect the flow of information into and of out of the Cloud resources.

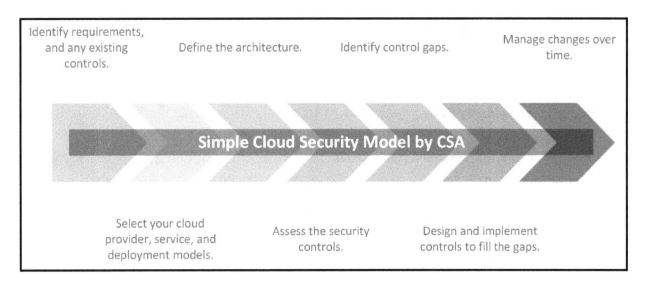

Figure 1-3: Simple Cloud Security Model by CSA

The infrastructure of cloud platform is secured by the service provider itself. Whereas the services availed by the customers from the providers are secure with shared responsibilities manner. Cloud services providers run compliance programs with accreditation bodies, CSA recommends the following models:

- CSA Enterprise Architecture
- CSA Cloud Controls Matrix
- Cloud Computing Security Reference Architecture (NIST Special Publication 500-299)
- ISO/IEC FDIS 27017 Information technology – Security techniques – Code of practice for information security controls based on ISO/IEC 27002 for Cloud services.

Privacy

The capacity of cloud computing to sufficiently address privacy regulations has been called into inquiries. Associations today face various diverse necessities attempting to protect the privacy of individual's information, and it is not clear (i.e., not yet established) whether the cloud computing model gives adequate protection of such information, or whether associations will be found in violation of regulations because of this new model.

As we know, Cloud is a highly distributed infrastructure. Each operational position of cloud technology has to pay strong attention to the privacy and compliance implications.

It is the responsibility of cloud service providers to ensure customer data is not exposed to employees or other administrators using technical and process controls. Cloud providers should enforce the compliance standards, rules and regulations upon their customers.

Cloud users should consider use of data masking or obfuscation when considering a service that does not meet security, privacy, or compliance requirements

Resiliency

Resiliency is the capacity to deal with failures gracefully and recover the whole system. This is a huge a challenge for services and applications where the components rely upon internal or external segments/services that should be always functional and available for all processes. Planning will help to identify, fix, log and recover from these failures.

There are three essential techniques which are used to expand the strength of a Cloud system:

- Continuous checking and monitoring
- Checkpoints, Recovery points and System restoring
- Replication

Governance

Governance is a general term which defines how a governing process will run. Governing a cloud computing includes policies and controls that comprise how an organization is run. Governance is the ability to govern and measure the functionality, risk and production including legal precedence of breaches, responsibilities to secure sensitive information and much more. Following are the types of governance:

- **ISO/IEC 38500:2015 - Information Technology - Governance of IT for the organization:** ISO/IEC 38500:2015 provides guiding principles for members of governing bodies of organizations (which can comprise owners, directors, partners, executive managers, or similar) on the effective, efficient, and acceptable use of information technology (IT) within their organizations.
- **ISACA - COBIT - A Business Framework for the Governance and Management of Enterprise IT:** The COBIT 5 framework is built on five basic principles which includes extensive guidance on enablers for governance and management of enterprise IT.
- **ISO/IEC 27014:2013 - Information Technology - Security techniques - Governance of Information Security:** ISO/IEC 27014:2013 provides guidance on concepts and principles for the governance of information security, by which organizations can evaluate, direct, monitor and communicate the information security related activities within the organization.

Maintenance and Versioning

Cloud-based Computerized Maintenance Management Systems (CMMS) can be accessed by a web browser or application. This implies that support staff can recover relevant information wherever they are found. Maintenance can be planned, monitored, scheduled

and automated from a web browser. It is a software package that maintains a computer database of information about an organization's maintenance operations.

Auditability

Auditability is a detail for the presentation of information about how a cloud computing service provider organization tends to control frameworks. The objective of Cloud Audit is to provide service providers with an approach to make their execution and security data readily accessible for potential customers. The specification provides a standard method to present and share detailed, automated statistics about performance and security.

Security Concepts Relevant to Cloud Computing

Cryptography

In Cloud computing, the idea of cryptography that employs encryption methods to secure data in motion or at rest. It enables users to conveniently and securely access shared cloud services, as any data that is hosted by cloud providers is secured with encryption. Cryptography secures sensitive data without delaying information exchange.

Encryption

Encryption is an important security measure that is used in not only on-premises environment but necessarily in cloud-based environments. Encryption secures both states of data, data at rest and data in motion. Data in motion is typically secured with Internet Protocol (IP) Security Protocol (IPSec), Virtual Private Network (VPN), or Transport Layer Security/Secure Sockets Layer (TLS/SSL). Similar to data in motion, encryption techniques used for data at rest are AES and RSA. Data encryption, which prevents data visibility in the event of its unauthorized access or theft, is commonly used to protect data in motion and increasingly promoted for protecting data at rest. In these models, Cloud storage providers encrypt data upon receipt, passing encryption keys to the customers so that data can be securely decrypted when needed.

Encryption is one of the most effective approaches to data security, scrambling the substance of any system, file, or database in such a way that it's impossible to decipher without a decryption key. By applying encryption and practicing secure encryption key management, companies can guarantee that only approved users have access to sensitive data.

<u>Advantages of Cloud Encryption:</u>

The advantage of Cloud encryption is same as application of encryption.

- Encrypted data is only readable for authorized parties with access to the decryption keys. Encrypting data guarantees that if that data falls into the wrong hand, it is useless as long as its keys stay secure.
- Cloud encryption is critical for industries that need to meet regulatory compliance requirements

In-Motion

Data in-motion is data moving from one location to another such as between source to destination across the public internet or a private network or in between processes of different applications. Data security in motion is the insurance of this data while it is travelling from network to network or being transferred from a local storage device to a Cloud storage device.

Encryption plays an important role in data assurance and is a popular instrument for securing data both in motion and at rest. For protecting data in motion, enterprises often choose to encrypt sensitive data preceding to moving and/or use encrypted connections (HTTPS, TLS, FTPS, SSL, etc) to protect the contents of data in motion.

At Rest

Data at rest, is data that is not effectively moving from device to device or network to network such as data stored on a hard drive, flash drive, laptop, or stored in some other way. Data protection at rest, aims to secure in active data stored on any devices or network.

For protecting data at rest, enterprises can essentially encrypt sensitives files prior to storing them and/or choose to encrypt the storage drive itself.

Key Management

Key management is the process whereby the keys in a cryptosystem are managed, including their generation, exchange, disposal and use. This incorporate various protocols that intend to keep the keys secure consistently, granting access to them only to authorised entities.

When implementing a key management system, one needs to think about where the encryption keys must be stored. These keys may be stored in one of three main locations.

<u>Placing keys in an enterprise data center:</u>

When using an enterprise data center to store the keys, these are maintained with large amounts of security, ensuring that these are not compromised.

<u>Using SaaS to manage keys:</u>

Keys may alternatively be stored using SaaS key management solution where the application provider will manage and store the keys. This high reliance upon the provider raises various security concerns, including the possibility of having the keys unavailable in case of an outage.

<u>Using IaaS to manage keys</u>

A third approach is to use the encryption and key management services provided by IaaS. Like the SaaS option, such a system results in strong dependence upon the provider if the customer decides to enable the provider to deal with the keys. However, some IaaS providers also provide their customers with the chance to deal with the encryption keys themselves, bringing about better separation of duties. Amazon S3 Storage (Amazon Web Services) is an example.

Access Control

Access Control is a security method that controls the person who may view or use assets in a computing environment. It is a basic concept in security that reduces risk to the business or organization. The main purpose of access control is to reduce the risk of unauthorized access to logical and physical systems. Access control is a basic part of security compliance programs that protect security technology and access control policies in place, to ensure confidential information, for example customer data.

Features of Cloud Based Access Control:

There are lot of features in cloud based access control to make its use convenient. The processes are managed remotely following as:

- Adding new users to the access control
- Verification of the system operation
- Changing user's rights
- Revoking rights to access certain facilities
- Access point reprogramming

Security of remote sites can be put under one umbrella, because of data received from each source is saved in one single place. By having a cloud based physical access control system turn capital expenses into operational ones. There are no high costs connected with the purchase of servers and wiring that will associate all the parts of access control.

Access Control offers verity of features to keep your cloud account and resources safe from unauthorized access or abuse. This includes credentials for access control, HTTPS endpoints for coded data transmission, the creation of separate Identity and Access

Management (IAM) user accounts, and user activity logging for security check. You can take benefit from all these security tools, no matter which service you are associated with. To ensure only authorized user and processes access the resources, many types of credentials for authentication are employed. These include passwords, digital signatures, cryptographic keys, and certificates. Cloud service provider also provides the option of requiring Multi-Factor Authentication to log in. Some credentials are defined below:

- Username/Password
- Multi-Factor Authentication (MFA)
- Access key
- Key pair
- X.509 Certificates

Data and Media Sanitization

The fundamental concern about media and data sanitization is securely disposing the information and sanitizing the media from recorded information. The security concern i.e. confidentiality about information, media disposal process should securely and completely be removing the sensitive information that is recorded intentionally or unintentionally on a storage media. This activity may be for maintenance reasons, system upgrades, or during a configuration update. The process of media sanitization should be irreversible i.e. removing the information from the media permanently.

Media sanitization is the key element in assuring confidentiality. Confidentiality is "Preserving authorized restrictions on information access and disclosure, including means for protecting personal privacy and proprietary information" In order for organization to have appropriate controls on the information they are responsible for safeguarding, they must properly dispose of used media.

There are two types of media are as follow:

1. **Hard Copy:**

Hard copy media is the physically recorded information such as documents, files, printouts, drums and platens.

This type of media is often the most uncontrolled. Information tossed into the recycle bins and trash containers exposes a significant vulnerability to "dumpster divers", and overcurious employees, risking accidental disclosures.

2. **Soft Copy:**

Softcopies are the digital information such as data in a digital form, digital document, pictures, videos, recordings, and other digital form of data stored in an electronic media

in bits and bytes. Electronic media holding softcopies may include hard drives, Random Access Memory (RAM), Read-Only Memory (ROM) and disks.

Types of Sanitization

The key in deciding how to manage media in an organization is to first consider the information, then the media type. The security categorization of the information, along with internal environmental factors, should drive the decisions on how to deal with the media. The key is to first think in terms of information confidentiality, then by media type.

There are different types of sanitization for each type of media as:

Disposal: Disposal is the act of discarding media with no other sanitization considerations.

Clearing: Clearing information is a level of media sanitization that would protect the confidentiality of information against a robust keyboard attack. Clearing should not allow information to be retrieved by data, disk, or file recovery utilities. It should be resistant to keystroke recovery attempts executed from standard input devices and form data scavenging tools. Such as, overwriting is an acceptable method for clearing media.

Purging: Purging information is a media sanitization process that protects the confidentiality of information against a laboratory attack. For some media, clearing media would not suffice for purging. A laboratory attack would involve a threat with the resources and knowledge to use sub-standard systems to conduct data recovery attempts on media outside their normal operating environment.

Destroying: Destruction of media is the ultimate form of sanitization. After media is destroyed, it cannot be reused as originally intended. Physical destruction can be accomplished using a variety of methods, including disintegration, incineration, shredding and melting.

Disintegration, Incineration, Pulverization and Melting these sanitization methods are designed to completely destroy the media. They are typically carried out at an outsourced metal destruction or incineration facility with the specific capabilities to perform these activities, securely, and safely

Shredding: Paper shredders can be used to destroy flexible media such as diskettes, once the media is physically removed from their outer containers. The shred size should be small enough that there is reasonable assurance in proportion to the data confidentiality level that the information cannot be reconstructed.

Cryptographic Erase

As media has expanded over time, new technologies such as solid-state storage has come into widespread use. Organizations have sought to minimize the time required to perform

sanitization, even on devices having sanitization commands. The increasing use of encryption for data at rest, has provided a very fast technique of cryptographic erase.

Cryptographic erase basically involves destroying the encryption key for the data and thus forcing an adversary to conduct an attack against the cryptologic implementation in order to gain access to the sanitized data. Another advantage of cryptographic erase is its high granularity.

For example, it is theoretically possible to cryptographically erase a single field in a database by encrypting it under a random key that is immediately sanitized.

Cryptographic erase may also be the only effective technique for sanitizing certain types of media (such as flash-based solid-state storage).

Though it sounds deceptively easy to implement and very attractive because of its speed, there is a number of critical requirements to be met:

- Encryption must be applied before any data is written to the drive- this requirement assures that there is no data on the media in clear-text form.
- High-pedigree encryption is required. This requires that the cryptographic algorithms themselves and their implementation must be reliable. This is to assure that there are no weakness in the implementation that would make it easier for an adversary to access the encrypted information.
- Effective key management is required. In order to conduct cryptographic erase, all copies of the relevant key must be sanitized.
- Proof of encryption is required. For cryptographic erase to be accepted as a sanitization method, it should be reliably documented that the data was encrypted appropriately in the first place

Virtualization Security

Virtualization is the process of hosting a number of operating systems or softwares virtually on a single hardware instead of hosting an OS on a physical device. This virtualization can be deployed on an on-premises server or on a remotely server hosted on cloud. Each virtual instance is known as Virtual Machine (VM). The operating system providing the virtualization environment is called Hypervisor. There are two types of hypervisor.

1. Hypervisor type-1 is referred as bare-metal hypervisor which runs directly on a host physical machine. Hypervisors such as VMware ESXi, Microsoft Hyper-V server and open source KVM are examples of Type 1 hypervisors.
2. Hypervisor type-2 is referred as hosted-hypervisor that is installed on the top of existing operating system. Type 2 hypervisors include VMware Fusion, Oracle VM

Virtual Box, Oracle VM Server for x86, Oracle Solaris Zones, Parallels and VMware Workstation.

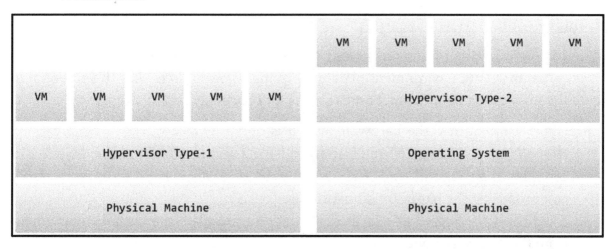

Figure 1-4: Hypervisor Type-1 and Type-2

Virtualization is a trending and cutting-edge technology because of the rapid growth and demand of Cloud computing. The two types of virtualization architecture are Hosted Virtualization and Native Virtualization

In Native or Hardware Virtualization the hypervisor-type 1 runs directly on the hardware providing all hardware resources to be available for virtualization. In a Hosted virtualization, the hypervisor runs on a hosted OS. With the implementation of the Virtualization in a Cloud, four new fundamental characteristics are present in the system that change the way security mechanism can be utilized.

1. Virtualization creates a new management layer with the hypervisor.
2. Because of the nature of virtualization, a concentration of VMs on each machine is present.
3. VMs have variable states compared to continuous running physical machines.
4. VMs mobility allows them to move from physical locations easily.

The secure solutions based on virtual architecture aim to provide secure virtual environment by considering security of all virtualization components. Hypervisor security is the first line of defense.

Hypervisor Security

There are several virtual machines running in a virtual environment which may have independent security zones or deployed in isolated manner so that they are not accessible from other virtual machines. A hypervisor is the core operator of this virtual environment and the security of hypervisor is even more imporatant concern as it is the controlling agent

for everything in virtual environment. Any modification or compromise in hypervisor can affect all of the virtual machines running within the virtualization host.

Advantages of Hypervisor Security:

Hypervisor-based virtualization technology is the best choice of implementing methods to achieve a secure Cloud environment. Its ability to manage resources, has the potential to secure the infrastructure of Cloud. Some reasons for choosing this technology:

- Hypervisor controls the hardware, and it is only way to access it. This capability allows hypervisor-based virtualization to have a secure infrastructure. Hypervisor can act as a firewall and will be able to prevent malicious users to from compromising the hardware infrastructure.
- The hypervisor is used as a layer of abstraction to isolate the virtual environment from the hardware underneath.
- Hypervisor is implemented below the guest OS in the Cloud computing hierarchy, which means that if an attack passes the security systems in the guest OS, the hypervisor can detect it.
- The hypervisor- level of virtualization controls all the access between the guests OSs and shared hardware underside. Therefore, hypervisor is able to simplify the transaction-monitoring process in the Cloud environment.

Common Threats

There are common threats to Cloud computing such as

Accountability and Data Risk:

In cloud computing, several organizations are opting for the public cloud for their business, where the cloud service provider has the control over the data security, not the data owners.

The lack of control on the hand of data owner will increase the risk of sensitive data. Most of the cloud service providers are using the multi-tenancy storage architecture, which allows the multiple customers to store their data in one place. There is a chance for cross data harvesting in case the storage architecture is not stable.

How to mitigate:

- The organization should be clear about the data recovering procedure of the providers to make sure the attackers should not be able to recover the deleted data in cloud
- The provider should ensure proper backup process.
- Data should be maintained in encrypted format both at rest and in transit.
- The operator should use different encryption keys for different users.

User Identity Federation:

In an event when an association is moving their services and application, starting with one cloud service provider to another, it must have legitimate control over their user's credentials. Rather than enabling the cloud provider to keep up identities making authentication overhead users, associations are utilizing user identity federation. The methodology includes SAML, an open source protocols that permits single sign-on over various cloud service providers. It kills different identities assigned to an individual user.

There are a lot of advantages of user identity federation, but this methodology accompanies with it some security challenges.

- It includes risk of the unauthorized access, on the off chance that the services allowing access to the user are inappropriately configured.
- Any attack on the SAML can enable the attackers to increase unauthorized access by taking user credentials.
- Moreover, the single sign-on ability builds up the chances of a single purpose of failure.

How to mitigate

- The organization must be clear in how the user identities & AAA protocols like SAML are implemented.
- The federation partners must follow the security policies and standards.
- Single sign-on in the enterprise
- Federated identity with multiple partners
- Federated identity in SaaS applications
- If there's more than one identity provider configured for the STS, it must detect which identity provider the user should be redirected to for authentication. This process is called home realm discovery.

Regulatory Compliance:

Data is stored at a random place in cloud-based solution. In most of the cases, customers are not even aware where they are hosted. Following different regulatory rules at different countries, the data that is supposed to be protected in one country is not supposed to be protected in another country.

As a result of the lack of transparency in the execution, data owners discover hard to show compliance. There is a lack of consistent standards and in addition, necessities for the worldwide regulatory compliance. For example, the US nationalist act gives no limitations to the government organizations to access to the corporate data. Then again, the European

Union has strict privacy laws, consequently the data stored in the US according to the US compliance appear to be compliance violation in Europe.

<u>How to mitigate</u>

- Ensuring the provider made a contractual commitment in order to obey the local privacy requirements.
- To avoid compliance violation, the organization must make sure that their Cloud service provider is storing their data in specific jurisdictions.

Business Continuity & Resilience:

The organization must ensure that their business can be performed even in an accidental situation to achieve business growth. In Cloud computing, it is essential to make sure that data will be available even in an unexpected incident occurs.

An ongoing research shows that blackouts of most cloud services portray that 100 % availability may not be guaranteed. In cloud computing, the duty of business continuity and resilience goes to cloud providers rather than the organization. This will expand the chance of risk due to not providing suitable business continuity when a disaster happens.

<u>How to Mitigate</u>

- The organization has to make sure the RTOS (Recovery Time Objectives) are clearly defined in the contractual agreement
- Ensure the provider comprise approved business continuity policy in place.

User Privacy and Secondary Usage of Data:

The accessibility of information especially Personal Identifiable Information (PII) and Personal Health Information (PHI) are the most critical security concern. This is a sensitive stored personal information and is at direct risk of confidentiality. As PII represents the hobbies, daily routine, personal interest whereas PHI represents records of wellness, illness and test results. The probability of secondary use of these information is a confidentiality and privacy concern.

<u>How to mitigate</u>

- The organization must re-ensure that their provider is not using their user's private data for any secondary purpose.
- Enforce policy for privacy and acceptable usage, consent and secondary usage.

Service and Data Integration:

The security of data in transit must be a great concern to every organization. In the cloud computing solution, the data is transmitted between the end user and cloud data center.

While utilizing cloud, the transmission is carried over the internet, where there is an increase in risk for the organization.

As like the traditional computing model, the transmission of secure data is vulnerable to interception and compromise.

<u>How to Mitigate:</u>

- The provider must ensure that the data transferred between the end user and data center over the internet are appropriately protected.
- They must ensure that they are suing SSL or other stronger encryption protocols for securing data in transit.

Multi-Tenancy & Physical Security

Most organizations prefer cloud computing because of its multi-tenancy feature, that is they can share resources like networking, storage, computing as well as functionality related components.

Risk in Multi-Tenancy

In a multi-tenant environment, security dependencies are more on logical segregation instead of physical resource separation. The inadequate logical security control, the chance of the presence of ignorance or malicious tenants, and co-mingled tenant dataincreases the security risk.

<u>How to Mitigate</u>

- Organizations should provide transparency to tenants.
- Make sure the tenants are provided with the proper knowledge on administrative access to their resources.

Incidence Analysis & Forensics Risk

When security breaches, policy violation or attack occurs, it is important to analyze that incident and conduct a forensic investigation. The existing incident handling and forensics principle is commonly intended for the off-line investigation.

Risk in Incident Analysis & Forensics

The evidence of the incident is likely to be stored in a place beyond the instant control of the investigator. Since the logging is distributed over multiple hosts and cloud data centers are placed in various countries, thereby governed by various laws, it is difficult to investigate the incident. As well as multiple customers are storing the data in same shared hardware and data center, issues in law enforcement will arise during forensic recovery.

How to Mitigate

- Maintain comprehensive logging without any compromise in performance.
- Employ enthusiastic forensic VM images.

Infrastructure Security:

The security of the data present in Cloud is influenced greatly by the infrastructure component's security, which sets up the application platform. Failure to consider the best practices to ensure security can lead to loss of reputation, data and availability.

Risk in Infrastructure Security

Failure to keep the system and network device up-to-date might compromise the system's security. Running of services that includes security-related bugs will enhance the possibility of infrastructure becoming a target for the security exploit.

How to mitigate

- Isolate infrastructure component
- Employ tired solution architecture
- Enforce role-based administrative access and regular vulnerability assessments

Non-production Environment Exposure

Organizations generally use non-production environment internally to design, develop and test their software or application. This environment is not as much secure as the production environment. Hence, there is a minimum risk in security when compared to a cloud-based solution where the non-production environment is beyond the control of the organization.

Risk in Non-Production Environment

In cloud computing, there is a risk of malicious user accessibility in the non-production environment. This environment often includes generic authentication credentials which may not be aligned with the standard password policy of the organization. Hence, it makes it effortless to achieve unauthorized access. With unauthorized access, attacker can make the environment useless or they can even delete it entirely.

How to mitigate

- Enforce strong credentials which are aligned with the same standards of production environment for accessing as the non-production environment.
- Make sure the non-production environment does not include the sensitive data that is present in the production environment

Security Considerations for Different Cloud Categories

As we know, there are different cloud categories for difference nature of requirements. There is no way to cover all conceivable security options. Following are the best practices for securing data within various Cloud models.

SaaS

In Software as a Service, most of the control of the environment is ceded to the provider. Cloud customer will not have ownership of the hardware or the software, because the customer only supplies and processes data to and in the system. The cloud provider is responsible for all security counter-measures, system maintenance, and the vast majority of policy affecting the data. Cloud provider performs background checks and continual monitoring of all personnel with access to the data center, extreme physical security measures at data center location, assignment of contractual liability to the provider, and encryption of data processed and stored in Cloud. It is important to remember that the residual risk of loss of data to physical access will always exist.

PaaS

In Platform as a Service (PaaS), Cloud customer loses still more control of the environment as to the Cloud provider is responsible for maintaining, installing, and administering OS. This will demand more adjustment of the security policy and additional efforts to guarantee regulatory compliance. The responsibilities for updating and maintaining the software will also be shared by the customer. Updates and administration of the OS falls under the provider's responsibilities.

PaaS security includes four main areas such as system and resource isolation, user access management, user level permission, and protection against malware, backdoors and Trojans.

User Access Management

It allows the users to access resources, IT services, data, and other assets. Access management helps to ensure the Confidentiality, Integrity and Availability (CIA) of these assets and resources, protecting that only those authorized users can access them. In recent years, traditional standalone access control methods have developed less consumed, with more holistic methods to unite the authentication of users becoming favoured. (This includes single sign-on.) For successful functioning of user access management processes and controls, it is important to agree upon execution of the rules, and organizational policies for access to data and assets. The basic components of user access management include authentication, authorization, administration, intelligence.

User-Level Permissions:

Each occasion of a service must have its own notion of user-level entitlements (permissions). If the instances share mutual policies, suitable counter-measures and controls must be allowed by the Cloud security professional to reduce authorization creep or the inheritance of permissions over time.

System and Resource Isolation:

PaaS tenants must not have shell access to the servers running their instances (even while virtualized). The rationale behind this is to maximise the chance and likelihood of configuration or system changes affecting multiple tenants. Where possible, administration facilities must be restricted to siloed containers to decrease this risk. Careful consideration must be given before access is provided to the basic infrastructure hosting a PaaS instance. It takes time and effort to undo tenant-related fixes to their environments.

Protection against Malware, Backdoors, and Trojans:

The challenge with these is that once backdoors are generated, they offer a constant vector for attackers to target and possibly increase access to the relevant PaaS resources. You have heard of the story in which attackers increased access through a backdoor, only to create additional backdoors whereas removing the legitimate backdoors, basically holding the systems, resources and associated services, hostage. More recently, attackers have used embedded and hardcoded malware as a way of obtaining unauthorized access and retaining this access for a prolonged and extended period. Most particularly, malware has been placed in point-of-sale (PoS) devices, handheld card-processing devices, and other platforms, thus divulging large amounts of sensitive data (including credit card numbers, customer details, and so on).

Since PaaS is so differing, it may not cover every single potential options are following list:

- *Client/application Encryption:* Data is encoded in the PaaS application, or the customer accessing to the platform.
- *Database Encryption:* Data is encoded in the database utilizing encryption worked in and supported by the database platform.
- *Proxy Encryption:* Data passes through an encryption intermediary before being sent to the platform.
- *Other:* Additional alternatives may incorporate APIs incorporated with the platform, external encryption services, and different varieties.

IaaS

In Infrastructure as a Service, cloud customer has the most responsibility and authority of all possible cloud models. The customer, however, is incharge of everything, from the operating system and up, all software will be installed and administered by the customer, and the customer will supply and manage all the data. In terms of security, the cloud customer is quiet behind some of the control featured in the legacy situation. For instance, the customer obviously does not acquire to select the particular IT assets, thus the security of the acquisition process (during which we normally vet vendors and suppliers) must be assigned to the cloud provider. The cloud customer may also lose some capability to monitor network traffic inside the data center—the cloud provider might not be willing to enable the customer to place monitoring equipment or sensors on the provider's infrastructure, and also might refuse to share traffic data they, the provider, have collected themselves. This makes auditing difficult, which also affects security policy and regulatory compliance. An organization migrating to the cloud will necessarily have to significantly adapt its security policy to reflect the new limits, and will have to find some way to offer the required deliverables to appease regulators. This must be negotiated at the outset of migration, and early communication with regulators is highly suitable.

Understand Design Principles of Secure Cloud Computing

Before we can discuss specific data security controls, we need a model to understand and manage our information. In the *data security* section, we discuss the specific technical controls and recommendations to monitor and enforce this governance.

Cloud Secure Data Life Cycle

The Data Security Life Cycle is different from Information Life Cycle Management, reflecting the different needs of the security audience.

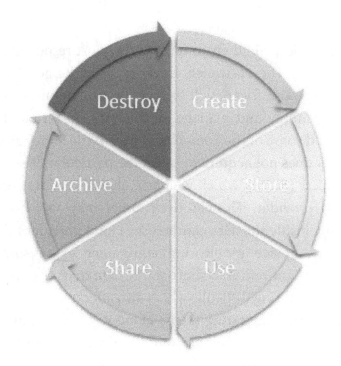

Figure 1-5: Cloud Secure Data Life Cycle

There are six stages, from creation to destruction, in the concept of life cycle. However, we display it as a linear progression, once created, data can bounce between phases without limitation, and may not pass across all stages (such as, not all data is eventually destroyed).

Create:

Data will most often be created by the users accessing cloud remotely. Create applies to creating or changing a data/content element, not just a document or database. It is the generation of new digital content, or the alteration/updating of existing content.

Store:

From the perspective of the life-cycle diagram, the store stage takes place right after the create stage, and before the use and share stages. Store is the act committing the digital data to some sort of storage repository, and typically occurs nearly simultaneously with creation.

Use:

Data security in the use requires considering other operational aspects as well. Data is viewed, processed, or otherwise used in some sort of activity.

Share:

Information is made accessible to others, for example, between users, to customers, and to partners.

Archive:

Archive is the stage for long-term storage, and we necessarily must consider this for longer time-frame when planning security controls for the data.

Destroy:

Data is permanently destroyed using physical or digital means (e.g., crypto-shredding). Crypto-shredding is the only feasible and thorough means currently available for the purpose, in the cloud environment.

Crypto-shredding or digital shredding is the encryption of data before being disposed of Important aspect of data protection method, crypto-shredding is the procedure of deliberately destroying the encryption keys that are used to encrypt the data originally.

Cloud Based Business Continuity/Disaster Recovery Planning

Business continuity management is the process where risks and threats to the on-going business functions, availability of services, and the organization are dynamically managed and reviewed at set intervals as part of the overall risk-management process. The main purpose of business continuity is to keep the business operating and functioning in the event of interference.

Disaster Recovery Plan (DRP) is the process of recovering access to data, hardware and software necessary to continue critical business operations after a human-induced or natural disaster (such as storm, flood, tornado, etc.). The main purpose of DRP is to rapidly re-establish, or recover critical areas or element of the business after a disaster or similar incident. DRP is part of a larger process known as business continuity planning.

From cloud customer's point of view, business continuity elements contain the related security pillars of availability, integrity, and confidentiality. The availability of the related resources and services is regularly the key requirement, along with the uptime and capability to access these on demand. Failure to guarantee these, results in major impacts including loss of opportunities, loss of earnings, and loss of confidence between the customer and the provider. Many security professionals struggle to retain their business continuity processes. once they have started to use cloud-based services. Similarly, many fail to effectively update, adjust, and keep their business continuity plans up to date in terms of whole coverage of services. This may be because of a number of factors, but the root factor contributing to it is that business continuity is continually operated, mostly at set intervals and is not integrated as a continuous process into on-going business operations. That is, business continuity events are performed only annually or biannually, which may not take into account the prominent changes in business operations (such as cloud) within related business units, systems, or sections.

Two critical success factors for business continuity while using cloud-based services are:

To understand your responsibilities compared to the CSP's responsibilities

- Customer responsibilities
- CSP responsibilities
- Understanding any interdependencies or third parties (supply chain risks)
- Order of restoration (priority)
- Suitable frameworks and certifications held by the facility, services, and processes
- Right to audit and make regular assessments of continuity capabilities
- Communications of any issues or limited services
- Understanding the need for backups to be held on-site or off-site or with another CSP

The following components of business continuity and disaster recovery are covered as

- Penalties and compensation for loss of service
- RTOs and RPOs
- Loss of integrity or confidentiality
- Points of contact and escalation processes
- Failure to keep compliance
- Changes being communicated in a timely manner
- Clearly defined responsibilities
- Where usage of third parties is prerequisite per the agreed-upon SLA

The cloud customer should adhere to the agreement after he/she is completely satisfied with all the details relating to BCDR (with recovery times, responsibilities, and more), prior to signing any documentation or agreements that show acceptance of the terms for system operation.

Cost Benefit Analysis

There appears to be exceptional cost-cutting advantages in using Cloud computing services. Investment and operating costs reduction, high service elasticity and greater flexibility are few most apparent advantages. On the other hand, it is non-trivial to adopt Cloud computing in business environments. Cost-cutting is often referred to as the key component for adopting Cloud computing. The challenge of making decisions on costs savings alone or exclusively, can bring back the aspect of risk for any company that does not take into account the relevant consequences.

The model that would be used by organizations to conduct the cost-benefit analysis is in three layers.

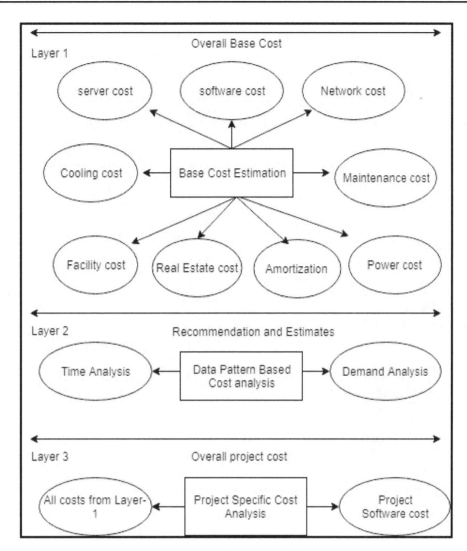

Figure 1-6: Standard Architecture of Disaster Recovery

Layer 1 is base cost optimization. As we know that, now a days Cloud computing use on-demand pricing so you can customize and maintain the cost of Infrastructure (in-house). For most of the components, the concept of Total Cost of Ownership (TCO) is used. TCO is the determination of the real cost attributing to owning and managing IT infrastructure. A number of 9 components including Amortization, Server costs, Networking costs, Power costs, Software costs, cooling costs, Immovable costs, Installation cost and Support and Maintenance costs are considered in the base cost estimate.

- *Amortization* - For servers and other facilities the amortization parameter will be calculated, in order to achieve fair cost allocations for different IT resources (hardware / programming). The cost of amortization for each item of construction considered must be calculated on a monthly basis.

- **Cost of servers** - Servers are usually installed on racks, with similar configurations assumed for all servers. This is assumed to facilitate server cost calculations.
- **Network Cost** - It deals with the cost of switches, ports, cables and the implementation costs.
- **Power Cost** - Power is the single largest cost. In an organization, IT infrastructure contributing to the power consumption comprises computer infrastructure (servers, switches, etc.), physical infrastructure of critical networks, transformers, continuous supply, suppliers, air conditioners, pumps, lighting, etc.
- **Software Cost** - It includes cost of installation of OS patches and resources for load balancing. It is included in base cost optimization because of licence payment. Software cost divide into two Class A include OS and Class B include other software.
- **Cooling Cost** - It represents the energy consumed by the 1W heat dissipation cooling equipment.
- **Real Estate Cost** - It deals with monthly cost of real estate used by infrastructure.
- **Facility Cost** - These are tangible as well as intangible components that are essential to normal equipment functioning. These installations are wrapped in racks containing the servers. Components such as PDU, KVM (keypad / video / mouse), cables, etc. may be included.
- **Support and Maintenance Cost** - It includes cost of maintenance.

Layer 2 deals with data size, time required for computational resources, predicted demand, actual demand and amount of server that meet the demand. It has two analysis; Time analysis and Demand estimation. Time analysis will recommend that cloud computing be adopted based on the time needed to process and compare data of in-house with cloud. Demand analysis will provide the advantages and disadvantages of cloud computing resource provisioning for demand of an organization.

Layer 3 shows overall project cost. This cost is obtained by using all the cost components in layer 1. Instead of the total servers in-house for an organization, the number of estimated servers required for a project under consideration would be the input to cloud computing cost estimation model. With this you can identify that whether the existing infrastructure would be beneficial to execute for future project. In this layer cost of project software cost is also included which is the cost of software used in design, deployment and development of project.

Functional Security Requirements

Portability:

The concept of portability provides the ability to be easily carried or moved. Portability in cloud ensures application and it's components to continue their functions in the same way when moved. Cloud environment to another without any changes. A portable part can be moved easily and re-used regardless of the provider, operating system, platform, storage or other elements of surrounding environment.

Portability of applications means that application running on one cloud platform can be moved to a new cloud platform and operate as before without having to be re-designed, re-coded, or re-compiled. If the new cloud platform is a different operating platform for example, when an application moves from a Windows host to a Linux host, the application will run without any requirement of changes/modification.

There are number of issues standing in the path of moving to cloud. Portability considerations and recommendations that impact upon moving to cloud include:

Security integrations also includes End-to-End security to ensure compliance and data confidentiality. Cloud introduces unique portability concerns for maintaining security, including:

- Authentication and identity mechanisms for user or process access to systems now must operate across all components of a cloud system. Single sign-on using authentication against an enterprise Active Directory may pose a risk when outside components cannot authenticate to an internal LDAP repository. Ensuring authentication extends appropriately to the divergent systems required for a cloud application.
- Access controls must extend from the internal environment to cloud. Preventing access to users within the corporate perimeter is an established practice today. cloud applications running on the internet now require access management to appropriately restrict access for anyone using the internet.
- Data encryption must be applied to data moving to cloud. The systems one which your data resides will not be owned by your organization, and they will most often be managed and maintained by outside parties. To ensure there is no loss of control of sensitive data or risk of falling out of compliance, encrypt data before it moves to cloud. Remove risks to portability by placing data into universally portable secure formats that are published such as OpenPGP or ZIP.
- Encryption keys should not be turned over to the cloud providers.

Interoperability:

The concept of interoperability, as it applied to cloud computing, is at its simplest; the necessity for the components of a processing system to work together to accomplish their intended result. Components should be replaceable by new or different components from different providers and continue to work. Components that make up a system consists of the hardware and software elements required to build and operate it. Typical components required of a cloud system include:

- Hardware
- Operating systems
- Virtualizations
- Networks
- Storage
- Software
- Data security

In security, applications and data in cloud reside on systems you do not own and likely have only limited control over. A number of important items to consider for interoperable security include:

1. Make sure authentication controls for system and client account access to certifications are perfect to ensure continued and steady system access to security and integrity.
   - This incorporates maintaining similar authentication factor level (for example single versus double).
   - Assess whether client or process authentication needs an adjustment in credentials
   - If Smart card or other removable key storage is used, ensure support is given, or use roaming credentials.
2. The most important approach to ensure sensitive data moved to Cloud is through encryption
   - Encrypting the data before storing into Cloud. It will ensure that it cannot be accessed and disclosed to unauthorized users.
   - Use only interoperable encryption, that is accessible through distributed particulars, for example, ZIP or OpenPGP, that directly and persistently ensure data and documents to the platform, storage systems, or area where it resides.
3. Data integrity measures ensures the data to remain unaltered while stored in Cloud.
   - Use watermarks where proper to distinguish ownership
   - Increase the utilization of digital signing of files and reports to approve data identity and integrity

- Incorporate time-stamps on digital signatures to settle content and integrity checks in time.
- Where native document format does not support digital signing, ensure documents in interoperable organizations that do. Such as ZIP and OpenPGP. Both of these configurations give digital signing to file or document.

4. Log file data must be handled with indistinguishable dimension of security from every single other data moving to cloud. Log files contain vital data for system analysis and investigation and frequently containhighly sensitive information that should be secured.
   - Investigate how log files are made and managed within the cloud environment where preparing happens.
   - Determine how log analysis devices interoperate with existing log management to ensure the standard log management proceeds without interruption or determine what new instruments are required to help logging prerequisites for a cloud service.

Encryption of log file data must occur. choose an encryption strategy that is interoperable crosswise over platform. It is prescribed to utilize secure ZIP compression on all log files to ensure them and to store them effectively. Log files commonly have a high compression factor, frequently as high up to 90%.

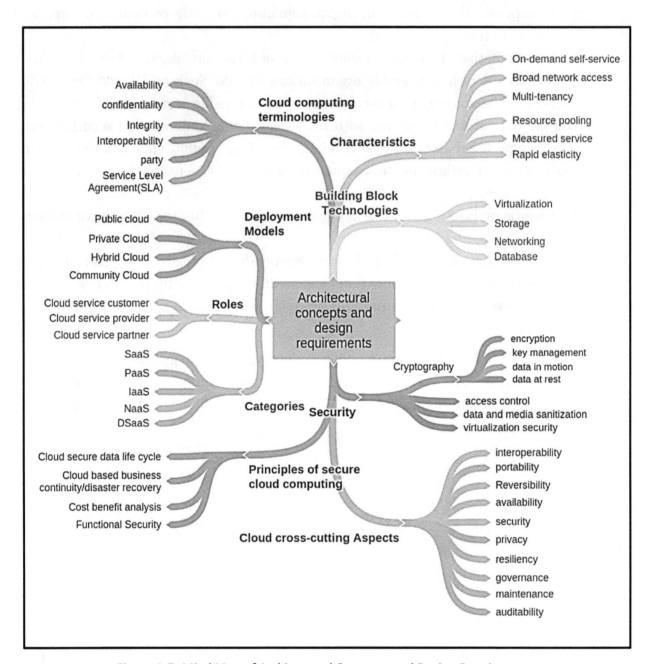

Figure 1-7: Mind Map of Architectural Concepts and Design Requirements

Practice Questions

1. What is Cloud computing? (Choose the best answers)
   a) It is a new operational model and set of technologies for managing shared pools of computing resources.
   b) It is the practice of using a network of remote servers hosted on the internet to store, manage and process data rather than using a local server or personal computer.
   c) It is the on-demand delivery of computing resources through a Cloud services platform with pay-as-you-go pricing.
   d) None of the above

2. What are the advantages of Cloud computing?
   a) Increase speed and agility
   b) Go global in minutes
   c) Stop spending money on running and maintaining data centers
   d) Benefit from massive economies of scale
   e) All of the above

3. Which of the following statement that ensuring that information is not subject to unauthorized modification?
   a) Availability
   b) Integrity
   c) Confidentiality
   d) None of the above

4. Which role in cloud environment offers cloud-based platform, application, infrastructure, or storage services?
   a) Cloud Service Partner
   b) Cloud Service Provider
   c) Cloud Service Customer
   d) Cloud Service Provider and Cloud Service Partner

5. Which of the following are key cloud computing characteristics?
   a) Broad network access
   b) Multi-tenancy
   c) On-demand self service
   d) None of the above

6. Which of the following statement is true that resources are accessible over the network and available through standard devices including laptops and mobile devices?
   a) On-demand self service
   b) Broad network access
   c) Resource pooling
   d) Multi-tenancy

7. What is on-demand self-service?
   a) Accessible over the network and available when required.
   b) Manually scaling up or down as per requirement.
   c) Auto-scaling of resources.
   d) None of the above

8. What is Virtualization?
   a) Virtual versioning of servers, storages or an operating system.
   b) Resources pooling to serve various end-users with various physical and virtual resources.
   c) A technology providing broad network accessibility.
   d) None of the above.

9. What are the advantages of virtualization technology?
   a) Isolation
   b) Resource sharing
   c) Dynamical resources
   d) All of the above

10. Which of the following are cloud service models?
    a) SaaS
    b) PaaS
    c) Iaas
    d) None of the above

11. Which of the following statement introduces another path to deploy, operate, and manage distributed enterprise networks through cloud?
    a) Storage
    b) Database
    c) NaaS

d) Virtualization

12. What are the advantages of cloud database?
    a) No hardware provisioning
    b) Cost effective estimated 20% to 75% lower cost
    c) No software licensing
    d) All of the above

13. What is cloud database?
    a) Primary backup of an organization stored on cloud
    b) Secondary backup of an organization stored on cloud
    c) Cloud based database service for customers
    d) None of the above

14. What is the acronym of DSaaS?
    a) Data Storage as a Service
    b) Database Software as a Service
    c) Data Security as a Service

15. A category of cloud computing services that provides a platform allowing customers to develop, run, and manage applications without the complexity of building and maintaining the infrastructure?
    a) SaaS
    b) PaaS
    c) IaaS

16. What is DSaaS?
    a) Cloud based data security service encrypting the data before storing it on cloud.
    b) Data Storage service for cloud customers with flexible, pay-as-you-go pricing and scalability
    c) Cloud based data sharing service.
    d) None of the above.

17. What are the advantages of Cloud encryption?
    a) Encrypted data is only readable for authorized parties with access to the decryption keys. Encrypting data guarantees that if that data falls into the wrong hand, it is useless as long as its keys stay secure.

b) Cloud encryption is critical for industries that need to meet regulatory compliance requirements
c) Both of them
d) None of the above

18. Which of the following data is effectively moving from one location to another such as across the internet or through a private network?
a) Data at rest
b) Data in motion
c) Both of them
d) None of the above

19. Which of the following is a type of Sanitization?
a) Purging
b) Clearing
c) Disposal
d) All of the above

Chapter 02: Cloud Data Security

Data security is the main component of cloud security. Cloud Service Providers (CSP) will often share the responsibility for security with the customer. Roles such as the Chief Information Security Officer (CISO), Chief Security Officer (CSO), Chief Technology Officer (CTO), Enterprise Security Architect, and Network Administrator may all play a part in providing elements of a security solution for the enterprise.

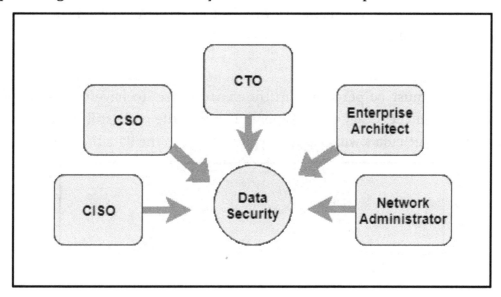

Figure 2-1: Cloud Data Security

The goal of the cloud data security is to provide a knowledge of the types of controls necessary to administer several levels of availability, confidentiality, and integrity about securing data in cloud.

The most significant part of any system or application is the data contained within it; the data holds the most value for any organization or company. While several principles of protection and data security are the same within a cloud environment as in a traditional data center, there are some challenges and differences unique to the cloud environment.

Cloud Data Life Cycle (CSA Guidance)

The Data Security Life Cycle, as introduced in the Cloud Security Alliance (CSA) guidance, enables the organization to map the different phases in the data life cycle against the required controls that are important to each phase.

The life cycle contains the following steps:

- Map the different life cycle phases.
- Integrate the access types and different data locations.
- Map into actors, controls, and functions.

The data life cycle guidance provides a framework to map significant use cases for data access while assisting in the development of proper controls within each life cycle stage.

The life cycle model serves as a reference and framework to provide a standardized approach for data life cycle and data security. Not all implementations or situations will align fully or comprehensively.

Phases

Data in the cloud must be perceived, in the general case, to have the same needs and properties as data in the legacy environment. The data life cycle still has a purpose; only the implemented particulars will change. Typical stages in the data life cycle are shown:

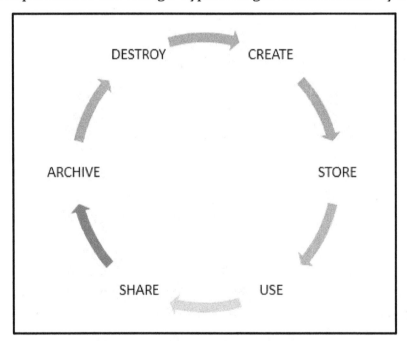

Figure 2-2: Cloud Data Life Cycle

Create

Cloud customers generate, alter or modify the information on Cloud. Depending on the use phase, the data may be created locally or internally. Externally, creation can be performed on remote workstations, and then uploaded onto the cloud. Creation phase is more important because it is an appropriate time to classify the sensitivity of the created

information and its value to an organization. This classification is an important factor to apply proper security controls.

Data Created Remotely

Data created by the user must be encrypted before uploading to the cloud. We need to protect against apparent vulnerabilities, including man-in-the-middle attacks and insider threat at the cloud data center. The cryptosystem used for this purpose should have a high work factor and listed in the **FIPS 140-2** approved crypto solutions. We must implement good key management practices as well.

The connection used to upload the data should also be secure, preferably with an IPSec VPN solution.

> **Note:** "The Federal Information Processing Standard (FIPS) Publication 140-2, (FIPS PUB 140-2), is a U.S. government computer security standard used to approve cryptographic modules."

Data Created within the Cloud

Similarly, data created within the cloud through remote manipulation must be encrypted upon creation, to obviate unnecessary access or view by data center personnel.

Store

After the data is created, it must be stored in a way that is useable to the application or system. Data can be stored in several ways. Storage methods include data written to a database, remote object storage in a cloud and files on a file system. All storage of data should be complete by the data classification determined during the Create phase.

The store phase is the first place where the security control can be implemented to secure the data at rest, and the cloud security professional should make sure that all storage methods employ whatever technologies are necessary for its data classification level, including the auditing, encryption, access controls, monitoring and logging. The use of appropriate redundancy and backup methods also comes into play immediately in the store phase to protect the data on top of the security controls.

Use

In use phase, data is accessed, processed, viewed and being involved in some sort of activity other than modification and alteration. Being in process, the data is in its most vulnerable state because it is more exposed, decrypted, might be transported to unsecure location and increase the chance of leak or compromise. At this time, when the state of data is transiting from rest to motion, controls must be employed to secure the data such as Data Loss

Prevention (DLP) policy, Information Right Management (IRM), databases and file access monitoring to record and audit data access and prevent unauthorized access.

Using the information or data is only possible when it is in decrypted state. As we discussed in storage phase to encrypt the data while storing, exposing unencrypted state of data in use phase requires logging and auditing. Additionally, granting least privileges considering read-only mode ensures that no further modification or alteration is possible.

Share

In sharing phase, the data is available for use between users, partners and customers. It depends upon the nature of data if it is to be shared with all or among selected ones. It is a big challenge to make sure that proper protections are in place, once the data leaves the system and is shared. Unlike the Use phase, the data is being allowed to be accessed and used by contractors, partners, customers, and other associated groups, and once the data leaves the central system, it is no longer under the employed security control mechanisms. Technologies such as **DLP (Data Loss Prevention)** and numerous rights management packages can be utilized to detect either additional attempt or sharing to prevent modification. However, neither method is entirely secure.

Archive

In the archive phase, data moves to long-term storage, thus removing it from being active within a system. The archiving process can range from moving data to a lower storage tier that is slower and not as redundant but still accessible from the system, all the way up to removing it from the active system entirely and placing it on different media altogether. Additionally, the data can be recovered and read by the system again, but typically will involve more time, effort, or cost to do so. In many cases where the data is completely removed from the active system, it is also stored offsite for disaster recovery reasons— sometimes even being hundreds or thousands of miles away. More than one overlooked aspects of archiving data are the ability to recover and retrieve as well.

Destroy

Destroy phase is the phase in which the data is removed by the Cloud provider. This phase can be interpreted into different technical meanings according to data content, usage, and applications used. Data destruction can mean logically erasing pointers or permanently destroying data using digital or physical means. Consideration must be made according to regulation, the type of Cloud is used (SaaS vs. IaaS), and the classification of the data.

Relevant Data Security Technologies

Cloud Security Models (CSM)

Cloud Security Models are tools to help guide security decisions. It can consist of some of the following types:

Conceptual Models or Frameworks

It includes descriptions and visualizations used to explain principles and Cloud security concepts such as the Cloud Security Alliance (CSA) logical model.

Controls Models or Frameworks

It can categorize and detail specific cloud security controls or categories of controls, such as the CSA Cloud Controls Matrix (CCM).

Reference Architectures

It is a template used for implementing cloud security, typically generalized (e.g., an Infrastructure as a service (IaaS) security reference architecture). They can be very conceptual, intellectual, abstract, or quite detailed, down to specific functions and controls.

Design Patterns

It is a re-usable solution to specific problems. Insecurity, an example is IaaS log management. As with Reference Architectures, they can be inherently specific or abstract, common implementation patterns on specific Cloud platforms.

Recommended CSA Security Models

CSA Enterprise Architecture

BUSINESS OPERATION SUPPORT SERVICES (BOSS)	INFORMATION TECHNOLOGY OPERATION & SUPPORT (ITOS)	PRESENTATION SERVICES	SECURITY & RISK MANAGEMENT
		APPLICATION SERVICES	
		INFORMATION SERVICES	
		INFRASTRUCTURE SERVICES	
(SABSA)	(ITIL)	(TOGAF)	(Jericho)

Table 2-1: CSA Enterprise Architecture

CSA Cloud Controls Matrix (CCM)

- Provides a fundamental security principle to guide Cloud vendors and to assist prospective cloud customers in assessing the entire security risk of a cloud provider.
- The CSA CCM are aligned to the Cloud Security Alliance guidance in 13 domains.
- Customized relationship to important industry security standards, guidelines, and controls frameworks such as the ISACA COBIT, ISO 27001/27002, PCI, NIST, Jericho Forum and NERC CIP
- CCM provides organizations with the needed structure, in details and clarity and relatied information security tailored into the Cloud industry.
- Provides operational risk management and standardized security, and seeks to normalize security expectations, Cloud taxonomy, and terminology.
- It has the following versions:
    - Cloud Control Matrix v3.0.1
    - Cloud Control Matrix v3
    - Cloud Control Matrix v1.4
    - Cloud Control Matrix v1.3
    - Cloud Control Matrix v1.2
    - Cloud Control Matrix v1.1
    - Cloud Control Matrix v1.0

NIST SP 500-299

NIST SP 500-299 is a Cloud Computing Security Reference Architecture. A framework that identifies a fundamental security component that can be implemented in the Cloud ecosystem.

ISO/IEC 27017

This standard gives guideline for information security controls applicable to the provision and use of Cloud services by providing additional implementation guidance for relevant controls specified in **ISO/IEC 27002**.Also, provides additional control with implementation guidance that relates explicitly to Cloud services.

This Recommendation and International Standard provides controls and implementation guidance for both Cloud service providers and Cloud service customers.

Cloud Data Storage Architectures

NIST recommends three service models, which define the different foundational categories of Cloud services:

- IaaS (Infrastructure as a Service)

- PaaS (Platform as a Service)
- SaaS (Software as a Service)

Infrastructure as a Service (IaaS)

IaaS provides access to a resource pool of basic computing infrastructures, such as computer, network, or storage. IaaS has the following storage options:

- **Content Delivery Network (CDN):** It is also known as a content distribution network. A content is stored in object storage, which is distributed to various geographically distributed nodes to increase Internet consumption speeds.
- **Object Storage:** Object storage is referred to as file storage. Instead of a virtual hard drive, object storage is similar to a file share accessed through a web interface or Application Programming Interface (API).
- **Raw Storage:** This type of storage includes the physical media where the data is stored. It can be mapped for direct access in specific private cloud configurations.
- **Volume storage:** This type of storage includes volumes attached to IaaS instances, usually as a virtual hard drive. Volumes usually use data dispersion to support resiliency and security.

Platform as a Service (PaaS)

PaaS provides and relies on an extensive range of storage options, including:

PaaS may provide:

- **Application Storage**: This includes storage options built into a PaaS application platform and consumable through APIs that does not fall into other storage categories.
- **Big Data as a Service**: This application is offered as a cloud platform. Data is stored in object storage or another distributed file system. Data needs to be close to the processing environment and can be moved temporally if needed for processing.
- **Database as a Service(DBaaS)**: A multi-tenant database architecture that is directly consumable as a service. Users consume the database through direct SQL calls or APIs, depending on the offering. Each customer's data is separated and isolated from other tenants. Databases may be relational, flat, or any other common structure

PaaS may consume:

- **Databases:** Content and information may be directly stored in the database (as text or binary objects), or as files referenced by the database. The database itself may be a collection of IaaS instances sharing common back-end storage.

- **Object/File Storage**: Files or other data are stored in object storage, but only accessed via the PaaS API.
- **Volume Storage**: Data may be stored in IaaS volumes attached to instances dedicated to providing the PaaS service.

Software as a Service (SaaS)

As with PaaS, SaaS uses an extensive range of storage and consumption models. SaaS storage is accessed through a web-based user interface or server/client application. If the storage is accessible through API, then it is considered as a PaaS. Numerous SaaS providers also offer PaaS APIs. The two most common storage types are:

- **Information Storage and Management**: Data is arrived into the system through the web interface and stored within the SaaS application (with a back-end database application).
- **Content and File Storage**: A File-based content is stored in the SaaS application such as documents, reports, image files, and made accessible through a web based user interface.

Examples of IaaS, PaaS, SaaS

IaaS	DigitalOcean, Linode, Rackspace, Amazon Web Services (AWS), Cisco Metapod, Microsoft Azure, Google Compute Engine (GCE)
PaaS	AWS Elastic Beanstalk, Windows Azure, Heroku, Force.com, Google App Engine, Apache Stratos, OpenShift
SaaS	Google Apps, Dropbox, Salesforce, Cisco WebEx, Concur, GoToMeeting

Table 2-2: Examples of IaaS, PaaS, SaaS

Storage Types (e.g., long-term, ephemeral, raw-disk)

Long-term Storage

Few vendors provide a Cloud storage service tailored to the needs of data archiving. These include features such as data life cycle management, guaranteed immutability, and search.

For Example:

HP Autonomy Digital Safe Archiving Service

This service uses an on-premises appliance, which connects to customers' data stores via API and allows the user to search.

Digital Safe offers read-only Write Once Read Many (WORM), e-discovery, legal hold, and all the features associated with enterprise archiving. Its appliance carries out data deduplication before transmission to the data repository.

Ephemeral Storage

Ephemeral storage is significant for IaaS instances and exists only if its instance is up. It is usually used for swap files and other temporary storage needs. It is terminated with its instance.

Raw-Disk

Raw Device Mapping (RDM) is a method of disk virtualization in VMware to enable a storage **Logical Unit Number (LUN),** is to be directly connected to a virtual machine (VM) from the **Storage Area Network (SAN).** In a Microsoft's Hyper-V platform, this is accomplished using pass-through disks.

Swap-File: A file on a hard disk that is used to provide space for programs which have been transferred from the processor's memory.

Data Deduplication: It is a technique for eliminating duplicate copies of repeating data.

Threats to Storage Types (e.g., ISO/IEC 27040)

There are many threats to storage types defined by the ISO/IEC 27040.

- **Unauthorized Usage:** In the cloud environment, data storage can be implemented into unauthorized usages, such as by account hijacking or uploading illegal content. The multi-tenancy of the cloud storage makes tracking unauthorized usage more challenging.
- **Unauthorized Access:** This can happen due to hijacking, non-regulated permissions in a multi-tenant's environment, or an internal cloud provider employee.
- **Liability due to Regulatory Non-Compliance:** Certain controls such as encryption might be required for specific regulations, some cloud services enable all relevant data controls.
- **Distributed Denial of Service (DDoS) and Denial of Service (DoS) attacks on storage:** Availability is a definite concern for cloud storage. Without data, no instances can be launched.
- **Corruption or Modification and Destruction of Data:** A wide variety of sources can cause this: human errors, hardware or software failure, events such as fire or flood, or intentional hacks. It can also affect a particular portion of the storage or the entire array.

- **Data leakage or Data breaches:** Customers always have to be aware that cloud data is exposed to data breaches. Maybe external or coming from a cloud provider employee with storage access. Data tends to be replicated and moved into cloud, which increases the likelihood of a leak.
- **Theft/Accident Loss of Media:** This threat applies to portable storage, but as cloud datacenters grow and storage devices are getting smaller, there are increasingly more vectors for them to experience theft or similar threats as well.
- **Malware Attack:** The objective of almost every malware is eventually reaching the data storage.
- **Improper Treatment:** End of use is more challenging and complex in cloud computing since most often, we cannot enforce physical destruction of media. However, the dynamic nature of data, where data is kept in different storages with multiple-tenants, mitigates the risk where digital remnants are located.

Technologies Available to Address Threats

A significant approach and concept employed in a cloud environment to protect data are called Data Loss Prevention (DLP) and also known as data leakage prevention.

Data Loss Prevention:

DLP is a set of controls and practices used to make sure that data is only accessible and exposed to those systems and users authorized to have it. The objective of a DLP strategy for an organization is to manage and minimize risk, maintain compliance with regulatory requirements, and show due diligence on the part of the application and data owner. However, it is vital for any organization to take a **holistic** view of DLP and not focus on individual systems or hosting environments. The DLP strategy must involve their entire enterprise, particularly with hybrid cloud environments, or those where there is a mixture of traditional and cloud data center installations.

DLP Components

DLP consists of three components:

- **Discovery and Classification:** This is the first component of DLP, also a recurring process, and the majority of cloud-based DLP technologies are predominantly focused on this component. The discovery process usually maps data in cloud storage services and databases. It enables classification based on data categories such as classified data, credit card data, and public data.
- **Monitoring:** Data usage monitoring forms the key function of DLP. Effective DLP strategies monitor the usage of data across locations and platforms while enabling administrators to define more than one usage policies. The ability to monitor data

can be executed on gateways, servers, and storage as well as workstations and endpoint devices. Recently, the increased adoption of external services to assist with DLP "as a service" has increased, along with many cloud-based DLP solutions. The monitoring application must be able to cover most sharing options available for users (email application, portable media, and internet browsing) and alert them of policy violations.

- **Enforcement:** Many DLP tools provide the capability to interrogate data and compare its location, use, or transmission destination against a set of policies to prevent data loss. If a policy violation is detected, specified appropriate enforcement actions can automatically be performed. Enforcement option can include the ability to alert and log, block data transfer, or re-route them for additional validation, or to encrypt the data before leaving the organizational boundaries.

DLP Architecture

DLP tool implementations typically conform to the following topologies:

- **Data in Motion (DIM):** This referred to a gateway or network-based DLP. In this type of topology, the monitoring engine is deployed near the organizational gateway to monitor outgoing protocols such as FTP, HTTP/HTTPS, and SMTP. The topology can be a combination of proxy-based, bridge, network tapping, or SMTP relays. To scan encrypted HTTPS traffic, proper mechanisms to enable SSL interception/broker is required to be integrated into the system architecture.
- **Data at Rest (DAR):** This referred to as storage-based data. In this type of topology, the DLP engine is installed where the data is at rest, typically more than one storage sub-systems, also file and application servers. This topology is very useful for data discovery and for tracking usage but may require integration with network or endpoint based DLP for policy enforcement.
- **Data in Use (DIU):** This referred to as a client or endpoint-based data. The DLP application is installed on the user's workstations and endpoint devices. This topology offer insight into how the data is used by users, with the ability to add the protection that the network DLP may not be capable of providing. The challenge with client-based DLP is the time, complexity, and resources to implement across all the endpoint devices, often across multiple locations and a significant number of users.

Cloud-Based DLP Considerations

Some important considerations for cloud-based DLP include:

- **Data in the Cloud tend to move and replicate**: Whether it is between locations, backups, data centers, or backward and forward into the organizations, the movement and replication can present a challenge to any DLP deployment.
- **Administrative access for enterprise data in the cloud could be tricky:** Ensure that you could understand how to perform discovery and classification within cloud-based storage.
- **DLP technology can affect overall performance:** Gateway or network DLP, which scans all traffic for pre-defined content, could affect network performance. Customer-based DLPs scan all workstation access to data; this should have a performance impact on the workstation's operation. The overall impact should be considered during testing.

> **Note**: A holistic approach means thinking about the big picture. Whether you are doing holistic website design, holistic parenting, or holistic medicine, know that each change you make to one part affects the entire approach.

Data Security Strategies

Many technologies and tool sets are commonly used as data security strategies:

Encryption

As we know, encryption is a process of encoding a message or an information in a way that it can only be decrypted by authorized parties. Plain text data is readable information by users or applications whereas an encrypted data also known as Cipher text is a random and meaningless piece of code. Decryption key is required to decrypt the data back to plain text. Encryption across the enterprise architecture could reduce the risks associated with unauthorized data access and exposure but may raise performance issues as every piece of information is encrypted at sender's end and decrypted at destination end.

It is a responsibility to a CSP to implement encryption within the enterprise in such a way that it provides the most security benefits, safeguarding the mission-critical data while minimizing system performance issues as a result of the encryption.

Encryption Implementation

Encryption can be implemented within different phases of the data life cycle:

- **Data in Motion (DIM):** Encrypting data in motion are mature and include IPSEC or VPN, TLS/SSL, and other same types of protocols.

- **Data at Rest (DAR):** When the data is archived or stored, different encryption techniques must be used. The encryption mechanism itself may vary in the manner it is deployed, dependent on the timeframe or indeed the period for which the data will be stored, such as extended retention versus short-term storage, data located in a database versus a file system, and so on.

- **Data in Use (DIU):** Data that is being shared, processed, or viewed. This stage of data life cycle is less mature than other data encryption techniques and typically focused on IRM/DRM solutions.

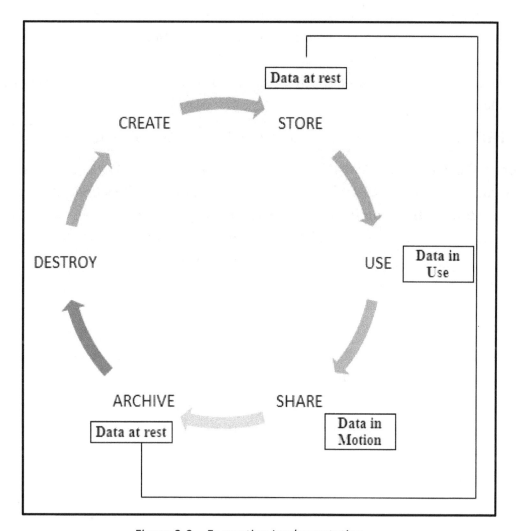

Figure 2-3 – Encryption Implementation

Sample Use Cases for Encryption

There are following some use cases for encryption:

- Inbound and Outbound traffic to cloud- for archiving, sharing, or processing- we use encryption for data in motion methods such as VPN or SSL/TLS to avoid data leakage or information exposure while in motion.
- You are protecting data at rest such as application components, archiving, backup applications, database information, and file storage.
- Objects or files should be protected when stored, shared, or used in Cloud.
- While complying with regulations such as **HIPAA** and **PCI-DSS**, which in turn requires proper protection of data traversing of untrusted networks, along with the protection of specific data types.
- Protection from third-party access through a lawful interception.
- Increased mechanisms or creating enhanced for logical separation between different clients' data in the Cloud.
- Logical destruction of data when physical destruction is not technically possible or feasible.

> **Note: HIPAA** is a US' Health Insurance Portability and Accountability Act.

Payment Card Industry Data Security Standard (PCI DSS): Payment Card Industry Data Security Standard (PCI-DSS) is a global information security standard created by *"PCI Security Standards Council,"* It was created for organizations to develop, enhance and assess security standards required for handling cardholder information and payment account security. PCI Security Standards Council develops security standards for payment card industry and provides tools required for enforcement of these standards like training, certification, assessment, and scanning.

Founding members of this council are:

- American Express
- Discover Financial Services
- JCB International
- MasterCard
- Visa Inc.

PCI data security standard deals basically with cardholder data security for debit, credit, prepaid, e-purse, POS, and ATM cards. A high-level overview of PCI-DSS provide:

- Secure Network
- Strong Access Control
- Cardholder data security
- Regular Monitoring and Evaluation of Network
- Maintaining Vulnerability program
- Information security policy

Cloud Encryption Challenges

There are many factors influencing encryption, considerations and associated implementation in the enterprise. Using encryption should always be directly concern to the business considerations, regulatory requirements, and additional constraints that the organization may have to address. There are many different techniques will be used based on the location of data at rest, in transit, or use-while in the Cloud.

Different options could be applied when dealing with specific threats, such as protecting **Personally Identifiable Information (PII)** or legally regulated information, or when defending against unauthorized access and viewing from systems and platform administrators.

Encryption Challenges

The following challenges are associated with encryption:

- The integrity of encryption is heavily dependent on the control and management of the relevant encryption keys, including how they are secured. If the cloud provider holds the keys, then not all data threats are mitigated against, as unauthorized actors may gain access to the data through the acquisition of the keys via a search warrant, legal ruling, or theft and misappropriation. Equally, if the customer is holding the encryption keys, this presents different challenges to make sure they are protected from unauthorized usage as well as compromise.

- Encryption can be challenging to implement effectively when a cloud provider is required to process the encrypted data. This is true even for simple tasks such as indexing, along with the gathering of metadata.

- Data in the cloud is highly portable. The data can be replicated, copied, and backed up extensively, making encryption and key management a challenge.

- Multi-tenant cloud environments and the shared use of physical hardware present challenges for the protection of keys in volatile memory such as RAM caches.

- Secure hardware for encrypting keys may not exist in cloud environments, and software based key storage is often more vulnerable.

- Storage-level encryption is typically less complicated and can be most easily exploited (given sufficient time and resources). The higher you go up towards the application level, the more it becomes to deploy and implement encryption. However, encryption implemented at the application level will technically be more effective in protecting the confidentiality of the relevant resources or assets.

- Encryption can negatively affect performance, especially high-performance data processing mechanisms such as data warehouses and data cubes.

- The nature of cloud environment typically requires us to manage more keys like API keys, access keys, encryption keys, and shared keys.

Note: Multi-tenancy is an architecture in which a single instance of a software application serves multiple customers. Each customer is called a tenant.

Data Cube: "It is a multi-dimensional array of values."

Object Storage Encryption

Most of the object storage services offer server-side storage-level encryption. This kind of encryption offers limited effectiveness, with the recommendation for external encryption mechanisms to be encrypting the data before its entrance within the cloud environments. Potential external mechanisms include:

- **Application-level Encryption**: In this mechanism, the encryption engine resides in the application that is using the object storage. It could be integrated into the application component or by a proxy that is responsible for encrypting the data before moving to the cloud. The proxy can be implemented on the client gateway or as a service residing at the external provider.
- **File-level Encryption**: Such as Digital Rights Management (DRM) or Information Rights Management (IRM) solutions, both of which can be very efficient when used in conjunction with sharing services and file hosting that typically rely on object storage. The encryption engine is generally implemented at the client side and will preserve the format of the original file.

Database Encryption

There are following database encryption:

- **Application-level Encryption**: The encryption engine resides at the application that is using the database.
- **File-level Encryption**: Database servers reside on volume storage. For this deployment, we are encrypting the folder or volume of the database, with the encryption engine and keys residing on the instances attached to the volume. External file system encryption secures from lost backup, media theft, and external attack but not secure against attacks with access to the application layer, the instances OS, or the database itself.
- **Transparent Encryption**: Various Database Management Systems (DBMS) contain the ability to encrypt the entire database or specific portions, such as tables. The encryption engine resides within the DB, and it is transparent to the application. Keys typically reside within the instance, although processing and managing them

might be offload to an external Key Management System (KMS). This encryption can provide sufficient protection from backup system intrusions, media theft, and specific database and application level attacks.

Key Management

Key management is the most challenging components of any encryption implementation. Although new standards such as Key Management Interoperability Protocol (KMIP) are protection keys, emerging and appropriate management of keys are still the most difficult tasks you will need to engage in when planning cloud data security.

Common challenges with key management are:

- **Access to the keys:** Best practices coupled with regulatory requirements might set particular criteria for key access, along with restricting or not permitting access to keys by cloud Service Provider employees or personnel.
- **Replication and Backup:** The nature of cloud results in data replication and backups across some different formats. This can impact the ability for long and short-term key management to be managed and maintained adequately.
- **Key Storage:** Secure storage for the keys is crucial to protect the data. In traditional environments, keys were able to be stored in secure dedicated hardware. This might not always be possible in cloud environments.

Key Management Considerations

Considerations when planning key management include:

- Lack of access to the encryption keys will result in a lack of access to the data.
- Random number generation must conduct as a trusted process.
- Throughout the life cycle, cryptographic keys could never be transmitted in the clean environment and always remain in a "trusted" environment.
- Where possible, key management functions must be conducted separately from the cloud provider to enforce separation of duties and force collusion to occur if unauthorized data access is attempted.
- When considering key management or key escrow "as a service," carefully plan to take into account all relevant regulations, laws, and jurisdictional requirements.

> **Note:** Key escrow is an arrangement in which the keys required to decrypt encrypted data are held in escrow so that, under desirable conditions, an authorized third party might gain access to those keys.

Key Storage in the Cloud

It is generally implemented using more than one of the following approaches:

- **Externally Managed**: In this approach, keys are maintained separately from the data and encryption engine. They can be on a similar cloud platform, internally within the organization, or on a different cloud platform. The actual storage can be a separate instance (hardened especially for this specific task) or on a Hardware Security Module (HSM). When implementing external key storage, consider how the key management system is integrated with the encryption engine and how the entire life cycle of key creation through to retirement is managed.

- **Internally Managed:** In this approach, the keys are stored on the application component or virtual machine that is also acting as the encryption engine. This type of key management is typically used in storage-level encryption, internal database encryption, or backup application encryption. This approach can be helpful for mitigating against the risks associated with lost media.

- **Managed by a Third Party**: This is when a trusted third party provides key escrow services. Key management providers use specifically developed secure infrastructure and integration services for key management. You should evaluate any third-party key storage services provider that might be contracted by the organization to make sure that the risks of allowing a third party to hold encryption keys are well understood and documented.

Key Management in Software Environments

Cloud Service Providers (CSP) secure keys using software-based solutions to avoid the additional cost and overhead of hardware-based security models.

Software-based key management solutions do not meet the physical security requirements specified in the National Institute of Standards and Technology (NIST) Federal Information Processing Standards Publication FIPS 140-2 or 140-3 specifications." The ability for software to provide evidence of tampering is unlikely. The lack of FIPS certification for encryption might be an issue for U.S. Federal Government agencies and other organizations.

Masking

Data masking is the process of replacing, hiding, or omitting sensitive information from a specific dataset. Data masking is also known as Data Obfuscation.

Data masking is usually used to secure specific datasets such as PII or commercially sensitive data or to comply with specific regulations such as HIPAA or PCI-DSS.

Data masking is also widely used for test platforms where suitable test data is not available. Both techniques are usually applied when migrating, developing testing or protecting production environments from threats such as data exposure.

The primary methods of masking data are:

Static Masking	Dynamic masking
A new copy of the data is created with the masked values. It is usually effective when creating clean non-production environments.	It referred to as "on-the-fly" masking, adds a layer of masking between the application and the database. The masking layer is responsible for masking the information in the database on the fly" when the presentation layer accesses it. This type of masking is efficient when protecting production environments. It can hide the full credit card number from customer service representatives, but the data remains available for processing.

Table 2-3: Method of Masking Data

Conventional approaches to data masking include:

- **Algorithmic Substitution**: The value is replaced with an algorithm generated value (this usually permits for two-way substitution).
- **Deletion**: Uses a null value or deletes the data.
- **Masking**: Uses particular characters to hide certain parts of the data. Commonly applies to credit cards data formats: XXXX XXXX XX65 5432
- **Random Substitution:** The value is replaced with a random value.
- **Shuffle**: Shuffles different values from the dataset. Commonly from a similar column.

Tokenization

It was initially introduced by the Payment Card Industry (PCI) as a means to secure credit card information, but tokenization is now used to protect all types of sensitive data.

Tokenization is the method replacing sensitive data with a unique identification code, referred to as a token. The token is a collection of random values with the form and shape of the original data placeholder and mapped back to the original data by the tokenization solution or application.

Tokenization is not encryption and presents different challenges and benefits. Encryption is using a key to obfuscate data, while tokenization removes the data entirely from the database, replacing it with a mechanism to identify and access the resources.

Tokenization is used to protect the sensitive data in a protected, secure, or regulated environment

Tokenization can be implemented internally where there is a need for safe, sensitive data internally or externally using a tokenization service.

Tokenization can assist with:

- Complying with laws or regulations.
- Fewer risks of storing sensitive data and reducing attack vectors on that data
- Reducing the cost of compliance

Emerging Technologies

It often seems that the cloud and the technologies that make it possible are evolving in multiple directions, all at once. It is hard to keep up with all of the new and innovative technology solutions that are being implemented across the cloud landscape.

Bit Splitting

Bit splitting typically involves splitting up and storing encrypted information across different cloud storage services. Depending on how the bit-splitting system is implemented, some or all the dataset are required to be available in order to be decrypted and read.

If a **RAID 5** solution is used as part of the implementation, then the system can provide data redundancy as well as confidentiality protection, while ensuring that a single cloud provider does not have access to the entire dataset.

Benefits:

- Bit splitting between different jurisdictions/ geographies may make it harder to gain access to the complete dataset through a **subpoena** and other legal processes.
- Improvements to data security relating to confidentiality.
- It can be scalable, might be incorporated into secured cloud storage API technologies, and might reduce the risk of vendor lock-in.

Challenges

- The whole dataset may not be required to be used within the same geographies that the cloud provider stores and processes the bits within, leading to the need to ensure data security on the wire as part of the security architecture for the system.
- Processing and re-processing the information to encrypt and decrypt the bits is a CPU-intensive activity.

- Storage requirements and costs are usually higher with a bit splitting system. Depending on the implementation, bit splitting can generate availability risks, since all parts of the data may need to be available when decrypting the information.

Bit splitting can use different methods, a large amount of which is based on "secret sharing" cryptographic algorithms:

- **Secret Sharing Made Short (SSMS)**: Uses a three-phase process-encryption of information; use of Information Dispersal Algorithm (IDA), which is designed to split the data using care coding into fragments efficiently; then splitting the encryption key itself using the secret sharing algorithm.
- **All-or-Nothing Transform with Reed-Solomon (AONT-RS)**: Integrates the AONT and remove or delete the coding. This method initially encrypts and transforms the information and the encryption key into blocks in such a way that the information cannot be recovered without using all the blocks, and then it uses the IDA to splitting the blocks into many shares that are distributed to different cloud storage services (As similar as in SSMS).

Redundant Array of Independent Disks (RAID): RAID storage uses many disks to provide fault tolerance, to improve overall performance, and to increase storage capacity in a system. It has many standard levels, and **Level 5** is block interleaved distributed parity.

Subpoena: It is a legally binding order for the delivery of evidence.

Homomorphic Encryption

This type of encryption enables processing of encrypted data without the need to decrypt the data. It allows the cloud customer to upload data to a Cloud Service Provider (CSP) for processing without the requirement to decipher the data first.

The advantages of homomorphic encryption are sizeable, with Cloud-based services benefitting most, as it enables organizations to protect data in the Cloud for processing while eliminating most confidentiality concerns.

Note that homomorphic encryption is a developing area and does not represent a mature offering for most use cases. Many of the current implementations represent "partial" implementations of homomorphic encryption; however, these are typically limited to particular use cases involving small amounts or volumes of data.

Data Discovery and Classification Technologies

Data Discovery

It is a departure from traditional business intelligence. In that it emphasizes interactive, visual analytics rather than static reporting. The goal of data discovery is to work with and enable people to use their intuition to find meaningful and essential information in data. This process usually consists of asking questions of the data in some way, seeing results visually, and refining the questions.

Contrast this with the traditional approach, which is for information consumers to ask questions, which causes reports to be developed, which are then fed to the consumer, which may generate more questions, which will generate more reports.

Data Discovery Methodologies

Developing companies consider data to be strategic assets and understand its importance to drive innovation, differentiation, and growth. However, leveraging data and transforming it into the real business value requires a holistic approach to business intelligence and analytics. This means going beyond the scope of various data visualization tools, and it's dramatically different from the Business Intelligence (BI) of recent years.

These trends are driving the continuing evolution of the data discovery in the organizations and the cloud:

Agile Analytics and Agile Business Intelligence:

Business intelligence teams and data scientists are adopting more agile, iterative methods of turning data into business value. They perform data discovery processes more often and in ways that are more diverse.

For example:

When profiling new datasets for integration, seeking answers to new questions emerging present week based on previous week's new analysis, or finding alerts about emerging trends that can be warranted new analysis work streams.

Big Data:

This type of projects, data discovery, is more critical and challenging. Not only the volume of data should be efficiently processed for discovery is more significant, but the diversity of source and formats presents challenges that make various traditional methods of data discovery is fail. In a big data cases, initiatives also involve rapid profiling of high-velocity big data that makes data profiling are complicated and less feasible using existing tool sets.

<u>Real-time Analytics:</u>

The ongoing shift towards real-time analytics has created a new class of use cases for data discovery. These use cases are valuable but need data discovery tools that are faster, more adaptive, and more automated.

Different Data Discovery Techniques:

Data discovery tools differ by technique and data matching abilities. Assume you wanted to find credit card numbers. Data discovery tools for databases use a couple of methods to find and then identify information. Most use unique login credentials to scan internal database structures, itemize tables and columns, and then analyze what was found. There are three basic analysis methods are employed:

Content analysis	Metadata	Labels
In this form of analysis, we examine the data itself by employing pattern matching, hashing, statistical, lexical, or other forms of probability analysis	This is data that describes itself, and all relational databases store metadata that describes tables and column attributes.	When data elements are joined with a tag that describes the data, this can be completed at the same time the data is created, or tags can be added over time to provide additional references and information to describe the data. In multiple ways, it is just similar to metadata but slightly less formal.
Credit Card Example: When we search a number that looks like a credit card number, a standard method is to perform a **LUHN** check on the number itself. This is a simple numeric checksum used by credit card	**Credit Card Example:** We would examine column attributes to determine whether the name of the column or the size and data type, looks like a credit card number. If a column is a 16-digit number or the name is	**Example:** Some relational database platforms provide mechanisms to create data labels. However, this method is more usually used with flat files, becoming increasingly useful as more firms move

companies to verify if a number of a credit card is valid. If the number, we discover passes the LUHN check, then it is a very high possibility that we have discovered a credit card number. Content analysis is a growing trend and one that is being used successfully in data loss prevention (DLP) and web content analysis products.	something like "Credit Card" or "CC#," then we have a high possibility of a match. Moreover, the effectiveness of each product will vary depending on how well the analysis rules are implemented. This remains the most common analysis technique.	to **Indexed Sequential Access Method (ISAM)** or quasi-relational data storage, such as **Amazon's SimpleDB**, to handle fast-growing datasets. This form of discovery is same as to a **Google search**, with the higher number of same labels, the greater the possibility of a match. Effectiveness is dependent on the use of labels.

Table 2-4: Data Discovery Techniques

LUHN: The LUHN algorithm, also called as the modulus 10/mod 10 algorithms, is a simple checksum formula used to validate a type of identification numbers, such as IMEI numbers, credit card numbers, Canadian Social Insurance Numbers.

ISAM: It is a method for creating, maintaining, and manipulating indexes of key-fields extracted from random data file records to achieve fast recovery of required file records. IBM developed ISAM for mainframe computers.

Problems in Data Discovery:

There are following problems in data discovery:

Dashboards

In the dashboard, these are the following problems that may appear:

- Is the data accurate on the dashboard?
- Is the analytical method accurate?
- Most importantly, can important business decisions be based on this information?

Users modify data and fields with no audit trail, and there is no way to recognize who changed what. This disconnect can lead to uneven insight and flawed decisions, increase administration costs, and inevitably create numerous versions of the truth.

Security also poses issues with data discovery tools. IT staff usually have little or no control over these types of solutions, which means they cannot protect sensitive information. This

can result in unencrypted data that is to be cached locally and viewed by or shared with unauthorized users.

Hidden Costs

A typical data discovery technique is to put all of the data into server RAM to take advantage of the fundamental input/output rate improvements over the disk.

Poor Data Quality

Data visualization tools are only as good as the information that is inputted. If organizations want an enterprise-wide data governance policy, they might be relying on incomplete or inaccurate information to create their charts and dashboards.

Having a big enterprise data, governance policy will help to lower the risk of a data breach. This consists defining rules and processes related to dashboard creation, distribution, ownership, and usage; creating restrictions on who can access what data; and make sure that employee follows their organizations' data usage policies.

Data Discovery Challenges in the Cloud

There are many challenges with data discovery in the Cloud that are:

Accessing Data:

Not all the data stored in the Cloud can be accessed easily. Sometimes customers do not have the necessary administrative rights to access their data on demand. Long-term data can be visible to the customer but not accessible to download in acceptable formats to use offline.

The lack of data access might require specific configurations for the data discovery process, which in turn might result in additional time and expense for the organization. Data access requirements and capabilities can also change during the data life cycle. Archiving, DR, and backup sets tend to offer less control and flexibility for the end user. Also, metadata such as indexes and labels might not be accessible.

Identifying Data:

The ability to have data available on-demand, across almost any platform and access mechanism, is an incredible advancement concerning end-user productivity and collaboration. However, at the same time, the security implications of this level of access confound both the enterprise and the CSP, challenging them to find ways to secure the data that users are accessing in real time, from many locations, across many platforms.

Not knowing where data is, where it is going, and where it will be at any given moment with assurance presents significant security concerns for enterprise data and the

confidentiality, integrity, and availability that is required to be provided by the Cloud Security Professional.

<u>Maintenance and Preservation:</u>

Ensure that preservation requirements are documented and supported by the Cloud provider as part of the Service Level Agreement (SLA).

If the time required for preservation exceeds what has been documented in the provider SLA, the data might be lost. Long-term preservation of data is possible and can be managed through an SLA with a provider as well. However, the issues of data granularity, access, and visibility all could need to be considered when planning for data discovery against long-term stored datasets.

Classification

Data classification as a part of the Information Life Cycle Management (ILM) process can be defined as a tool for categorization of data to enable or help the organization in a very effective way.

Data classification is a process that is recommended for implementing data controls such as encryption and DLP. Data classification is also a requirement of specific regulations and standards, such as ISO 27001 and PCI-DSS.

Types of Data Classification

There are different reasons for implementing data classification and therefore many different parameters and categories for the classified data. Also, some of the generally used classification types are:

- Business constraints or contractual
- Context
- Data type (structure, format)
- Jurisdiction (of domiciled, origin) and other legal constraints
- The obligation for retention and preservation
- Ownership
- Trust levels and source of origin
- Criticality, sensitivity, and value (to the organization or the third party)

The classification categories should match the data controls to be used.

For example

When using encryption, data can be classified as "not to encrypt" or "to encrypt." For DLP, other types such as "limited sharing" and "internal use" that could be required to classify the data correctly.

Classification and labelling relationship—data labelling is commonly referred to as tagging the data with additional information such as creator, department, and location. One of the labelling options can be classified according to a specific criterion that is top secret, secret, and classified.

Therefore, classification is typically considered as the part of data labeling. Classification can be manual or automatic based on policy rules.

Challenges with the Cloud Data

There are some challenges in this area consists of:

- **Classification Controls**: This could be administrative (as guidelines for users who are creating the data), compensating, or preventive.
- **Classification Data Transformation**: This could be placed to ensure that the relevant metadata or property can survive data object format changes and cloud imports or exports.
- **Data Creation**: The CSP needs to make sure that proper security controls are in place so that whenever data is modified or created by anyone, they are forced to update or classify the data as part of the creation or modification process.
- **Metadata**: Classifications can be made based on the metadata that is attached to the file, such as location or owner. This metadata could be accessible to the classification process to make the proper decisions.
- **Reclassification Consideration**: Cloud applications should support a re-classification process based on the data life cycle. Sometimes the new classification of a data object could mean enabling new controls such as retention or encryption and disposal.

Jurisdictional Data Protections for Personally Identifiable Information (PII)

Data Privacy Acts

Privacy and Data Protection (P&DP) issues are often cited as a concern for cloud computing scenarios. The P&DP regulations affect not just those organization whose personal data is processed in the cloud but also those organizations who are using cloud computing to process others' data and indeed those providing cloud services used to process that data. The world wide economy is suffering an information explosion; there has been an enormous growth in the complexity and volume of global data services: personal data is now vital source, and its privacy and protection have become essential aspects to enabling the acceptance of cloud computing services.

The following ways in which different countries and regions around the world are addressing the varied legal issues they face.

Global P&DP Laws in the United States

There is no single federal law, privacy is recognized differently in individual states and specific circumstances.

- **COPPA**: Children's Online Privacy Protection Act 1998
- **ECPA and SCA:** Electronic Communication Privacy Act and Stored Communications Act, from 1986. It is older law in the US that means to limit wiretaps.
- **FERPA**: Family Educational Rights and Privacy, to protect student data
- **HIPAA**: Health Insurance Portability and Accountability Act — Dept Health & Human Services
- **GLBA**: Gramm-Leach-Bliley Act, a.k.a. Financial Modernization Act of 1999, run by Federal Deposit Insurance Corporation (FDIC).
- **SOX**: Sarbanes-Oxley — created in response to Enron corporate corruption, for publicly-traded companies
- **Safe Harbor Program**: Developed by Dept of Commerce and EU, now discontinued, replaced by EU-U.S. Privacy Shield.

Global P&DP Laws in the European Union (UN)

Data Protection Directive 95/46/EC: This act applies to paper records and electronics but does not apply to purely household or personal activities, or in operations related to state security or public safety.

GDPR: General Data Protection Regulation, it is updated 95/46/EU to include:

- Access requests
- Consent
- Role establishing of the data protection officer
- Home state regulation
- Increased sanctions
- Transfers abroad
- The right to be forgotten

Global P&DP Laws in APEC

Asia-Pacific Economic Cooperation: It is a privacy framework that makes sure the free flow of information and open conduct of business within the region while protecting privacy.

Difference between Applicable Law and Jurisdiction:

For P&DP, it is particularly important to distinguish between the concepts of:

Applicable law	Jurisdiction
This determines the legal regime applicable to a specific matter.	This typically determines the ability of a national court to decide a case or enforce a judgment or order.

Table 2-5: Applicable Law and Jurisdiction

Implementation of Data Discovery

The solutions provide an adequate foundation for useful application and governance for any of the P&DP fulfillments.

Customer's Perspective

The customer role of data controller has full responsibility for compliance with the P&DP laws obligations; therefore, the implementation of data discovery solutions together with data classification techniques provide him or her with a sound basis for operatively specifying to the service provider the requirements to be fulfilled and for performing effective periodic audit according to the applicable P&DP laws, also for demonstrating, to the competent privacy authorities, his due accountability according to the applicable P&DP laws.

Service Provider's Perspective:

The service providers, in the role of data processor, have to implement and can demonstrate they have implemented in a clear and objective way the rules and the security measures to be applied in the processing of private data on behalf of the controller; thus data discovery solutions jointly with data classification techniques provide an effective enabler factor for their ability to comply with the controller P&DP instructions.

Additionally, the service provider will particularly benefit from this approach:

- Its service provider responsibility to operatively support the controller when a data subject exercises his/her rights. Thus, it is required information about which data is processed or to implement actions on this data (e.g., correct or destroy the data).
- For its duty to detect, promptly report to the controller, and adequately manage the personal data breaches concerning the applicable P&DP obligations.
- When the service provider has to support the controller in any of the P&DP obligations concerning the application of rules or prohibitions of personal data transfer through many countries.

- When the service provider involves sub-service providers, in order to clearly trace and operatively transfer to clients. The P&DP requirements according to the process assigned by the service provider.

Classification of Discovered Sensitive Data

For compliance with the applicable **Privacy and Data Protection (P&DP)**, laws play an essential part in the adequate control of the elements that are the feeds of P&DP fulfillments. This means that not only the "nature" of the data could be traced with classification but its relationship to the **P&DP Act** in which the data itself could be processed as well.

The P&DP fulfillments, and especially the security measures required by these laws, can always be expressed at least regarding a set of primary entities:

The Purpose and Scope of Processing:

It represents the main impression that effects the entire set of typical P&DP fulfillments.

For example

Processing for accounting and administrative purposes requires fewer fulfillments when compared with the processing of traffic telephone or Internet data for the purpose of mobile payment services, since the cluster of data processed (personal data of the subscriber, his/her billing data, the kind of purchased objects) assumes a more critical value for all the stakeholders involved. The P&DP laws consequently require more obligations and a higher level of protection.

Categories of Personal Data to be Processed:

Data means here the type of data as identified for a P&DP law, and usually, it is entirely different from the "nature" of the data, that is, its intrinsic and objective value. In this sense, data categories include

- Personal data
- Sensitive data (health, political belief, religious belief, etc.)
- Biometric data
- Telephone or Internet data
- Categories of the processing to be performed

From the perspective of the P&DP laws, the processing means an operation or a set of combined operations that can be materially applied to data; therefore, in this sense processing can be one or more of the following operations:

- Collection
- Recording
- Organization
- Selection

- Retrieval
- Comparison
- Communication
- Dissemination
- Erasure

In the derivation of these, a secondary set of entities is relevant for P&DP fulfillments:

- Data location allowed.
- According to the applicable P&DP laws, there are prohibitions or constraints to be observed, and this could be accurately reflected in the classification of data to act as a driver in allowing or blocking the moving of data from one location to another one.

Categories of users allowed

Accessibility of data for a specific category of users is another essential feature for the P&DP laws.

For example

The role of the backup operator should not be able to read any data in the system, even though the operator role will need to be able to interact with all system data to back it up.

Data-retention constraints

The majority of the categories of data processed for specific scopes and purposes must be retained for a determined period (and then erased or anonymized) according to the applicable P&DP laws.

For example

Data-retention periods are to be respected for access logs concerning the accesses made by the role of system administrator, and there are data-retention periods to be respected for the details concerning the profiles defined from the "online behavior" of Internet users for marketing. Once the retention period has ended, the legal ground for retention of the data disappears, and therefore any additional processing or handling of the data becomes unlawful.

Security Measures to be Ensured

The type of security measures can widely vary depending on the purpose and data to be processed. Typically, they are expressed in terms of

- Accurate classification of the data regarding security measures will provide the basis for any approach of control based on data leakage prevention (DLP) and data-protection processes.
- Necessary security measures to make sure a minimum level of security regardless of the type of data/purpose/processing
- Specific measures according to the type of data/purpose/processing
- Measures identified regarding output from a risk analysis process, to be operated by the Controller or processor considering the risks of a specific context. It may be technical or operational, and it cannot be mitigated with the measures of the previous points.

Data Breach Constraints

Several P&DP laws around the world already provide for specific obligations regarding a data breach. These obligations essentially require to do the following:

- Notify the competent DPA within tighter time limits and also notify some specific cases set forth by law, the **data subjects**
- Follow a specific process of Incident Management, including activation of measures aimed at limiting the damages to the concerned data subjects
- Handle a secure archive concerning the occurred data breach

Therefore, data classification that can take into account the operational requirements coming from the data breach constraints becomes essential, especially in the Cloud services context.

> **Note:** A Data Subjects is any person whose personal data is being collected, held or processed.

Status

As a consequence of events such as a data breach, data might be left in a specific state that may require various necessary actions or a state where specific actions are prohibited. The precise identification of this status regarding data classification might be used to direct and oversee any further processing of the data according to the applicable laws.

Summary

It provides the primary input entity for data classification about P&DP.

Sets	Input Entities
Primary Set	<ul><li>P&DP law</li><li>Scope and purpose of the processing</li><li>Categories of the personal data to be processed</li></ul>

	<ul><li>Categories of the processing to be performed</li></ul>
Secondary Set	<ul><li>Data location allowed</li><li>Categories of users allowed</li><li>Data-retention constraints</li><li>Security measures to be ensured</li><li>Data breach constraints</li><li>Status</li></ul>

Table 2-6 - Main Input Entities for Data Classification for P&DP Purposes

Mapping and Definition of Controls

There are various requirements to be mapped out in privacy acts, a central role of the Cloud Security Professional is the mapping of those requirements to the actual security controls and processes in place with both the application and the Cloud environment under the responsibility of the Cloud provider. For large applications that could span various jurisdictions and privacy act, this will be of specific importance. The Cloud customer and Cloud provider will need to work together through proper contractual or SLA requirements to make sure compliance for both parties regarding the requirements for regulatory bodies or applicable privacy acts.

Application of Defined Controls for PII (in consideration of customer's Data Privacy Acts)

The efficient application of the defined controls for the protection of PII is generally affected by the cluster of providers or sub-providers involved in the operation of specific Cloud service; therefore, any attempt to provide guidelines for this can be made only at a general level.

Since the application of data-protection measures has the ultimate goal to fulfill the P&DP laws applicable to the controller, any constraints arising from specific arrangements of a Cloud service operation will be made clear by the service provider to avoid any consequences for unlawful personal data processing.

For example

About servers located across numerous countries, it could be challenging to make sure the proper application of measures such as encryption for sensitive data on all systems.

Additionally, the service providers might benefit from making explicit reference to standardized frameworks of security controls expressly defined for Cloud services.

Cloud Controls Matrix (CCM)

An essential and up-to-date security controls framework is addressed to the Cloud community and stakeholders. A fundamental richness of the CCM is its ability to provide mapping or cross relationships is widely accepted in industries' security standards, regulations, and controls frameworks such as the **ISO 27001/27002, ISACA's COBIT, and PCI-DSS.**

The CCM can be seen as an inventory of Cloud service security controls, arranged in the following separate security domains:

- Application and Interface Security
- Audit Assurance and Compliance
- Business Continuity Management and Operational Resilience
- Change Control and Configuration Management
- Data Security and Information Life Cycle Management
- Data Center Security
- Encryption and Key Management
- Governance and Risk Management
- Human Resources
- Identity and Access Management
- Infrastructure and Virtualization Security
- Interoperability and Portability
- Mobile Security
- Security Incident Management, E-Discovery, and Cloud
- Supply Chain Management, Transparency, and Accountability
- Threat and Vulnerability Management

Although all the CCM security controls can be considered applicable in a specific CS context, from the privacy and data-protection perspective, some of them have greater relevance to the P&DP fulfilments.

Therefore, the selection and implementation of controls for a specific Cloud service involving processing of personal data will be performed:

- Within the context of information security managed system: this requires at least the identification of law requirements, risk analysis, design and implementation of security policies, and related assessment and reviews.

Data Rights Management

Data right management is an extension of normal data protection, where additional control and ACLs are placed on the data sets that require additional permission or condition to access and use beyond just simple and traditional security controls. This is encapsulated with the concepts of **Information Right Management (IRM).**

Data Rights Objectives (e.g., provisioning, users and roles, role-based access)

Information Rights Management (IRM) is not only the use of standard encryption technologies to provide confidentiality for data; it also provides use cases and features as well:

IRM adds a layer of access controls on top of the document and data object. The Access Control List (ACL) determines who can open the document and what they can do with it and provides granularity that flows down to copying, printing, saving, and similar options. Because IRM contains ACLs and is embedded into the actual file, IRM is agnostic to the location of the data, distinct other preventative controls that depended on file location. IRM protection will travel with the file and provide continuous protection.

IRM is useful for securing sensitive organization content such as financial documents. However, it is not securing to only documents; IRM can be implemented to protect database columns, emails, web pages, and other data objects. Also, it is useful for setting up a baseline for the default Information Protection Policy, that is, all documents created by a specific user, at a specific location, will receive a specific policy.

IRM Cloud Challenges

IRM requires that all users with data access should have matching encryption keys. This requirement means robust identity infrastructure is necessary when implementing IRM and the identity infrastructure have to expand to partners, customers, and any other organizations with which data is shared.

- IRM needs that each resource will be provisioned with an access policy. Each client accessing the resource will be provisioned with account and keys. Provisions could be made securely and efficiently for the implementation to be successful. Automation of provisioning of IRM resource access policy can help in implementing that goal. Automated policy provision can be based on file location, the origin of the document or keywords.
- Access to resources can be granted per user bases or according to user role using an **RBAC model**. Provisioning of users and roles must be integrated into IRM policies. Since in IRM most of the classification is in the user responsibility, or based on automated policy, implementing the right RBAC policy is essential.

- Identity infrastructure can be implemented by creating a single location where users are created and authenticated or by creating federation and trust between different repositories of user identities in different systems. They carefully consider the most appropriate method based on the security requirements of the data.

- Many IRM implementations will force end users to install a local IRM agent either for key storage or for authenticating and retrieving the IRM content. This feature might limit certain implementations that involve external users and must be considered as a part of the architecture planning before deployment.

- When reading IRM-protected files, the reader software must be IRM-aware **Microsoft, and Adobe products** in their latest versions have high-quality IRM support, but other readers might encounter compatibility issues and have to be tested before deployment.

- The challenges of IRM compatibility with different operating systems and different document readers increase when the data needs to be read on mobile devices. The usage of mobile platforms and IRM have also be tested carefully.

- IRM can integrate into other security controls such as DLP and documents discovery tools, adding extra benefits.

Note: Data Rights Objectives like provisioning, users and roles, role-based access cover in the **IRM Cloud Challenges** section.

RBAC Model: Role-Based Access Control (RBAC) is an approach to restricting system access to authorized users

Appropriate Tools (e.g., Issuing and replication of certificates) Domain

Instead of focusing on specific software technologies or implementations for IRM, we will focus on the common attributes and features of those tool sets and what they can provide for IRM and security:

- **Auditing:** IRM technologies allow for robust auditing of who has viewed information, also provide proof as to when and where they accessed the data.

- **Expiration:** IRM technologies allow for the expiration of access to data.

- **Policy Control:** IRM technologies allow an organization to have very granular and detailed control over how their data is accessed and used.

- **Protection**: With the implementation of IRM technologies and controls, any information under their protection is always protected.

- **Support for Applications and Formats**: Most IRM technologies support a range of data formats and integration with application packages commonly used within organizations, such as e-mail and various office suites.

Data Retention, Deletion, and Archiving Policies

Protection Data policy should be active and ensure compliance with regulatory or corporate compliance requirements, the concepts of retention, deletion, and archiving are the most important. While other data policies and practices are focused on the security and production usage of data. These three concepts are typical of those that fulfill regulatory obligations, which can come in the form of legal requirements or mandates from certification or industry oversight bodies.

Data Retention Policies

It is a policy that is established within an organization, a protocol for saving information for regulatory or operational compliance needs. The goals of a data-retention policy are to save most crucial information for reference or future use, to organize information so it can be searched and accessed later, and to dispose of the information that is no longer needed. The policy balances the regulation, legal and business data archival requirements against data storage costs, complexity, and other data considerations.

A good data-retention policy should define **Retention periods**, **Data formats**, **Data security**, and **Data-retrieval procedures for the enterprise**. A data-retention policy for Cloud services must contain the following components:

Data Classification

Data classification is based on business usage, compliance requirements, locations, ownership, or in other words, its "value." It is used to decide about the proper retention procedures for the enterprise as well.

Data Mapping

Data mapping is a process of mapping all relevant data to understand data formats, data locations (databases, network drives, object, or volume storage), data types (structured or unstructured) and file types.

Data-Retention Procedure

For each data category, the data-retention procedures must be followed based on the proper data-retention policy that governs the data type. How long the data is to be saved, where (physical location, and jurisdiction), and how (which technology and format) must all be spelled out in the policy and implemented through the procedure. The procedure must include backup options, retrieval requirements, and restoration procedures, as required and necessary for the data types is to be managed as well.

Monitoring and Maintenance

It is a procedure for ensuring that the entire process is working, including a review of the policy and requirements to ensure that there are no changes.

Legislation, Regulation, and Standard Requirements

Data-retention considerations are entirely dependent on the data type and the required compliance regimes associated with it.

For example

According to the Basel II Accords for Financial Data:

"The retention period for financial transactions must be between three to seven years, while according to the **PCI-DSS version 3.0 Requirement 10**, complete access to network resources and cardholder data and credit card transaction data must be saved for at least a year with at least three months available online."

PCI-DSS version 3.0 Requirement 10: Clarified the intent and scope of daily log reviews.

Basel II: Basel II is the second of the Basel Accords offering recommendations on banking laws and regulations issued by the Basel Committee on Banking Supervision.

Data Deletion Procedures and Mechanisms

The primary objective of data-protection procedures is the safe disposal of data once it is becomes useless. Failure to do so may result in data breaches and compliance failures. Safe disposal procedures are designed to make sure that there are no files, pointers, or data remnants left behind in a system that can be used to restore the original data.

Reasons

A policy is required for the following reasons:

1.Technical and Business Requirements:

The business policy could require safe disposal of data. Process such as encryption may require safe disposal of clear text data after creating the encrypted copy.

2.Legislation or Regulation:

Certain regulations and laws need specific degrees of safe disposal records.

Restoring Data:

In a Cloud environment, restoring deleted data is not an easy job for an attacker because Cloud-based data is distributed, usually is to be stored in a different physical location with unique pointers. Achieving any level of physical access to the media is a challenge.

On the other hand, it is still an actual attack vector that you must consider when evaluating the business requirements for data disposal.

Data Disposal

To save a deletion of electronic records, the following options are available:

Degaussing: Using strong magnets for scrambling data on magnetic media such as tapes or hard drive.

Overwriting: Writing random data over the actual data. The more times the overwriting process occurs, the more thorough the destruction of the data is considered to be.

Physical Destruction: Physically destroying the media by shredding, incineration or other means.

Encryption: To use an encryption method to rewrite the data in an encrypted format to make it unreadable without the encryption key.

Crypto-Shredding

Since the first three data disposal options are not entirely suitable for Cloud computing, the only remaining suitable method is the encryption of data. The process of encrypting the data to be disposed of. It is known as **crypto shredding or digital shredding**.

Crypto-shredding is the process of deliberately destroying the encryption keys that were used to encrypt the data initially. Since the data is encrypted with the keys, the result is that the data is made unreadable (at least until the encryption protocol used can be broken or is capable of being brute-forced by an attacker).

To perform a proper crypto-shredding, consider the following points:

- The data must be completely encrypted without leaving any clear text remaining.
- The technique should ensure that the encryption keys are entirely unrecoverable. This can be hard to achieve if an external Cloud provider or other third party manages the keys.

Data Archiving Procedures and Mechanisms

A process of identifying and moving **inactive data** out of existing Cloud environment and into specialized long-term archival storage systems. Moving inactive data out of Cloud environment optimizes the performance of resources required there. Specialized archival systems store information more efficiently and provide for retrieval when needed. A policy for the Cloud must contain the following elements:

Ability to perform eDiscovery and Granular Retrieval

Archive data can be subject to retrieval according to specified parameters such as authors, dates, subject, etc. The archiving platform must provide the ability to do eDiscovery on the data to decide which data must be retrieved.

Backup and Disaster Recovery Options:

All the needs for data backup and restore must be specified and documented. It is essential to make sure that the business continuity and disaster recovery plans are updated and aligned with whatever procedures are implemented.

Data-Encryption Procedure:

Long-term data archiving with encryption could present a challenge for the organization about key management. The encryption policy should consider which media is used, the restoral options, and what the threats are that should be mitigated by the encryption. Bad key management could lead to the destruction of the entire archive and therefore requires attention.

Data Format and Media Type:

The format of the data is a significant consideration because it might be saved for an extended period. Proprietary formats can modify, thus leaving data in a useless state, so selecting the suitable format is most important. The similar consideration should be made for media storage types as well.

Data Monitoring Procedure:

Data stored in the Cloud tend to be replicated and moved. To maintain data governance, it is necessary that all data access and movements be tracked and logged to ensure that all security controls are to appropriately applied throughout the data life cycle.

Data Restoration Procedure:

Data restoral testing must start periodically to ensure that the whole process is working. The trial data restore must be made into an isolated environment to lesser risks, such as restoring an old virus or accidentally overwriting existing data.

Inactive data is data that does not "show up" in your file tree, also known as your data structure or directory. Even though, this data resides on your hard drive, it cannot be accessed by the operating system and therefore it can no longer be maintained by it.

eDiscovery: Electronic discovery is a method in which electronic data is sought, secured, located, and explored with the intent of using it as evidence in a criminal or civil legal case.

Auditability, Traceability, and Accountability of Data Events

Events can be defined as things that happen. Not all events are important, but many are, and being able to discern which events you need to pay attention to can be a challenge.

Definition of Event Sources

Event sources are monitored to provide the **raw data** on events that will be used to clarify a system to be monitored. Event attributes are used to identify the type of information and data that are associated with an event that you would want to capture for analysis. Depending on the number of events and attributes being tracked, a large volume of data will be produced. This data will be stored and then analyzed to uncover patterns of activity that might identify vulnerabilities or threats, existing in the system that have to be addressed.

Security Information and Event Management (SIEM)

SIEM systems are used to collect and analyze the data flow from several systems, allowing for the automation of this process.

Events are essential and available for capture, will vary and depend on the particular Cloud service model employed. These include IaaS, PaaS, and SaaS.

IaaS Event Sources:

With an IaaS environment, Cloud Service Provider (CSP) usually will have control of, and access to event and diagnostic data. More or less all infrastructure level logs will be visible to the CSP, along with detailed application logs. To maintain a reasonable investigation auditability, traceability, and accountability of data, it is suggested that you specify the required data access requirements in the Cloud Service Level Agreement (SLA) or contract with the CSP.

The following logs could be essential to examine at some point but could not be available by default:

- API access logs
- Billing records
- Hypervisor and host operating system logs
- Logs from DNS servers
- Management portal logs
- Network or Cloud provider perimeter network logs
- Packet captures
- Virtual machine monitor (VMM) logs

PaaS Event Sources:

With a PaaS environment, the user usually will have control of, and access to event and diagnostic data. A few infrastructure-level logs will be visible to the CSP, along with detailed application logs. Because the applications that will be monitored are being built and designed by the organization directly, the level of application data that can be extracted and monitored is up to the developers.

To maintain reasonable investigation auditability, traceability, and accountability of data, it is suggested that you work with the development team to understand the capabilities of the applications under development and to help design and implement monitoring regimes that will maximize the organization's visibility into the applications and their data streams.

OWASP recommends the following application events is logged:

- Authentication successes and failures
- Authorization (access control) failures
- Application errors and system events, such as syntax and runtime errors, etc.
- Application and related systems start-ups, logging initialization (starting, pausing or stopping) and shut-downs.
- Legal such as permissions for mobile phone capabilities, terms and conditions etc.
- Output validation failures such as invalid data encoding and database recordset mismatch.
- Session management failures such as cookie session identification value modification.
- Use of higher-risk functionality such as network connections, addition or deletion of users, changes to privileges, assigning users to tokens, adding or deleting tokens, Data Event Logging, etc.

SaaS Event Sources:

With a SaaS environment, the user will usually have minimal control of, and access to event and diagnostic data. Most of the infrastructure level logs will not be visible to the CSP, and they will be limited to the high-level, application-generated logs that are located on a client endpoint. In order to maintain a reasonable investigation capabilities, auditability, and traceability of data, it is suggested to identify required data access requirements in the Cloud SLA or contract with the CSP.

The following data sources play a significant role in event examination and documentation:

- Application server logs
- Billing records
- Database logs

- Guest operating system logs
- Host access logs
- Network captures
- SaaS portal logs and Virtualization platform logs.
- Web server logs

Note: Raw data, also known as primary data, is data (e.g., numbers, instrument readings, figures, etc.) collected from a source.

Identity Attribution Requirement

To be able to perform efficient audits and examinations, the event log must contain as much as possible of the relevant data for the processes that are being examined as possible. OWASP recommends the following data event logging and event attributes to be integrated into event data.

When:	Where:	Who (Any user):	What:
Log date and time (international format).	Application identifiers, such as name and version	Source address, including the user's device/machine identifier, user's IP address, mobile telephone number	Type of event
Event date and time. The event time stamp might be different to the time of logging,	Application address such as port number, workstation identity, and local device identifier	User identity (if authenticated), including the user database table primary key value, username, and license number	The severity of the event (0=emergency, 1=alert, ..., 7=debug), (fatal, error, warning, info, debug, and trace)
Interaction identifier	Service name and protocol		Security-relevant event flag (if the logs contain non-security event data too)
	Geolocation		Description

	Window/page/forms, such as entry point URL and HTTP method		
	Code location, including the script and module name		

Table 2-7: Shows an Identify Attributes

Storage and Analysis of Data Events

"A process to maintain and safeguard the integrity and original condition of the potential digital evidence" defined by **ISO 27037:2012**

With the volume of logs created and collected for any application or system, there is a need for a method or technology to catalog and make those events reportable or searchable. Without having a system in place to synthesize and process the event data, there could mainly be a large amount of data collected that does not serve any meaningful or useful purpose, and that is not accessible for the fulfillment of regulatory and auditing requirements.

The most important techniques used for this type of operation is called a **Security and Information Event Management (SIEM)** system.

Security and Information Event Management (SIEM):

SIEM is a term for product services and software that merges **Security Information Management (SIM)** and **Security Event Management (SEM)**. SIEM technology provides real-time analysis of security alerts generated by network hardware and applications.

Figure 2-4 – Security and Information Event Management

SIEM is sold as appliances, software, or managed services and is also used to log security data and generate reports for compliance purposes.

The security management segment that deals with real-time monitoring, correlation of events, notifications, and console views is called **Security Event Management (SEM)**. The second part provides analysis, long-term storage, and reporting of log data. It iscalled **Security Information Management (SIM)**.

SIEM systems will usually provide the following capabilities:

Alerting

The automated analysis of correlated events and production of alerts, to inform recipients of instant issues. Alerting can be to a dashboard or sent through third-party channels such as email.

Correlation

Looking for linking events and common attributes together into meaningful bundles. This technology provides the ability to perform a variety of correlation techniques to integrate different sources, to turn data into useful information. Typically, correlation is a function of the **Security Event Management, part** of a full **SIEM solution**.

Compliance

Applications can be employed to automate the gathering of auditing processes, compliance data, governance, and producing reports that adapt to existing security.

Data Aggregation

Log management aggregates data from numerous sources, including applications, databases, network, security, servers, and providing the ability to consolidate monitored data to help avoid missing important events.

Dashboards

Tools that can take event data and turn it into informational charts to assist in seeing patterns or identifying activity that is not creating a standard pattern.

Forensic Analysis

The ability to search across logs on different nodes and periods based on specific criteria. This should aggregate log information in your head or having to search through thousands of logs.

Retention

Employing long-term storage of old data to facilitate correlation of data over time and to provide the retention necessary for compliance requirements. Long-term log data retention is essential in forensic examinations as it is unlikely that the discovery of a network breach being at the time of its action.

Continuous Optimizations

To support continuous operations, the following principles have to be adopted as part of the security operations policies:

New Event Detection

The objective of auditing is to identify new information security events. Policies have to be created that define what a security event is and how to address it.

Adding New Rules

Rules are built to permit detection of new events. Rules permit for the mapping of expected values to log files to detect events. Mode of continuous operation, rules have to be updated to address new risks.

Reduction of False Positives

The continuous operations audit logging quality is reliant on the ability to decrease over time the number of false positives to maintain operational effectiveness. This requires continuous improvement of the rule set in use.

Chain of Custody

Chain of custody is the protection of evidence and preservation from the period it is collected till the time it is presented in court. In order for evidence to be considered admissible in court, documentation should exist in many ways such as collection, condition, possession, transfer, and location. Its access and analysis performed on an item from acquisition through eventual final disposition. This concept is referred to as the "chain of custody" of evidence.

Creating a verifiable **chain of custody for evidence** within a Cloud-computing environment where there are several data centers spread across different jurisdictions can become challenging. Sometimes, the only way to provide for a chain of custody is to include this provision in the service contract and make sure that the Cloud provider will comply with requests relating to chain of custody issues.

Non-repudiation

Nonrepudiation is the ability to confirm the origin or authenticity of data to a high degree of certainty. This usually is complete through hashing and digital signatures, to make sure that data has not been changed from its actual form. This idea plays directly into and complements chain of custody to make sure the integrity and validity of data.

Summary:

In this chapter, Cloud data security covers a wide range of areas focused on the concepts, structures, principles, and standards used to monitor and secure assets. Also, the controls used to apply numerous levels of availability, confidentiality, and integrity across IT services through the organization. Cloud Security Professionals focused on Cloud security need to use and apply standards to make sure that the systems under their protection are maintained and supported correctly.

Security specialists understand the different security frameworks, standards. They adopt best practices leveraged by numerous methodologies and how they may be used together to make systems stronger. Information security governance and risk management have enabled information technology to be used safely, responsibly, and securely in environments like never before. The ability to establish strong system protections based on standards and policy and to assess the level and efficacy of that protection through auditing and monitoring is vital to the success of Cloud computing security.

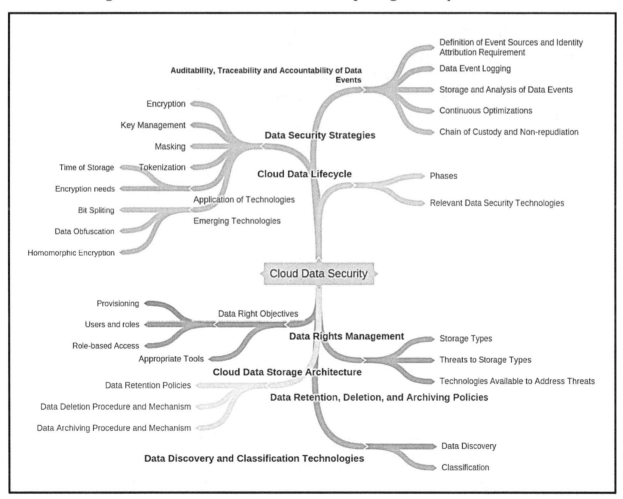

Figure 2-5: Mind Map of Cloud Data Security

Practice Questions

1. Which of the following are storage types used with an Infrastructure as a Service (IaaS) solution?
   a) Volume and block
   b) Structured and object
   c) Unstructured and ephemeral
   d) Volume and object

2. Which of the following can be deployed to help make sure the confidentiality of data in the cloud? (Choose two)
   a) Encryption
   b) Service Level Agreement(s)
   c) Masking
   d) Continuous monitoring

3. When using transparent encryption of a database, where does the encryption engine reside?
   a) At the application using the database
   b) On the instance(s) attached to the volume
   c) In a key management system
   d) Within the database

4. In the context of privacy and data protection, what is a controller?
   a) One who cannot be identified, directly or indirectly, in particular by reference to an identification number or other factors specific to his/her physical, physiological, mental, economic, cultural, or social identity
   b) The natural or legal person, public authority, agency, or any other body which alone or jointly with others, determines the purposes and means of processing of personal data
   c) A natural or legal person, public authority, agency, or any other body, which processes personal data on behalf of the customer.
   d) None of the above

5. Which of the following are common capabilities of Information Rights Management solutions?
   a) Persistent protection, dynamic policy control, automatic expiration, continuous audit trail, and support for existing authentication infrastructure

b) Persistent protection, static policy control, automatic expiration, continuous audit trail, and support for existing authentication infrastructure

c) Persistent protection, dynamic policy control, manual expiration, continuous audit trail, and support for existing authentication infrastructure

d) Persistent protection, dynamic policy control, automatic expiration, intermittent audit trail, and support for existing authentication infrastructure.

6. Which of the following methods for the safe disposal of electronic records can always be used within a cloud environment?
   a) Physical destruction
   b) Encryption
   c) Overwriting
   d) Degaussing

7. What are the three things that you must understand before you can determine the necessary controls to deploy for data protection in a cloud environment?
   a) Management, provisioning, and location
   b) Function, location, and actors
   c) Actors, policies, and procedures
   d) Life cycle, function, and cost

8. Which of the following data storage types are used with a Platform as a Service (PaaS) solution?
   a) Raw and block
   b) Structured and unstructured
   c) Unstructured and ephemeral
   d) Tabular and object

9. Where would the monitoring engine be deployed when using a network-based data loss prevention system?
   a) On a user's workstation
   b) In the storage system
   c) Near the gateway
   d) On a VLAN

10. What are three analysis methods used with data discovery techniques?
    a) Metadata, labels, and content analysis
    b) Metadata, structural analysis, and labels

    c) Statistical analysis, labels, and content analysis

    d) Bit splitting, labels, and content analysis

11. What is the Cloud Security Alliance Cloud Controls Matrix?
   a) A set of regulatory requirements for cloud service providers
   b) An inventory of cloud service security controls that are arranged into separate security domains
   c) A set of software development life cycle requirements for cloud service providers
   d) An inventory of cloud service security controls that are arranged into a hierarchy of security domains

12. What are the four elements that a data retention policy should define?
   a) Retention periods, data access methods, data security, and data retrieval procedures
   b) Retention periods, data formats, data security, and data destruction procedures
   c) Retention periods, data formats, data security, and data communication procedures
   d) Retention periods, data formats, data security, and data retrieval procedures

13. To support continuous operations, which of the following principles have to be adopted as part of the security operations policies?
   a) Application logging, contract/authority maintenance, secure disposal, and business continuity preparation
   b) Audit logging, contract/authority maintenance, secure usage, and incident response legal preparation
   c) Audit logging, contract/authority maintenance, secure disposal, and incident response legal preparation
   d) Transaction logging, contract/authority maintenance, secure disposal, and disaster recovery preparation

14. Which of the following is NOT a type of storage used within a cloud environment?
   a) Structured
   b) Volume
   c) Container
   d) Object

15. Which of the following logs could be exposed to a cloud customer in a Software as a Service environment, if the contract allows it?

a) Billing records
b) Management plane logs
c) Network captures
d) Operating system logs

16. Where would the DLP solution be located for data-in-use monitoring?
a) On the application server
b) On the user's device
c) On the network boundary
d) Integrated with the database server

17. Which of the following is NOT a feature of a SIEM solution?
a) Monitoring
b) Aggregation
c) Alerting
d) Dashboards

18. Which of the following law in the United States governs the protection of health data?
a) SOX
b) HIPAA
c) Dodd-Frank
d) DACA

19. Which of the following is NOT a key feature of an IRM solution?
a) Expiration
b) Policy control
c) Chain of custody
d) Auditing

20. Which cloud model gives responsibility of the physical environment to the cloud customer?
a) IaaS
b) PaaS
c) SaaS
d) None of the above

Chapter 03: Cloud Platform & Infrastructure Security

Cloud Infrastructure Components

Cloud infrastructure is composed of many components, each with their own significance. These components include virtualization, physical environment, network and communications, compute, storage and the management plane.

Physical Environment

While a lay person may think that data being "in the Cloud" mean that it is in some virtual "other dimension," the Cloud has a physical environment. This physical environment is designed considering lowest chances of failure, high availability and security considerations to deploy a scalable, flexible, highly available, secure and multi-tenant environment to be acceptable for Cloud infrastructure.

Data Center:

Basically, Data centers are the physical environment where the Cloud infrastructure resides. Cloud data centers are designed to support protect security and availability of customer's data. There are many physical environment characteristics that require to be considered such as:

- Convenient floor space
- Convenient rack space/cages
- Expensive hardware
- Network connectivity
- Geographic considerations
- Availability of electricity
- Natural disaster considerations
- Political risks: Civil unrest, rioting and so forth.

Data Center Design:

Another most common and very important consideration in data center desgin is Redundancy. Data center designing mostly revolves around redundancy in its design considering all failures should be replicated eliminating the single point of failure. Multiple backup power supplies, independant cooling and ventilation units, Power Distribution Units (PDU), multiple network links, entrance and emergency exits ensures a redundant data center design.

External redundancy:

- Power feeds/lines
- Power substations
- Generators
- Generators fuel tanks
- Network circuits
- Building access points
- Cooling/chilling infrastructure

Internal Redundancy:

- Power distribution units
- Power feeds to racks
- Cooling chillers and units
- Networking
- Storage units
- Physical access points

Network and Communications

As we know data centers have several servers running for client services. Data centers requires high bandwidth for uploading and downloading data for its servers to be readily available anytime. Therefore, requirement of reliable network connection and smooth communication is a primary focus for data center deployment. Clients and endpoints must have ease of access to their respective applications running in a data center. Traffic filtering is another important of network and communication where network administrator has to filter-out all undesired traffic not only to avoid network congestion but also to prevent malicious and untrusted traffic. These concerns include:

- Rate limiting
- Bandwidth allocation
- Filtering
- Routing
- Software defined networking

Software-Defined Networking:

The usage of Software-Defined Networking (SDN) is an essential aspect of cloud computing. With SDN, the decisions concerning where network traffic is filtered or sent and the real forwarding of traffic are totally isolated from each other. With cloud computing, this isolation is imperative because it permits the administrators of the cloud network to rapidly and progressively change network flows and resources depend on the

current needs and requests of the cloud customers. with the level of access provided and the sorts of resources accessible to control, a high level of security requires to be attached to any SDN implementation, with access firmly controlled and monitored regularly.

Compute

A cloud server's computation relies on the quantity of CPUs and the amount of RAM associated with the server. The ability to allocate these resources is an essential concern to avoid resource exhaustion. Within a cloud environment, considering resource pooling and multitenancy, the computing abilities become increasingly complex in both planning and management.

These three factors that affect resource allocation:

- Reservations
- Limits
- Shares

Reservations:

When a shared resource in cloud is demanded by several consumers concurrently and the resource is not capable to accommodate all cloud consumers, this situation leads into a critical condition called resource constraints. Resource constraint condition may degrade the performance or result into unavailability if it is not properly planned before encounter.

Resource reservation is a solution which keeps the services available using tenants. Reservation makes the resource exclusively available for a designated cloud customer without actually sharing the resource. Resource reservation helps to avoid resource constraints and resource borrowing.

Limits:

Limits to implement most extreme usage of memory or processing by a cloud customer. These limits should either be possible at a virtual machine level or a comprehensive level for a customer. They are intended to ensure that huge cloud resources cannot be allocated or consumed by a single host or customer to the burden of other hosts and customers. Along with cloud computing components such as auto-scaling and on-demand self-service, limits can be either "hard" or "fixed," but can also be adaptable and permitted to change dynamically. Commonly, when limits are allowed to change, dependent on current conditions and utilizations, it is done by "borrowing" extra resources rather than making an actual improvement in the limits themselves.

Shares:

The concept of shares is another important feature which arbitrates the issue of resources contention in cloud. As we know, cloud services are accommodating too many requests from cloud consumers. This massive traffic creates contention situation and the actual resource may become unavailable. Shares prioritize and weighed against share values, higher the share value, larger the remaining resource is allocated to the user during contention period.

Virtualization

The utilization of amazing host machines providing shared resource pools to expand the number of guests is both a basic explanation of virtualization and the supporting of Cloud computing. In fact, Cloud computing would not be conceivable without virtualization. The most convincing arguments for the utilization of virtualization are:

- Increasing the efficiency and agility of hardware by sharing resources
- A reduction in personnel resourcing and maintenance, leading to easier management
- Virtualization also allows the abstraction from the hardware via the use of a hypervisor.

There are two types of hypervisors within virtualization:

1. Type 1
2. Type 2

Type 1 hypervisors: Type 1 Hypervisor is native execution that runs tied directly into the basic hardware. It also enables tighter security and controls because there are no extra applications or utilities running inside the hypervisor, other than those to satisfy its intended mission.

Type 2 hypervisors: Type 2 hypervisor varies from type 1 hypervisor in that it runs under a host operating system as opposed to directly tied into the basic hardware of the virtual host servers. With this type of executions, additional security and architecture concerns become possibly the most important factor as the interaction between the operating system and the hypervisor turns into a basic connection. It implies that any security concerns within the basic operating system can affect the hypervisor as well.

Storage

Storage in Cloud environment typically consists of spinning hard disk drivers or solid-state drivers (SSD). Requirement of redundancy with respect to storage can be fulfilled by grouping the disk drivers. For reliability, when storage is performed on a disk drive, the

method used is known as Redundant Array of Inexpensive Disks (RAID). Object storage is a prominently used storage solution offered by Cloud service providers. The redundancy with object storage comes by method of data storage across different object storage server.

Management Plane

Cloud management planes enable administrators to remotely deal all hosts rather than physically visiting each host server to install software or reboot/power on said hosts. The final result is automated control tasks. Administrator can control the whole Cloud infrastructure through the management plane.

Analyze Risks Associated to Cloud Infrastructure

A Cloud-based system should be managed and approached as other outsourced platforms, with the same types of concerns, risks, and audit/governance prerequisties as an external hosting environment. Eventually all risks related to a Cloud infrastructure must be customized for their individual needs. Risks to consider include

- Policy and organization Risks
- Loss of governance
- Provider lock-in
- Compliance challenges
- Provider exit

Risk Assessment/Analysis

A major risk in Cloud environment is sanitization of data. In a traditional data center, physical media can be destroyed to guarantee data destruction, which is not possible in a Cloud environment, so concepts of overwriting and cryptographic erasure are highly used. Data protection is the security of system images within a Cloud environment. The images themselves are just files on a file system without any physical partition of servers, shared with the possibility of malware being injecting into an image even when it is not running, their security becomes essential in a Cloud environment, where the Cloud provider bears sole duty for assurance.

Cloud service providers have a generally huge innovation scale, which influences risk. This one result relies upon the circumstance. considerations include:

- Larger scale platforms require more technical skill to manage
- Shifting control of techniceal risks towards Cloud service provider
- Consolidation of Cloud and IT infrastructure lead to consolidation of points of failure.

Cloud Attack Vectors

In Cloud Computing, the following are the most common attacks that are being used by an attacker to extract sensitive information such as credentials or gaining unauthorized access. Cloud Computing Attacks include: -

- Service Hijacking using Social Engineering Attacks
- Session Hijacking using XSS Attack
- Domain Name System (DNS) Attack
- SQL Injection Attack
- Wrapping Attack
- Service Hijacking using Network Sniffing
- Session Hijacking using Session Riding
- Side Channel Attack or Cross-guest VM Breaches
- Cryptanalysis
- Dos / DDoS Attacks

Service Hijacking using Social Engineering Attacks

Using Social Engineering techniques, the attacker may attempt to guess the password. Social Engineering attacks result in unauthorized access exposing sensitive information according to the privilege level of the compromised user.

Service Hijacking using Network Sniffing

Using Packet Sniffing tools by placing himself in the network, an attacker can capture sensitive information such as passwords, session ID, cookies, and another web service-related information such as UDDI, SOAP, and WSDL

Session Hijacking using XSS Attack

By launching Cross-Site Scripting (XSS), the attacker can steal cookies by injecting malicious code into the website.

Session Hijacking using Session Riding

Session riding is intended for session hijacking. An attacker may exploit it by attempting cross-site request forgery. The attacker uses currently active sessions and rides on it by executing the requests such as modification of data, erasing data, online transactions and password change by tracking the user to click on a malicious link.

Domain Name System (DNS) Attacks

Domain Name System (DNS) attacks include DNS Poisoning, Cybersquatting, Domain hijacking, and Domain Snipping. An attacker may attempt to spoof by poisoning the DNS server or cache to obtain credentials of internal users. Domain Hijacking involves stealing

Cloud service domain name. Similarly, through Phishing frauds, users can be redirected to a fake website.

Side Channel Attacks or Cross-guest VM Breaches

Side Channel Attacks or Cross-Guest VM Breach is an attack that requires the deployment of a malicious virtual machine on the same host. For example, deploying a malicious VM co-resident of target VM will result in resource sharing. Attacker can extract cryptographic keys. Similarly, attacker can also exploit shared high-level cache memory to launch side channel attacks. A malicious insider or an attacker can do installation by impersonating a legitimate user.

Similarly, there are other attackes that were discussed earlier, are also vulnerable to Cloud Computing such as SQL Injection attack (injecting malicious SQL statements to extract information), Cryptanalysis Attacks (weak or obsolete encryption), Wrapping Attack (duplicating the body of message), Denial-of-Service (DoS) and Distributed Denial-of-Service (DDoS) Attacks.

Virtualization Risks

Virtualization can expand the security of IT because it is easier to set up the correct network access controls between machines.

Layered based approach in virtualization also raises some risks which are not found in traditional servers based model. Compromising hypervisor layer will also compromise the hosted virtual machines because hypervisor is an authoritative layer over the hosts. As the hypervisor is hosting all the VMs on it, it is a single point of failure resulting in denial of services. Any unauthorized access to hypervisor can result into operational changes, access restrictions, service hijacking and much more. Similarly, installation of obsolete or unpatched or pre-configured virtual machines can also increase the risk in virtual environment. Additionally, some virtual environments are over allocated resulting in exhaust of resources.

Another risk of server virtualization is so called "**Resource Abuse**", where one guest (or tenant) is over-using the physical resources, in this manner keeping alternate guests of the resources required to run their workloads. This is also called the "noisy neighbour" issue. The hypervisor may have the capacity to limit the over usage of a guest, but the administrator must consider about restricting the large number of visitors on a single host. Few guests mean you are not saving money sufficiently.

- Numerous guests mean you risk performance issues.

With virtual servers, it becomes easy to clone, replicate, snapshot and stop images. Although there are benefits of using virtual servers, but with a probability of new risks. It

can prompt enormous sprawl or proliferation of server images that need to be stored somewhere. This can become difficult to manage and represent a security risk.

Counter-Measure Strategies

Cloud computing faces the same difficulties as other networks and infrastructures that use the internet, there are numerous ways in which counter-measures can avert the risks and threats that are manageable against cloud security.

There are various counter-measures that can be executed in the cloud infrastructure. These include:

- Access management
- Centralized directory
- Role-based access control
- Privileged user and access management
- User access certifications
- Identity and access reporting
- Separation of duties

Other counter-measures are conventional in order to prevent the use of attacks that include better techniques for transforming sensitive data over public cloud deployments. More significantly cloud servers need improved data portability and protection from external threats. This includes, creating an identity and access management guidanceEncryption should be increasingly unique and secure to protect files and other user data. Better encryptions permit for better methods in storage, provisions for security, acquisitions of data and information from service providers and vendors that support in regulations, dimensions and opportunities in cloud.

Cloud environments are of high availability in nature with redundancy, rapid elasticity, and auto-scaling. This architectural plan makes the maintenance, patching, and isolation of hosts in case of a conceivable security breach much easier because they can be removed from production pools. It also allows for scanning, updating, and making configuration changes without impacting the customer and users of a system or application, consequently reducing this risk to availability.

Security Controls

In order to protect a sound security policy and overall governance, the cloud security professional must concentrate on some different area, as discussed in this section.

Physical and Environmental Protection

The word physical and environmental security refers to measures taken to ensure the safety and security of an infrastructure against natural disasters, environmental effects, human attacks. While the access and technologies used with a cloud infrastructure offer a single set of services to customers, covered it is all is a classic data center model. While in most cases on a much larger scale. Because a cloud is a system that is accessible over broad networking, such as the public Internet, physical protection should also extend to those systems that are used to access the cloud.

The physical assets in the concrete data center include servers, physical racks, power distribution units, cooling units, as well as real physical facilities and the auxiliary systems located on the premises, for example, power conduits, battery backups, fuel tanks, generators. Outside the Data center property there are still further physical devices and infrastructure that are essential to the cloud security professional. These include the power and network conduits that the data center depends on, as well as the endpoints of access for the users and customers, for example, workstation, laptops, mobile devices.

Examples of relevant controls based upon one or more regulations:

- Procedures and policies recognized for maintaining the safe and secure working environments: includes offices, facilities, rooms and secure areas
- Restricted physical access of users and support personnel to information assets and functions.
- Physical security perimeters such as fences, guards, barriers, walls and so on.

Protecting Data Center Facilities

Data centers are essential to have a redundant, multi-layered way to deal with using access control. Controls are requisite to be at the facilities level, the computer floor level, and at the data center/facility staff level to guard against risk.

System and Communication Protection

Cloud computer run on physical systems which use services need protection. A number of these services are

- Hypervisor
- Volume management
- Storage controller
- IP address management
- Identity service
- VM image service
- Management databases

Other considerations for system and communication protections are:

- Detecting and logging of security events
- Responsibilities of protecting the Cloud: Cloud provider is responsible for underlying software and hardware regardless of cloud service model. Including knowing where the responsibility among cloud service provider and cloud customer.
- Automation of configuration

As with any application, the protection of data is a major concern, and different techniques are required for various conditions of data:

Data at rest: The major protection point for data at rest is the through the use of encryption techniques.

Data in transit/motion: With data in transit, the primary methods of protection are network isolation and the use of encrypted transport mechanisms such as TLS

Data in use: Data in use in protected through secure API calls and web services by means of the use of encryption, dedicated network pathways, or digital signatures.

Virtualization Systems Protection

Virtualization forms the foundation of any cloud infrastructure and allows a considerable lot of the feature that make cloud environment an interesting and popular technological platform. Given the essential role that virtualization plays, the components and systems that make up the virtualized infrastructure are the most obvious and attractive focuses for attackers.

Virtualization systems protection considers:

- Protecting the management plane
- Isolation of the management network from other networks
- Proper network design as well as properly operating components. such as, firewalls
- Use of trust zones

The management plane, with full organize over the environment and exposed APIs for allowing administrative tasks, is the most noticeable and essential aspect to completely protect. It is comprised of a series of APIs, exposed functions calls and services, as well as web portals or other client access to allow its use.

Maintaining cloud features such as resiliency and auto-scaling, the main function of virtualization environment and infrastructure is to support and maintain multitenancy. Allowing for multitenancy is a management task versus a technological task. From a virtualization standpoint, virtual machines are only host there is no dependency on what

type of customer they contain. where the significance of controls becomes an integral factor with multitenancy is the requirements to keep tenants separate and protected from each other. This includes both keeping system interaction and security isolated between tenants, but also resources and usage to guarantee that all tenants have what their specific systems and applications need to meet contractual and SLA requirements. While logging and auditing are certainly important to security, these are reactionary mechanisms and do not prevent an actual vulnerability from being exploited initially. Many of the same approaches and strategies that are used at the system level in a traditional data center also are adapted for a virtualization infrastructure in a cloud environment. A prime example is the establishment of trust zones, in the same manner a network separation between servers and systems would be implemented as a defensive layering strategy.

Trust zones can be established and segmented using many different strategies. The most common method involves separating out the different tiers of the system architecture such as applications, data zones of the infrastructure. Trust zones allows each zone to have its own protection and monitoring using tools and strategies that are relevant and specific to its actual needs and functions. It allows the application and data zones to be isolated from external network access and traffic.

Management of Identification, Authentication and Authorization in Cloud Infrastructure

Identity and Access Management innovation can be utilized to capture, record, initiate, and manage user identities and their access permissions. All users are authorized, authenticated, and evaluated according to policies and roles.

Cloud identity management is enhanced for integration across devices, applications, operating systems, and resources. This is basic as Cloud migration will open access to endpoints external of enterprise control and across locations. Cloud identity management can manage user access to WiFi networks, facilitates authentication, connect Cloud servers.

Authentication:

Authentication is the process for confirming the identity of the user. The ordinary authentication process enables the system to identify the user (username), and then validate their identity through user-provided evidence such as password. There are stronger techniques of authenticating the user, one-time password, including x.509 certificates, device fingerprinting. These can be mutual to provide a stronger combination of authentication factors.

Federated identity enables a user to access an application in one domain, such as Software as a Service (SaaS) application, using the authentication that occurred in another domain, such as corporate Identity Management (IdM) system.

Authorization:

Authorization is a permission or privileges assigned to a user. These privileges determine either the user is allowed to perform an action or not. These privileges are usually categorized as Roles. These roles are associated to the user defining the level of authorization. Authorization policy manages and controls the access of users regardless of location and other parameters. Authorization policy evaluates the user identity (in some cases, additional attributes are required) to govern and restrict the user under its authorization level.

Audit Mechanisms

The capacity for an enterprise to follow what applications users are accessing (and when) is a concern from both, a security and regulatory viewpoint. However, this has become a serious challenge since users and applications are no longer staying within the enterprise and working instead within cloud. Multiple failed authentication attempts of users accessing the resource will feature potential security and fraud related activities. Account lock-out control somehow prevents multiple failed authentication request and brute forcing. Regulated industries require audit trails to demonstrate that only authorized users have accessed or attempted to access certain confidential systems. Federation solutions provide the central gateway for users accessing cloud apps, computers or mobile device. This central point of access also provides a central point of reporting and auditing.

Plan Disaster Recovery and Business Continuity Management

Understanding of the Cloud Environment

It is major to understand the Cloud environment before developing a detailed plan of business continuity and disaster recovery. Firstly, understand the scenarios of Cloud environment.

1. On-premise Cloud as BC/DR Plan

Organizations often identify and select new cloud vendors, in this scenario. Therefore, they must increase a firm understanding of the functional and resource abilities necessary for an effective recovery in the incident of a disaster.

After a new cloud provider has been designated, a suspicious review of the Service Level Agreement (SLA) is required to ensure that all services, functionality and business requirements are sufficiently provided for, and any assumptions validated.

Consider the alteration of workloads on physical machines into virtual machines and how rapidly resources can be made accessible when needed

2. Cloud User, Primary BC/DR Cloud Provider

The enterprise infrastructure is now found in cloud, in this scenario. The risk of disaster of any quantity of the infrastructure, for example, regional failure, is mitigated. The business continuity strategy concentrates on service provisioning, restoration or failover to another quantity of the same cloud provider infrastructure. Whereas in this scenario, the concentration is located heavily on resources and abilities of the current cloud provider, one must carefully estimate the provider's abilities, as the BC/DR strategy may need new resources and functionality, for example, load-balancing performance and bandwidth obtainability among the redundant facilities of the cloud provider.

3. Cloud User, Alternative BC/DR Cloud Provider

This scenario is similar to scenario 2 , but in this case, service restoration is provided by a separate cloud provider. Therefore, the risk of whole cloud provider failure is mitigated.

In a situation when an organization selects a second cloud provider for service restoration, the speed of the transfer to the alternate cloud provider must be heavily evaluated. It is also possible that business users will feel the influence, as primary and secondary cloud provider functionalities may vary greatly. Consequently, it is worthwhile to include the business users as soon as conceivable, to assess the residual risks to their business.

Understanding of the Business Requirements

There are common concerns and business requirements particular to BC/DR and cloud, including legal and regulatory considerations, supply chain dependencies, loss of governance, and location risks, when developing a cloud-based strategy for BC/DR. Each of these concerns should be addressed when developing a complete strategy. BC/DR plan should be included in following items:

- Location and contact data of the business workforce, and business partners as well as third party providers
- Important assets that must to be protected and may must to be restored
- Recent location of these assets
- Network connectivity among the assets and sites of their processing
- Data and functionality repetition
- Failover ability

- Security and access concerns

Three big concepts to determine the business requirement of BC/DR, whether effected with a Cloud hosting model or traditional data center model:

Recovery Point Objective (RPO): It is the amount of data that a company would require to maintain and recover in order to function at a level suitable to management.

Recovery Time Objective (RTO): The period of time within which applications, systems, or functions must be recovered in the event of a disaster to the point where management's objectives for BC/DR are happened.

Recovery Service Level (RSL): Measures the percentage of the total, typical production service level that needs to be restored to meet BCDR purposes in the instance of a failure.

These three measures are all important in making a decision as to what needs to be covered under the BCDR strategy, as well as the method to take when considering possible BCDR solutions.

RTO and RPO are the two important measures which are the main objectives that must be achieved anytime assessing a great optimal in a given operating and capital cost.

Understanding of the Risks

With any BCDR plan, there are two sets of risks, those that require the implementation of the plan in the first place, and those that are realized as a result of the plan itself.

Many risks could need the implementation of the BC/DR plan, regardless of the specific result the company has selected to take. These risks include the following:

- Terrorists attacks, acts of war
- Natural disasters (earthquakes, hurricanes, floods, tornadoes, and so on)
- Equipment failures
- Data center or service provider failures or neglect
- Utility disruptions and failures

Disaster Recovery/Business Continuity strategy

It is time to create the BC/DR plan, the implementation steps and processes for it, and the partial testing and validation plan. The continual process of the BCDR strategy.

Define Scope:

This allows security to clearly define the roles and areas of concern during the planning and design phase and to guarantee that proper risk assessments are conducted and recognized by management along the approach.

Gather Requirements:

The purposes of critical systems and the time necessary to create operations in the incident of a BC/DR situation, requires the analysis and application of threats and vulnerabilities that pose a risk to the data and systems. Laws, policies, public relations, Regulations will all play a role in this purpose for possible solutions.

Analyze:

This step contains a thorough analysis of the current production hosting location for the application or system, a purpose of components that need to be replicated for a BCDR situation, and the areas of risk related with that. With moving to a new environment, new risks are certain due to changes in configurations and support models, as well as new hosting staff who do not have a history or understanding with the application or system. A main concern with moving to a secondary host provider for BC/DR reasons is whether they can handle the load and potentials for the system or application like the main production hosting arrangement does.

Assess Risk:

In IT system, regardless of hosting circumstances or providers, risk assessments are an ongoing and continual process to ensure security compliance and regulatory requirements. List of the main risks that are assessed:

- Load capacity at the BC/DR site
- Legal and contractual issues
- Migration of services

Design:

The design stage is where the real technical evaluation of BC/DR solutions is considered and matched to the company's requirements and policies. In many features, the requirements are the similar as what obtaining a primary production hosting arrangement would entail. Both the technical and support requirements need to be firmly recognised and articulated in SLAs, contracts, and policies. This contains identifying the owner and the hosting environments recognize their requirements and what preparations are necessary. Other completely important parts of the plan are how the testing of the plan will be conducted and how the restoration of services back to the steady manufacture state will be controlled once the appropriate time arrives.

Creation/Implementation of the Plan

The real production applications and hosting may need to be modified to provide abilities to allow the BC/DR plan to work. This can contain system configuration modifications to

bring the two hosting environment, or providing data replication and configuration replication services to the BC/DR host for continual updating and maintaining regularity. From this point forward, the BC/DR planning and strategy must be integrated as crucial component of current management of IT services and all change and configuration management activities.

A formal approval test will convey the BC/DR into production mode. This requires integration with all consistent IT service processes. Once in production mode, controls should be in place to guarantee that it will keep working.

The BC/DR plan must be tested at planned intervals or upon important organizational or environmental changes. An untested failover is improbable to end well. Ideally, a full-scale exercise will understand a full switch over to the DR platform. At the same period, this test must not pose a threat to the production user population. Risks that can manifest should be virtual and reacted to in the most realistic ways conceivable.

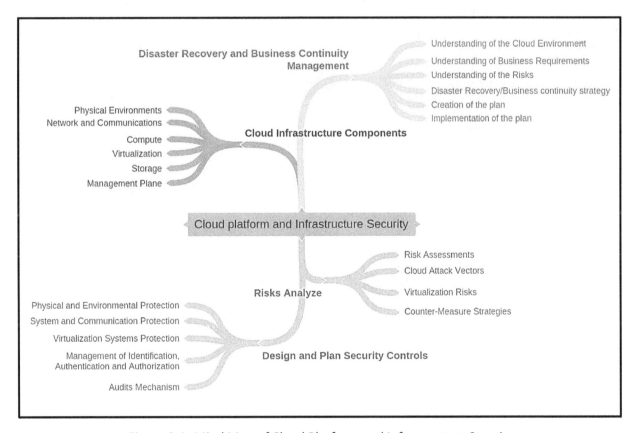

Figure 3-1: Mind Map of Cloud Platform and Infrastructure Security

Practice Questions:

1. What are the components of cloud infrastructure?
   a) Compute
   b) Network and communication
   c) Virtualization
   d) All of the above

2. Which of the following statement that are designed to support protect security and availability of customer data?
   a) Data center
   b) Storage
   c) Management plane
   d) None of the above

3. Which of the following options, provides the best way for customers and users to access their applications, systems, and software tools?
   a) Virtualization
   b) Management plane
   c) Network and communication
   d) None of the above

4. What is the acronym of SDN?
   a) Secure-Defined Networking
   b) Software-designed Networking
   c) Software-Defined Networking
   d) None of the above

5. How many types of hypervisors are there within virtualization?
   a) Two
   b) Three
   c) Four
   d) Five

6. What are the various counter-measures that can be executed in the cloud infrastructure?
   a) Separation of duties
   b) Identity and access reporting

c) Access management
d) All of the above

7. Which of the following options, is protected through secure API calls and web services by means of the use of encryption, dedicated network pathways, or digital signatures?
a) Data at rest
b) Data in use
c) Data in transit/motion
d) None of the above

8. Which of the following virtualization systems protection consideration?
a) Isolation of the management network from other network
b) Protecting the management plane
c) Use of trust zones
d) All of the above

9. Which of the following can be utilized to capture, record, initiate, and manage user identities and their access permissions?
a) Audit mechanisms
b) Identity and access management
c) Both of them
d) None of the above

10. Which of the following process for confirming the identity of the user?
a) Authentication
b) Identity management
c) Auditing
d) None of the above

11. What is federated Identity?
a) The capacity for an enterprise to follow what applications users are accessing (and when) is a concern from both a security and regulatory viewpoint.
b) It is enables a user to access an application in one domain, such as software as a Service (SaaS) application, using the authentication that occurred in another domain, such as corporate Identity Management (IdM) system.
c) It is enhanced for integration across devices, applications, operating systems, and resources.

d) None of the above

12. What is the acronym of RSL?
    a) Recovery Service Level
    b) Recovery System level
    c) Redundancy Service level
    d) None of the above

13. What is RPO?
    a) The period of time within which applications, systems, or functions must be recovered in the event of a disaster to the point where management's objectives for BC/DR are happened.
    b) It is the amount of data that a company would require to maintain and recover in order to function at a level suitable to management.
    c) Measures the percentage of the total, typical production service level that needs to be restored to meet BCDR purposes in the instance of a failure.
    d) None of the above

14. Which of the following statement that period of time within which applications, systems, or functions must be recovered in the event of a disaster to the point where management's objectives for BC/DR are happened?
    a) RPO
    b) RTO
    c) RSL
    d) None of the above

15. What are the Audit Mechanisms?
    a) It is enhanced for integration across devices, applications, operating systems, and resources.
    b) It enables a user to access an application in one domain, such as software as a Service (SaaS) application, using the authentication that occurred in another domain, such as corporate Identity Management (IdM) system.
    c) The capacity for an enterprise to follow what applications users are accessing (and when) is a concern from both a security and regulatory viewpoint.
    d) All of the above

Chapter 04: Cloud Application Security

The objective of the Cloud Application Security is to provide you better understanding and knowledge related to secure application development and deployment over cloud. Throughout an exploration of the *Software Development Life cycle (SDLC)*, the user will gain an understanding of utilizing secure software and understand the controls necessary for developing secure cloud computing and program interfaces.

You will gain knowledge in *Identity and Access Management (IAM)* solutions for the cloud application architecture to employ a layer of security to identify and manage the access to the application. You will also learn how to make sure data and application integrity, availability, and confidentiality through cloud software validation and assurance.

Application Security

Before we are going into cloud software assurance and validation, it is essential for a user to understand some basics about how a cloud application operates, along with some common pitfalls of getting into cloud development or migrating to a cloud environment from a traditional data center. The cloud security professional requires an excellent understanding of the common vulnerabilities facing cloud applications to properly advise on and implement security policies and best practices throughout the software development Life cycle.

Cloud Development Basics

A major difference between cloud systems and their operations versus a traditional data center is that cloud systems are heavily reliant on *Application Programming Interfaces (APIs)* for access and functions. APIs can be broken into many formats, but the most considerables are *Representational State Transfer (REST)* and *Simple Object Access Protocol (SOAP)*.

It is essential for developers to understand that in many cloud environments, access is acquired through the means of an Application Programming Interface (API). These APIs will consume tokens rather than traditional usernames and passwords.

Representational State Transfer (REST): REST is a software architecture style consisting of guidelines and best practices for creating scalable web services.

Simple Object Access Protocol (SOAP): A protocol specification for exchanging structured information in the implementation of web services in computer networks.

A high-level comparison of these two APIs are:

REST	SOAP
Representational State Transfer	Service Oriented Architecture Protocol
Uses Simple HTTP Protocol	Use the **SOAP envelope** and then HTTP (SMTP/FTP) to transfer the data.
Supports data format like XML, JSON, etc.	Support only XML format
Scalability and Performance are good and uses caching	Slower performance and scalability can be complicated and not uses caching
Used widely	Used where REST is not possible, SOAP provides **Web Services** feature

Table 4-1: Two APIs

Note: A SOAP message is an ordinary XML document containing the Envelope element that identifies the XML document as a SOAP message

Web Services: Web services are web application components that make themselves available over the internet and use a standardized XML messaging system. XML is used to encode all communications to a web service.

Common Pitfalls

The ability to communicate, identify, and plan for potential cloud-based application challenges proves an invaluable skill for project teams and developers. Failure to do so can result in failed projects, additional costs, and duplication of efforts as well as loss of efficiencies and executive support. While several projects and cloud journeys might have an element of unique or non-standard approaches, the pitfalls described in this section should always be understood and followed.

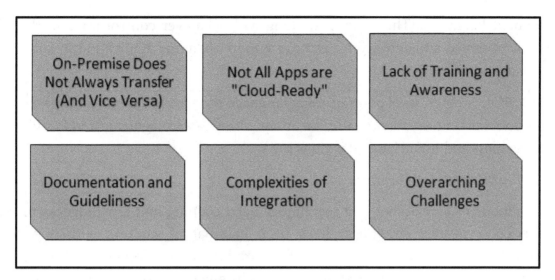

Figure 4-1: Common Pitfalls

On-Premise Does Not Always Transfer

Functionality and current performance might not be transferable. Applications and current configurations might be hard to replicate on or through cloud services. The rationale for this is two-fold.

- They were not developed with cloud-based services in mind. The continued evolution and expansion of cloud-based service offerings look to enhance technologies and development, not always maintaining support for more historical development and systems. Where cloud-based development has occurred, this may need to be tested against on-premise or legacy-based systems.

- Not all applications can be "forklifted" to the cloud. Forklifting an application is the technique of migrating an entire application, the way it runs in a traditional infrastructure with minimal code changes. Usually, these applications are self-contained and have few dependencies; however, transferring or utilizing cloud-based environments may introduce additional change requirements and additional interdependencies.

Not All Apps are "Cloud-Ready"

Where big data and high-level security controls are applied, cloud development and testing can become more challenging. This is because it is usually compounded by the requirement for such systems to be developed, tested, and assessed in traditional environments or on-premise to a level where integrity and confidentiality have been assured and verified. Numerous large size client-based applications come with different security and regulatory restrictions or rely on legacy coding projects, several of which may have been developed using **Common Business-Oriented Language (COBOL)**, as well as other more historical

development languages. These reasons, along with whatever control frameworks might have to be observed and adhered to, can cause more than one application to fail at being cloud-ready.

> **Note:** COBOL is a high-level programming language used for business applications. It was the first popular language designed to be an operating system agnostic and is still used in several business and financial applications today.

Lack of Training and Awareness

New development approaches and techniques need training and a willingness to utilize new service. Typically, developers have been habitual of working with SQL Server, Microsoft .NET or Java and other types of the traditional development platform. When cloud-based platform(s) is required or requested by any organization, this may introduce challenges (particularly if it is a platform or system with which developers are unfamiliar).

Documentation and Guidelines

Best practice needs developers to follow appropriate processes, methodologies, documentation, guidelines, and life cycles to reduce opportunities for heightened or unnecessary risk to be introduced.

Given the rapid implementation of evolving cloud services, it has created a disconnection between some developers and providers on how to make use of, integrate, or meet vendor requirements for development. Whereas various providers are continuing to improve levels of available documentation, the highly update guidance could not always be available, particularly for new releases and updates.

For these reasons, the cloud service provider needs to understand the basic concept of SDLC and what it can do for the organization. Essentially, SDLC is a sequence of phases, or steps, that provide a model for the development and life cycle management of a software or an application. The methodology within the SDLC process can vary across organizations and industries, but standards such as **ISO/IEC 12207** represent processes that develop a life cycle for software or application and provide a mode for the acquisition, development, and configuration of software systems.

The goal of an SDLC process is to help produce a product that is effective, cost-efficient, and of high quality. Usually, SDLC methodology contains the following stages:

- Planning
- Analysis
- Design
- Implementation
- Maintenance

Note that **ISO/IEC/IEEE 12207** Systems and software engineering – Software life cycle processes are an international standard for software life cycle processes.

Complexities and Integration

Integrating the cloud-based applications with the existing environment can be an essential part of the development process. When operational and developer resources do not have open or unrestricted access to supporting services and components, integration can be hard to implement, mainly where cloud providers manage applications, infrastructure, and integration platforms.

From a troubleshooting point of view, it can prove difficult to collect and track transaction and events across underlying or interdependent components.

In order to reduce these complexities, where possible, the cloud provider API has to be used.

Overarching Challenges

The developer should always remember two primary risks associated with applications that run in the cloud environment. These two risks are Third-party administrator and multi-tenancy.

It is also important that developers understand the security requirements based on the Services model (IaaS, PaaS, SaaS) and the deployment model (community, hybrid, public, private) that the application will run in

These two models will help in determining what security will be offered by the provider and what your enterprises or organizations are responsible for implementing and maintaining.

It is essential to find out who is responsible for security control across the deployment and services model. Consider creating an example responsibility matrix.

	IaaS	PaaS	SaaS
Security Governance, Risk and Compliance (GRC)	ER	ER	ER
Data Security	ER	ER	ER
Application Security	ER	ER	SR

Platform Security	ER	SR	CPR
Infrastructure Security	SR	CPR	CPR
Physical Security	CPR	CPR	CPR

Figure 4-2: Example security responsibility matrix for Cloud service models

ER = Enterprise Responsibility

SR = Shared Responsibility

CPR = Cloud Provider Responsibility

The developer should know that the metrics will always be needed and cloud-based application could have a higher dependency on metrics than internal applications to supply visibility into who is accessing the application and actions they are performing. This could need substantial development time to integrate said functionality and could eliminate a "forklift" approach.

Note: Forklift works exactly as its name implies, you pick up your existing environment and drop it into AWS Cloud. In this approach, elasticity and scalability of the cloud may not entirely be utilized. This option runs AWS Cloud like a virtual colocation environment.

Common Vulnerabilities

The applications run in cloud have to conform to best practice guidelines and guidance for the assessment and on-going management of vulnerabilities. The implementation of an application risk-management program addresses not only vulnerabilities but also risks associated with the applications.

The most common software vulnerabilities are found in the Open Web Application Security Project (OWASP) Top 10. There are OWASP 10 entries for 2017 along with the description of each entry.

Injections

Injection flaws are very prevalent, especially in the legacy code. Injection vulnerabilities are typically found in expression languages, LDAP, NoSQL queries, OS commands, ORM queries, SQL, SMTP headers, XPath, and XML parsers.

Injection flaws are to be recognized when examining the code. Fuzzers and scanners can assist attackers to search injection flaws.

Broken Authentication

Broken Authentication prevalence is widespread due to the design and implementation of most identity and access controls. Session management is the base of authentication and access controls and is existing in all stateful applications.

Attackers can detect broken authentication using manual means and exploit them to use automated tools with dictionary attacks and password lists.

Sensitive Data Exposure

Over the past years, this vulnerability has been the most common impactful attack. Usually, the flaw is just not encrypting sensitive data. When crypto is utilized, weak key generation and management, and weak algorithm, protocol, and cipher usage are familiar, particularly for weak password hashing storage techniques. For data in transit, server-side vulnerability is easy to detect but difficult for data at rest.

XML External Entities (XXE)

By default, various XML processors allow specification of an external entity, a URI that is evaluated and dereferenced during XML processing.

SAST tools can find out this issue by inspecting configuration and dependencies. DAST tools need extra manual steps to detect and exploit this issue. Manual testers require to be trained for how to examine for XXE, commonly as it not tested as of 2017.

Broken Access Control

This vulnerability is common due to the absence of automated detection, and lack of useful functional testing by application developers.

Access control detection is not usually amenable to automated static or dynamic testing. Manual testing is the secure way to detect weak or missing access control, including a controller, direct object references, HTTP method like GET, POST, etc.

Security Misconfiguration

This can occur at any level of an application stack, including the application server, database, custom code, frameworks, network services, platform, and pre-installed virtual machines, containers, or storage and web server. Automated scanners are useful for detecting misconfigurations, use of configurations or default accounts, legacy options, unnecessary services, etc.

Cross-Site Scripting (XSS)

In the OWASP Top 10 vulnerabilities, XSS is the second most prevalent issue and is found in around two-thirds of all applications.

Automated tools can search some XSS vulnerabilities automatically, particularly in developed technologies such as ASP.NET, JSP or J2EE, and PHP.

Insecure Deserialization

This vulnerability occurs when untrusted data is used to abuse the logic of an application. It inflicts a denial of service (DoS) attack, and also executes arbitrary code upon it being deserialized.

Using Components with Known Vulnerabilities

Components, such as frameworks, libraries, and other software modules, run with the same privileges as the application. If a vulnerable component is exploited, such as an attack can facilitate severe data loss or server takeover. APIs and Applications using components with known vulnerabilities could determine application defence and enable a range of possible attacks and impacts.

Insufficient Logging and Monitoring

One strategy for determining if you have sufficient monitoring is to inspect the logs following penetration testing. The testers' actions have to be recorded sufficiently to understand what damages they might have inflicted.

Cloud Software Assurance and Validation

As with any software development or implementation, those operating within a cloud environment should undergo testing, auditing, and validation to make sure that security requirements are to be appropriately employed and verified.

Cloud-based Functional Testing

Functional testing is a focused and specific test against a particular component or function of an application or system, as compared to **regression or full testing**, which is **holistic** and consists of the entire application with its full functionality. Software and Application development within a cloud environment has all the usual considerations that are part of any project or even additional considerations that are commensurate with the realities of cloud technologies. As part of security and testing, it is essential to consider every legal and regulatory requirement for the system when moved to cloud. The particular jurisdiction where the cloud is hosted and the authorities to which it is subjected should meet the similar requirements at minimum for the application. The cloud security professional needs to analyze the data being used and the application security needed around it, ensures that the cloud provider selected or being considered can meet those requirements.

Also, Functional testing software examines all the functions and features of the software and its interaction with hardware. For conducting functional testing, testers can use such tools as **Sauce Labs, Rapise, and TimeShiftX**. These cloud-based software testing tools use the following techniques:

- Acceptance testing
- Integration testing
- System testing

> **Note: Regression testing** is the process of testing changes in computer programs to ensure that the previous programming technique still applicable with the new changes.
>
> Also note that **Holistic** is an approach to IT management that is concerned with viewing and treating a complex computer system as a single entity.

Cloud Secure Software Development Life Cycle

The SDLC process is a set of stages or phases that drive a software development project from conception and requirement gathering through the phases of SDLC. The SDLC phases is **requirement, designing, development, testing, and maintenance**. Though the **SDLC** process is standardized and well known for all software development projects, adapting it for security within a cloud environment is an essential responsibility of the **Cloud Security Professional**.

SDLC has following the core stages.

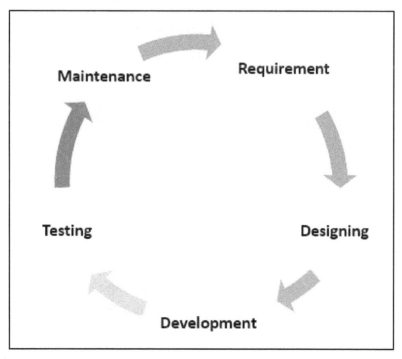

Figure 4-3: SDLC Process

The focus in this instance is adapting an organization's perspective and approach to the realities of a cloud environment, where many of the standard security controls and system architectures are not applicable or feasible. Both security and cloud components must be included in the SDLC process from the onset, and retrofitting them later in the process after coding has begun (or has been completed) should not be attempted.

Compared to a traditional SDLC process, the cloud SDLC process, much like most aspects of cloud computing in general, operates in a much faster way. This can often place considerable stress on established SDLC processes within an organization along with attempts to adhere to established timelines and development steps.

Security Testing

Some of the types of application security testing are followed within a Cloud environment, and for the most part, they have an essential intersection with testing in a traditional data center from a methodological perspective.

Static Application Security Testing (SAST)

Static Application Security Testing (SAST) is considered to be **white-box test**, where the application test performs an analysis of the application byte code, source code, and binaries without executing the application code. SAST is used to determine coding errors that are indicative of security weaknesses. SAST is typically used as a test method while the tool is under development.

SAST can find buffer overflows, cross-site scripting (XSS) errors, SQL injection, unhandled error conditions, and potential backdoors, etc.

By default, SAST typically delivers more comprehensive results than those found using DAST.

Dynamic Application Security Testing (DAST)

Dynamic Application Security Testing (DAST) is considered a **black-box test**, where the tool should find specific execution paths in the application being analyzed. Unlike SAST, which analyses code "offline" (when the code is not running), DAST is used against applications in their running state. DAST is also considered useful when testing exposed HTML and HTTP interfaces of web applications.

It is essential to understand that SAST and DAST play different roles and that one is not better than the other in any way. Static and dynamic application tests work together to improve the reliability of secure applications being created and used by organizations.

Pen Testing

Pen testing is also known as black box testing. It runs in a similar manner and with the similar toolsets as an attacker could attempt to use against an application. This security testing type is designed to actively attempt to attack and compromise ongoing (running) systems in real-world scenarios. The objective is to discover weaknesses and vulnerabilities using the similar approach a malicious user would employ against a system.

Use Verified Secure Software

A significant aspect of the selection of programming languages, application environments, development methodologies, and software development platforms is understanding the key components in a cloud environment that will promote and enforce security. Application code is developed on these frameworks and protocols, the decision to use toolsets and software packages that do not meet the security requirements in a Cloud environment will ultimately have a harmful impact on any software that is developed or implemented by an organization once it reaches its development stage.

Approved API

Application Programming Interfaces (API) is a massive part of Cloud application development because they allow other applications to utilize web services from the application, thereby expanding its capabilities.

Additionally, they provide for automation and integration with third-party tools, again aimed at increasing the functionality of the application. However, this does not come without risk. There are both providers and consumers of web services provided by APIs, and each of them presents special considerations.

When utilizing APIs, the developer is reliant on the API developer to have proper security controls and performs testing and validation to make sure of the integrity and security of application. However, it is impossible to ascertain this in advance.

One of the most crucial problems with using APIs is that not everyone who developed them uses the same level of scrutiny. APIs are sometimes coded with little or no validation or security testing. Consumption of these APIs without any type of validation can lead to data leakage, poor authentication, and authorization and application failure. Furthermore, manipulating an unsecured API might at worst, lead to a data breach. Besides, when an application is changed or updated, the API might expose items that were not exposed before.

One technique to overcome these issues is to make sure that processes are in place that allows for constant testing and review of APIs.

Community Knowledge

Software that has been openly tested and reviewed by the community at large is considered to be more secure by various security professionals as compared to the software that has not to gone through such a process. This can include open source software.

By moving toward leveraging standards such as **ISO 27034-1**, companies can be confident that partners have the same understanding of application security. This will increase security as organizations, regulatory bodies, and the IT audit community gain an understanding of the importance of embedding security during the processes required to create and utilize security.

> **Note: ISO 27034-1** is a standard which specify designing, developing, testing, implementing and maintaining security functions and controlling application systems.

Supply-Chain Management

It is crucial for organizations to consider the implications of non-secure software beyond their corporate boundaries. The ease with which software components with uncertain development processes can be combined to produce new applications has built a complex and highly dynamic software supply chain (API management).

We utilize softwares that are being developed by a third party or accessed with or through third-party libraries to enable or create functionality, without having a clear understanding of the origins of the software. This typically leads to a situation where there is complex and highly dynamic software interaction taking place between and among more than one services and systems within any organization and between organizations via Cloud.

This supply chain provides agility in the rapid development of applications to meet customer's demand. Therefore, it is important to assess all codes and services for accurate and secure functioning, no matter where they are sourced.

Software Development Life-Cycle (SDLC) Process

The SDLC process includes several steps in succession that form the framework for proper requirements analysis, designing, development, testing, and maintaining of software development projects.

Phases & Methodologies

Software development should be done for hosting in a Cloud environment or a traditional data center, the phases or steps for the SDLC are the same.

Requirement Analysis

This is the first stage in the SDLC process. It includes those requirements that go into determining the needs or conditions to meet for a new or altered software product, taking into account the possibility of conflicting requirements of the various stakeholders, such as users or beneficiaries.

Requirements analysis is significant to the success of a development project. Requirements should be measurable, actionable, testable, related to identified business needs or opportunities, and defined to a level of detail sufficient for system design. Requirements can be functional and non-functional.

Designing

This phase can take the formal requirements and specifications and change them into a structure and plan for the actual software coding, changing the requirements into an actual plan that can be applied to the programming language designated for the project. At this stage of the project, the formal security threats and the requirements for risk lessening and minimization are integrated with the programming designs.

Development

In this phase, the project plan is divided into pieces for coding, and then the actual coding is performed. As the requirements are converted into actual executable programming language, testing is done on each part of the phases to make sure that it compiles. This phase is typically the most significant phase of the SDLC process.

Testing

In this phase testing is performing against the requirements to ensure that the software product is solving the needs gathered during the requirements phase. Throughout this phase integration testing, unit testing, system testing, and acceptance testing are all conducted.

Maintenance

Once the software has been successfully tested and moved into production use, there will be continual updates for additional features, fixes bugs, and security patches for the lifetime of the software. This is an iterative and on-going process. It involves going through the complete SDLC process each time, progressing through requirements, design, development, and testing.

Business Requirements

It is a well-structured document of software requirement that defines the final deliverable of the project. The purpose behind developing this document is to drive the software

development process and assist the project management team. The comprehensive document holds the requirement of business and operation.

While developing a new project, client mentions their objective and the expectation in a document known as business requirement. The document helps us to define the functional requirement. The drive of a business requirement to functional requirement has more than one station which is known as a user requirement.

Software Configuration Management & Versioning

Once the application has been implemented using the SDLC process, the application moves in secure operations phase. Proper software configuration management and versioning are essential to application security. Some tools can be used to make sure that the software is configured according to specified requirements. Two tools that can be used:

Chef

With Chef, you can automate how you develop, implement, and manage your infrastructure. The Chef server stores your recipes along with other configuration data. The Chef client is installed on each server, container, virtual machine, or networking device you manage (called nodes). The client sometimes polls the Chef server for the latest policy and the state of your network. If anything on the node is outdated, the client promptly updates it.

Puppet

According to puppet labs, "**Puppet is a configuration management system that allows you to define the state of your IT infrastructure and then automatically enforces the correct state.**"

The objective of this application is to make sure that configurations are updated as required and if there is consistency in versioning. This phase calls for the following activities to take place:

- Activity monitoring
- Dynamic analysis
- Layer-7 firewalls (e.g., web application firewalls)
- Penetration testing and Vulnerability assessments

Apply the Secure Software Development Life-Cycle

To apply the Secure SDLC process, an understanding of Cloud-specific risks and the application of threat modeling to assess those risks is required along with specific vulnerabilities faced by an application.

Common Vulnerabilities

There are some vulnerabilities in the SDLC process, but some are defined in the common vulnerabilities OWASP Top 10 section, and some are defined here:

SQL Injection

This attack consists of injection or insertion of a SQL query through the input data from the client to the application. An effective SQL injection exploit can read sensitive data from the database, modify the data in the database such as Insert, Update or Delete, execute administration operations on the database (such as shutdown the DBMS), recover the content of a given file existing on the Database Management System (DBMS) file system and somtimes issues commands to the operating system. This attack is a type of injection attack, in which SQL commands are injected or inserted into data-plane input to affect the execution of predefined SQL commands.

Cross-Site Request Forgery (CSRF)

This attack forces a logged-on victim's browser to send a forged HTTP request, including the victim's session cookie and any other automatically included authentication information, to a weak web application. This allows the attacker to force the victim's browser to generate requests that the vulnerable application determines as legitimate requests from the victim.

Direct Object Reference

This can occur when a developer exposes a reference to an internal implementation object, such as a directory, file, or database key. Without an access control check or other protection, attackers can manipulate these references to access unauthorized data.

Buffer Overflow

This error is characterized by the overwriting of memory fragments of the process, which could have never been modified intentionally or unintentionally. Overwriting values of the Base Pointer (BP), Instruction Pointer (IP) and other registers causes exceptions, segmentation faults, and other errors to occur. Usually these errors end execution of the application in an unexpected way. This error occurs when we operate on buffers of **"char type."**

This can consist of overflowing the Heap overflow or Stack Overflow.

Cloud-Specific Risks

Cloud Security Alliance's (CSA) recommended the following risks in Cloud computing. These risks can be very high and found in many Cloud-computing environments.

Data Breaches

This risk is one of the significant risks associated with Cloud computing. A data breach is defined as the exposure of data like enterprise secrets, user information, etc. It is the most critical threat as it contains sensitive content and it can cause significant downfalls to enterprises along with the whole industry.

Solution

Data should always be encrypted. Typically when it is to be used by virtual machines. The user can use multi-factor authentication to provide more security features to confidential data stored in the Cloud as well.

Data Loss

The Cloud service provider must have a proper data recovery plan. The objective is that there is a high chance of data loss on Cloud services due to following reasons like Malicious attack, Natural disaster and Data removal by the provider.

An organization can lose valuable information as a consequence to lost data, and it could severely affect an organization. Hence, verifying the provider's data backup policy is of utmost importance as it is related to access, physical storage, and physical location of the data centers.

Account Hijacking

This risk is considered the highest risk in the IT industry due to an open access to Cloud platform. It has enhanced credential compromise like login details by attackers to make them successful in accessing sensitive user information in the Cloud. Additionally, they can manipulate the information using the hijacked user credentials. Sometimes, Hijackers use Cloud for stealing credentials by injecting cross-site scripting bug.

Insecure APIs

In a Cloud environment, APIs is a source to customize the features of Cloud services to improve the user experience. The developer creates their programs and integrates those applications within a Cloud service for improved performance. However, sometimes these APIs are used for accessibility, authentication, and encryption purposes, and that is where the vulnerability is created. This increases security risks.

Denial of Service (DoS)

This attack is a type of cyber-attack that does not target to breach the sensitive data. However, it carries long-term effects like making a website and servers unavailable. Moreover, sometimes it turns down firewalls to perform malicious actions.

Malicious Insiders

CERN defines an insider threat as "**A former or current employee, business partner or contractor who has or had authorized access to an organization's system, network, or data and intentionally exceeded or misused that access in a manner that negatively affected the availability, confidentiality, or integrity of the organization's information or information systems.**"

Abuse of Cloud Services

As Cloud leverages the extensive facility of services and storage, any organization whether small or large, host a massive amount of data in the Cloud. However, this storage solution also allows hosting illegal software and other digital contents. Therefore, it sometimes adversely affects the Cloud service providers and their users. In many cases, such contents include pirated books, music, videos or software.

Insufficient Due Diligence

Apart from the technical security concern, security risk can come up due to inefficient Cloud strategy. This means that when an organization is unclear about its objectives, policies, and resources, it causes insufficient due diligence which creates security risk for the organizations.

Shared Technology Issues

The Cloud security is a shared goal for the provider and the client. Here the partnership is between the provider and the client, where the client wants to take preventive measures to protect data. In many cases, this shared technology is omitted, there is a high chance of comprising security.

Quality of Service (QoS)

The QoS layer of service-oriented architecture (SOA) is focused on monitoring and managing both the IT systems levels and the business levels. On the IT systems level, QoS is focused on the security and health of systems, services, applications, networking, storage, and all other components that comprise the IT infrastructure. On the business level, QoS is focused on the measuring and monitoring of events, business processes, and key performance indicators (KPIs). QoS is also concerned with the monitoring and enforcement of business policies in all areas, including access, security, and data.

Threat Modelling

A threat model is a process that reviews the security of any web-based application, identifies problem areas, and determines the risk associated with each area.

Threat modeling is commonly used tool by software development teams as they integrate security into their development life cycle.

Threat modeling is performed once an application design is created. The objective of threat modeling is to determine any vulnerabilities in the application and the potential ingress, egress, and actors involved before it is introduced to production. It is the overall attack surface that is amplified by the Cloud, which the threat model has to take into account.

The Cloud Service Provider (CSP) always have to remember that the nature of threats faced by a system changes over time and that due to the dynamic nature of a changing threat landscape, constant vigilance and monitoring is a mandatory for overall application security in Cloud.

There are numerous threat modeling tools such as AS/NZS 4360, CVSS, DREAD, STRIDE, AND Trike. However, OWSAP recommended the STRIDE Model so that we will cover only the STRIDE model.

STRIDE Thread Model

STRIDE is an acronym of Spoofing, Tampering, Repudiation, Information, Disclosure, and Elevation. **Microsoft** creates this model.

STRIDE is a system for classifying known threats according to the types of exploit that are used or motivation of the attacker. In this model, the following six threats are considered, and controls are used to address the threats:

Threats	Description
Spoofing	Attacker assumes the identity of the subject
Tampering	An attacker alters Data or messages
Repudiation	Illegitimate denial of an event
Information disclosure	Information is obtained without authorization
Denial of service	Attacker overloads system to deny legitimate access
Elevation of privilege	Attacker gains a privilege level above what is permitted

Table 4-2: Threats and Description of STRIDE Threat Model

Specifics of Cloud Application Architecture

There are numerous tools, and additional technologies available that promote and make sure the highest levels of security within Cloud computing. These are based on a **defense-in-depth philosophy** and provide layered security to expand upon traditional host or application security controls to allow for different and additional types of security measures that exceed what can be supported by the application itself.

Supplemental Security Devices

These devices are used to add additional components and layers to a **defense-in-depth architecture**. The objective for a defense-in-depth architecture is to design using multiple overlapping and mutually reinforcing components and controls that will allow for the establishment of a robust security architecture. These devices include the following components:

WAF

A Web Application Firewall (WAF) helps to secure a web application by monitoring and filtering HTTP traffic between the Internet and a web application. It widely protects web applications from attacks such as cross-site-scripting (XSS), cross-site request forgery (CSRF), file inclusion, and SQL injection, among others. A WAF is a layer 7 protocol in the OSI model and is not designed to protect against all major types of attacks. This method of attack mitigation is usually part of a suite of tools, which together create a holistic defense against a range of attack vectors.

A Cloud-based WAF can be handy in the case of a denial-of-service (DoS) attack; several cases reported where a Cloud-based WAF was used to thwart DoS attacks of 350Gbs and 450Gbs successfully.

DAM

- Database Activity Monitoring (DAM) is a layer-7 monitoring device that identifies SQL commands.
- DAM is network-based (NDAM) or agent-based (ADAM).
- A DAM is to be used to detect and stop malicious commands from executing on an SQL server.
- Also, Database activity monitoring (DAM) is the process of monitoring, analysing and reporting a database's activities. Database activity monitoring tools use real-time security technology to monitor and analyze configured activities individually and without relying on the Database Management System (DBMS) auditing or logs.

XML Firewalls

"This is a specialized device used to protect applications exposed via XML based interfaces like Representational state transfer (REST), **Web Services Description Language (WSDL)**, and scan XML traffic coming in and out of an organization."

Besides, there are some points that further describe to XML Firewalls.

- An XML Firewall processes XML requests and responses over HTTP or HTTPS.

- An XML Firewall uses a single protocol and contains a processing policy with a set of the request, response, two-way and error rules.
- An XML Firewall provides a **rigid**, standards-based digital signature, signature verification capabilities and wire-speed.

API Gateway

- An API gateway is a device that filters API traffic; it can be installed as a proxy or as a specific part of your application's stack before data is processed.
- The API Gateway takes all the requests from the end-users, then routes them to the applicable **microservice** with request routing, protocol translation, and composition.
- API can implement access control, logging, metrics, rate limiting, and security filtering.

Cryptography

When working with Cloud computing, it is important to understand they are operating within and across trusted and untrusted networks. These can also be referred to as **semi-hostile and hostile environments**. As such, data held within and communications to and between services and systems operating in the Cloud must be encrypted.

Transport Layer Security (TLS)

Transport Layer Security (TLS) is a protocol that makes sure privacy between communicating applications and their users on the Internet. When a client and server communicate, TLS makes sure that no third party may tamper or **eavesdrop** any message. TLS is the successor to the Secure Sockets Layer (SSL).

Secure Socket Layer (SSL)

Secure Socket Layer (SSL) is the standard security technology for establishing an encrypted link between a browser and a web server. This link ensures that all data passed between the web server and browsers remain private and integral.

Virtual Private Network (VPN)

A network that is constructed by using public wires (such as the internet) to connect to a private network, such as a company's internal network. Some systems enable you to create networks using the Internet as the medium for transporting data.

All these technologies encrypt data to and from your data center and system communications within a Cloud environment.

> **Note: Hostile environments** is a particularly relevant application of pervasive computing. The technology can save lives by both eliminating the need for humans to work in these environments and supporting them when they do.
>
> **Eavesdropping** is the unauthorized real-time interception of private communication, such as a phone call, instant message, and videoconference or fax transmission.

Sandboxing

A sandbox separates and monitors the behaviour of only the intended elements while having proper separation from the remaining elements (i.e., the ability to store personal information in one sandbox, with corporate information in another sandbox). Within Cloud computing, sandboxing is widely used to run untrusted or untested code in a tightly controlled environment. Many vendors have begun to offer Cloud-based sandbox environments that can be leveraged by organizations to test applications thoroughly.

Most corporations use a sandbox environment to understand better how an application is properly working and thoroughly test applications by executing them and observing the file behavior for indications of malicious activity.

Application Virtualization

A technology that creates a virtual environment for an application to run. This virtualization essentially creates an encapsulation from the underlying operating system. Application virtualization can be used to isolate or sandbox an application to see the processes it performs.

There are many examples of application virtualization available:

- Windows XP mode in Windows 7.
- "Wine" allows some Microsoft applications to run on a Linux platform.

The primary objective of application virtualization is to test an application while protecting the operating system and other applications on a particular system.

Identity and Access Management (IAM) Solutions

Identity and Access Management (IAM) includes a system, process, and people that are used to manage access to organization resources by making sure that the identity of an entity is verified and then granting the proper level of access based on the protected resource, this assured identity, and other contextual information. There are many factors and elements to make up a complete IAM solution.

Federated Identity

A Federated Identity refers to the identity of a person in a single system that is linked to a similar person's identity in multiple other systems.

Federated identity provides the mechanisms, policies, and processes, which manage identity and trusted access to systems through the enterprises.

Federated identity is related to single sign-on (SSO), in which a user's single authentication token, or ticket, is trusted across many Information Technology systems and organizations.

The technology of federation is much similar of **Kerberos** within an **Active Directory** domain, where a user logs on once to a domain controller is eventually granted an access token and uses that token to gain access to systems for which the user has authorization. The main difference is that while Kerberos works well in a single domain, federated identities allow for the generation of tokens (authentication) in one domain and the consumption of these tokens (authorization) in another domain.

Generally, there are two types of federation

Web-of-trust model: Each member of the federation has to review and approve each other member for inclusion in the federation.

Third-party identifier: The member organizations outsource their responsibilities to review and approve each other to some external party that would take on this responsibility on behalf of all the members.

Federation Standards

There are some federation standards that exit but some are widely used.

Security Assertion Markup Language (SAML)

Security Assertion Markup Language (SAML) is XML based and consists of a framework for communicating authentication, authorization and attribute information through organizations. The latest version of SAML is SAML 2.0.

WS-Federation

An identity federation specification within the broader WS-security framework.

According to the WS-Federation Version 1.2 OASIS standard *"This specification defines mechanisms to allow different security realms to federate, such that authorized access to resources managed in one realm can be provided to security principals whose identities are managed in other realms. While the final access control decision is enforced strictly by the realm that controls the resource, federation provides mechanisms that enable the decision to be based on the declaration (or*

brokering) of identity, attribute, authentication, and authorization assertions between realms. The choice of mechanisms, in turn, is dependent upon trust relationships between the realms."

<u>OAuth</u>

OAuth is typically used in authorization with mobile apps, the OAuth framework provides third-party applications limited access to HTTP services.

<u>OpenID Connect</u>

This is an interoperable authentication protocol based on the **OAuth 2** specification. It allows developers to authenticate their users through applications and websites without having to manage usernames and passwords.

Identity Providers (IP)

IP is the entity that provisions and authenticates identity assertions such as validating users, provisioning user IDs and passwords, managing both, de-provisioning them, etc.

The IP holds all of the identities and generates a token for known users.

In Cloud computing, it is desirable that the organization itself continues to maintain all identities and act as the identity provider.

Single Sign-On (SSO)

This is widely used for facilitating inter-organizational and inter-security domain access to resources leveraging federated identity management.

SSO should not be confused with reduced sign-on (RSO). Generally, RSO operates through some form of credential synchronization. Implementation of an RSO solution introduces security issues which are not experienced by SSO, by default SSO eliminates usernames, passwords, and other sensitive data from traversing the network. As the foundation of federation relies on the existence of an identity provider (IP), reduced sign-on (RSO) has no place in a federated identity system.

Multi-factor Authentication (MFA)

MFA is a security system that requires one or more methods of authentication from independent categories of credentials to verify the user's identity for a login or other transaction. To be a multi-factor system, users must be able to provide two or more independent credentials: what they know (e.g., password), what they have (e.g., display token with random numbers displayed) and what they are (e.g., biometrics). The objective of MFA is to add an extra level of protection to verify the legitimacy of a transaction.

One-time passwords also fall under the banner of multi-factor authentication. The use of one-time passwords is strongly encouraged during provision and communication of first-login passwords to users.

Step-up authentication is an additional procedure or factor that validates a user's identity, usually prompted by high-risk transactions or violations according to policy rules.

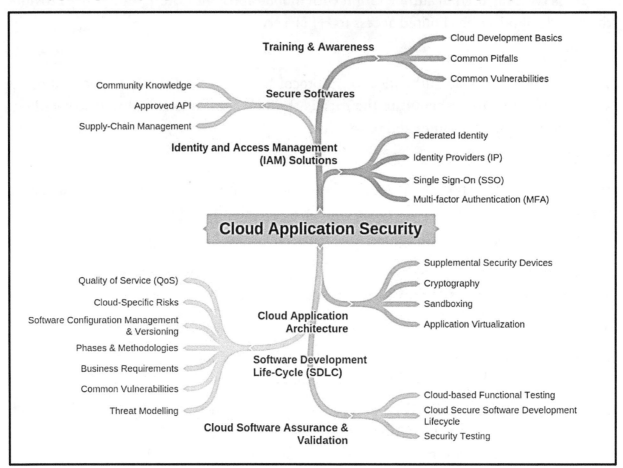

Figure 4-4: Mind Map of Cloud Application Security

Practice Questions

1. Which API is used the envelope?
   a) REST
   b) SOAP
   c) Both
   d) None of these

2. Which API provides a web services feature?
   a) REST
   b) SOAP
   c) Both
   d) None of these

3. Which security testing type is considered as white-box testing?
   a) SAST
   b) DAST
   c) Pen Testing
   d) None of the above

4. Which security testing type is considered as black-box testing?
   a) SAST
   b) DAST
   c) Pen Testing
   d) None of the above

5. Which security testing type works in a running application?
   a) SAST
   b) DAST
   c) Pen Testing
   d) None of the above

6. Which of the following is not a part of an OWASP Top ten list?
   a) Weak password requirements
   b) Injection attack
   c) Broken Authentication
   d) Sensitive Data Exposure

7. How many types of federations are there?

a) Two
b) Three
c) Four
d) Five

8. Which of the following is not a stage of SDLC process?
   a) Designing
   b) Development
   c) Reject
   d) Testing

9. Which of the following is not a part of the STRIDE model?
   a) Spoofing
   b) External Pen testing
   c) Repudiation
   d) Information

10. Database activity monitoring can be:
    a) Network base or agent-based
    b) Server-based or client-based
    c) Used in place of data masking
    d) Used in the place of encryption

11. Which layer in the OSI Model that WAF use?
    a) Layer 2
    b) Layer 4
    c) Layer 6
    d) Layer 7

12. Which device filters API traffic?
    a) WAF
    b) DAM
    c) XML Firewalls
    d) API Gateway

Chapter 05: Operations

The operations chapter is focused on how to plan, design, operate, run, manage, and monitor both the physical and logical components of a Cloud data center. These components are categorized in layers to be easy to manage and troubleshoot. We focus on the main components of each layer, including network devices, servers, and storage systems along with what makes them unique to a Cloud data center compared to a traditional data center. We will also examine the risk assessment process for a system, how it relates to Cloud systems, and the collection of forensic evidence, as well as the unique challenges and considerations that a cloud environment comprises.

Data Center Design

Data center's design and architecture have long formed an integral part of the information technology services for service providers. Over time these have often evolved and grown in line with Cloud computing developments and enhanced capabilities. Data center continues to be refined, enhanced, and improved globally; therefore, they remain dependent on the similar essential components to support their activities.

Implementing a secure design when developing a Cloud data center, involves numerous considerations. Before creating any design decision, work with senior management and other primary stakeholders to identify all compliance requirements for the Cloud data center. If you are developing a Cloud data center for public Cloud services, you will need to provide a higher level of security to your customers.

Logical Design

The logical design area contains the most profound differences between a traditional data center and a Cloud data center. Various main components of Cloud computing will drive key data center design decision, both with the design of the actual center along with the location of it.

Tenant Partitioning

As enterprises transition from traditionally dedicated server deployments to virtualized environments that leverage Cloud services, the Cloud computing networks that they are constructing need to provide security and segregate sensitive data and applications. In some cases, multi-tenant networks are a solution.

Briefly, Multi-tenant networks are data center networks that are logically divided into smaller isolated networks. They share the physical networking gear but operate on their network without visibility into other logical networks.

By default, in a Cloud deployment, multi-tenant needs a logical design that partitions and segregates customer's data. Failure to do so can result in an unauthorized access, view, or modification of tenant data.

Access Control

From a logical standpoint, some areas of access control are significant to consider in relation to the data center. In Cloud computing, you have the actual virtual machines to consider but also the management plane and hypervisor tiers. This sets a Cloud data center apart from a traditional data center because you are not only planning on accessing physical machines, but you also have to consider the layers that have supervisory and administrative control over other systems. Planning for early states to keep various layers separated allows the hypervisor and management plane layer to be completely shielded from systems and customer access, will promote stronger security control. Also planning for secure authentication and authorization controls, including strong verification requirements and multifactor authentication to be implemented at the very least for administrative access will ensure stronger security. As well as, secure access control designs, planning for robust logging, monitoring, and auditing for access control systems and mechanism from the initial phase of design is essential from a security perspective.

Physical Design

Data centers are the build-up of a standard set of equipment and components, same as servers and system, but all are different based on their requirements, purposes, and objectives, as set forth by the organizations constructing and maintaining the data centers. Many data center will look and function very similar to others, but each is unique with its problems and concerns.

Location

Location is the initial physical consideration of a data center, and it applies to various issues. The location of the data center will impact compliance decision and could further complicate the organization's ability to meet legal and regulatory requirements because the geographic location of a data center impacts its jurisdiction. Before selecting a location for the data center, an organization should have a clear understanding of requirements at the national, state or province and local levels. Contingency, failover, and redundancy involving other data centers in different locations are essential to understand.

The physical design of a data center also drives various design requirements based on the realities of threats posed from the physical requirement. Various locations have the threat or possibility of a natural disaster, which will directly impact many of the physical designs and protection requirements of the data center in different ways. The possibility of each natural disaster will influence the data center design along with the importance of business continuity and disaster recovery planning and testing. Various technologies can evolve to mitigate threats from natural disasters, such as **dikes, reinforced walls, and vibration control**.

Data centers need massive environmental and utility resources as well. These requirements include access to electrical grids that can handle the demands of a data center, access to water supplies, physical access for personnel, and access to telecommunication networks and the bandwidth that a data center needs.

Data center physical security is also a significant concern. Data centers should follow best practices for physical security and access. This means that border security such as fences, gates, walls, and so on, are all deployed in a layered approach along with monitoring capabilities. The location of a data center can significantly impact the types and layering of physical security available.

Buy/Build

The organization can build a data center, buy or rent some space in a data center. Regardless of the decision made by the organization, there are certain standards and concerns that must be considered and addressed through planning, such as data center tier certification, physical security level, and usage profile. As a Cloud Security Professional (CSP), you and the organization architect both play an essential role in ensuring these concerns are identified and addressed as part of the decision process.

If you build the data center, the organization will have the most control over the design and security of it. However, there is a significant investment that is necessary to build a robust data center.

Buying or renting space in a data center may be a cheaper alternative. With this option, there may be limitations to design impacts. The renting organization will include all security requirements in the **RFP** and contract.

When using a shared data center, physical separation of servers and equipment will be included in the design.

There are various standards available to select. Some of them are as follows:

- **Building Industry Consulting Service International Inc. (BICSI)**: The ANSI/BICSI 002-2014 standard covers cabling design and installation.

- **International Data Center Authority (IDCA):** **The Infinity Paradigm** covers data center location, facility structure, and infrastructure and applications.
- **National Fire Protection Association (NFPA):** The NFPA 75 and 76 standards specify how hot or cold aisle containment is to be carried out, NFPA standard 70 needs the implementation of an emergency power off button to secure first responders in the data center in case of emergency.

Note:

Dike: A dike, in geological usage, is a sheet of rock that is formed in a fracture in a pre-existing rock body.

RFP: A request for proposal (RFP) is a document that solicits proposal, often made through a bidding process, by an agency or company interested in procurement of a commodity, service, or asset, to potential suppliers to submit business proposals.

The Infinity Paradigm: The only all-in-one open standard framework for Data centers, Cloud, Big Data, IoT, IT, Facilities, and Infrastructure.

Environmental Design

The environmental design must account for adequate heating, ventilation, air conditioning, power with sufficient conditioning, and backup. Network connectivity must arise from many vendors and include many paths into the facility.

Heating, Ventilation & Air-conditioning (HVAC)

Heating, ventilation, and air conditioning (HVAC) refers to the different systems used for moving air between indoor and outdoor areas, as well as heating and cooling both residential and commercial buildings. They are the systems that keep you warm and cozy in the winter and feeling cool and fresh in the summer. They also are the systems that filter and clean indoor air to keep you healthy and maintain humidity levels at optimal comfort levels.

Its objective is to provide thermal comfort and acceptable indoor air quality (IAQ). HVAC system design is a study of mechanical engineering, based on the principles of thermodynamics, fluid mechanics and heat transfer.

In case of a Data center design, HVAC units are turned on and off based on return air temperature. **The American Society of Heating, Refrigeration, and Air Conditioning Engineers (ASHRAE)** recommends the Temperature and Humidity Guidelines that are specified in the table that will produce lower inlets temperature.

Temperature Type	Temperature Range
Low-end temperature	18°C (64.4°F)
High-end temperature	27°C (80.6°F)
Low-end moisture	40% relative humidity and 5.5°C (41.9°F) dew point
High-end moisture	60% relative humidity and 15°C (59°F) dew point

Table 5-1: Temperature Table

The Cloud Security Professional (CSP) should be aware that the lower the temperature in the data center, the higher the cooling would cost per month. Generally, the air conditioning system moves the heat generated by equipment in the data center outside, allowing the data center to maintain a stable temperature range for the operating equipment. The power requirements for cooling off a data center will be reliant on the amount of heat being removed along with the temperature difference between the inside of the data center and the outside air.

HVAC Design Consideration

Industry guidance ought to be followed to provide sufficient HVAC to secure the server equipment. Include the following considerations in your design:

- Backup power supplies must be provided to run the HVAC system for the time required for the system to stay up.
- Consideration has to be given to energy efficient systems.
- The local weather condition will affect HVAC design requirements.
- The HVAC system must provide air management that separates the cool air from the heat exhaustion of the servers.
- The HVAC system has to filter contaminants and dust.
- Redundant HVAC systems should be a part of the overall design.

Multi-Vendor Pathway Connectivity (MVPC)

Continuous service or access is essential to the daily operation and productivity of your business. With downtime translating directly to loss of income, data centers need to be designed for redundant, fail-safe reliability and availability.

The performance of the infrastructure also defines reliability of a data center. Cabling and connectivity backed by a reliable vendor with guaranteed error-free performance to help avoid poor transmission in the data center.

There must be redundant connectivity from numerous providers into the data center. This will guide to prevent a single point of failure for network connectivity. The redundant path has to provide the minimum expected connection speed for data center operations.

Note:

Thermal Comfort: It is the condition of mind that expresses satisfaction with the thermal environment and is assessed by subjective evaluation (ANSI/ASHRAE Standard 55).

Indoor Air Quality (IAQ): IAQ is the air quality inside and around the overall buildings and structures.

Mechanical Engineering: A discipline that applies engineering, engineering mathematics, physics, and materials science principles to analyse, design, manufacture, and maintain mechanical systems.

Thermodynamics: A branch of physics that deals with heat, temperature, and their relation to energy and work.

Fluid Mechanics: A branch of physics concerned with the mechanics of fluids that is liquids, gases, and plasmas and the forces on them.

Heat Transfer: A discipline of thermal engineering that concerns the generation, use, conversion, and exchange of thermal energy (heat) between physical systems.

ASHRAE: The American Society of Heating, Refrigerating and Air-Conditioning Engineers was founded in 1894, it has a huge number of members worldwide. ASHRAE is a global professional association seeking to advance heating, ventilation, air conditioning and refrigeration (HVAC&R) systems design and construction.

Physical Infrastructure for Cloud Environment

The physical infrastructure for a Cloud resolver around the significant components of networks, servers, and storage. All these components must go through careful planning to work together with the significant aspects of a Cloud compared to a traditional data center, done so with an eye towards security models and Cloud considerations.

Secure Configuration of Hardware Specific Requirements

A Cloud data center will have specific requirements that are unique to the Cloud environment, the appropriate securing of hardware and systems is the same as the traditional data center. Hardware and systems, much like applications and software, can carry a massive amount of configuration possibilities and requirements, due to the enormous amount of possible combinations of operating systems and hardware, along with the specific operating systems that run on appliance and hypervisor systems.

BIOS Settings

As with any physical hardware, virtualization hosts and **trusted platform modules (TPMs)** have BIOS settings that govern specific hardware configurations and security technologies to prevent access to them for manipulation.

Incorrect BIOS settings may reduce performance, so follow the vendor recommended guidance for the configuration of BIOS settings.

For Example:

If you are using **VMware Distributed Power Management (DPM)** technology, then you will need to turn off any power management settings in the host BIOS, as they may interface with the proper operation of DPM. It is essential to understand that the requirements for secure host configuration based on the vendor's platforms are being utilized in the organization.

Storage Controller

The following must be considered when configuring storage controllers.

- Switch off all unnecessary services, such as web interfaces and management services that will not be required or used.
- Validate the controllers that can meet the estimated traffic load based on vendor specifications and testing (1 GB, 10 GB, 16 GB, 40 GB).
- Deploy a redundant failover configuration such as a NIC team.
- You may also need to deploy a multi-path solution.
- Change default administrative passwords for configuration and management access to the controller.

Note that Vendor specifies different settings.

Network Controller

The two networking models that have to be considered are Traditional and Converged.

Traditional Networking Model

This model is a layered approach with physical switches at the top layer and logical separation at the hypervisor level. This model allows the use of network security tools. Maybe some limitations on the visibility of network segments between virtual machines (VM).

Converged Networking Model

This model is optimized for Cloud deployments and utilizes standard perimeter protection measures. The underlying storage and IP networks are converged to maximize the benefits

for a Cloud workload. This method facilitates the use of virtualized security equipment for network protection. It is essential to understand that a converged network model is a super network because it can carry a combination data, voice, and video traffic across a single network that is optimized for performance.

> **Note:**
>
> **Trusted Platform Module (TPM):** TPM is a computer chip (microcontroller) that can securely store artefacts used to authenticate the platform (your PC or laptop). These artefacts can include certificates, encryption keys, or passwords.
>
> **VMware's Distributed Power Management (DPM):** DPM is one feature that demonstrates the potential of VMotion -- not just visually but in hard cash. DPM, which is a piece of VMware's Distributed Resource Scheduler (DRS), and DRS do not get the exposure that they deserve. If every organization understood how well DRS and DPM minimize power consumption, these virtualization management tools would be considered mandatory for server infrastructure.
>
> **NIC Team:** In Windows Server, NIC teaming is a mechanism that allows multiple physical NICs to be bound together into a single logical NIC. That logical NIC has the capabilities of all the underlying physical hardware.

Virtualization Management Tools for the Host

Securely configuring the virtualization management toolset is one of the most critical phases when developing a Cloud environment. Compromising on the management tools may allow an attacker with unlimited access to the virtual machine, the host, and the organization network. Hence, you need to securely install and configure the management tools and then sufficiently monitor them.

All the management should take place on an isolated management network.

The virtualization platform will determine what management tools are needed to be installed on the host. The latest management tools must be installed on each host, and the configuration management plan has to include rules on updating these tools. Updating these tools may need server downtime, therefore, sufficient server resources have to be deployed to allow for the movement of virtual machines when updating the virtualization platform. You have to perform external vulnerability testing of the tools as well.

Follow the vendor security guidance when configuring and deploying these tools. Access to these management tools has to be role-based. You should also audit and log the management tools.

It is essential to understand what management tools are available by vendor platform, along with how to securely install and configure them in a proper way based on the configuration of the systems involved.

Best Practices

Regardless of the toolset used to manage the host, make sure that the following best practices are used to protect the tools and that only authorized users are given access when necessary to perform their jobs.

- **Access Control:** Secures the tool(s) and tightly controls and monitors to their access.
- **Auditing/Monitoring:** Monitors and tracks the use of the tool(s) throughout the organization to make sure that appropriate usage is taking place.
- **Defense in Depth:** Implements the tool(s) used to manage the host as part of a larger architectural design that mutually reinforces security at every level of the organization. The tool(s) should be seen as a tactical component of host management, one that is linked to an operational component such as procedures and a strategic component such as policies.
- **Maintenance:** Updates and patches the tool(s) as required ensuring compliance with all the vendor recommendations and security reports.

Run Physical Infrastructure for Cloud Environment

Running the physical infrastructure of a Cloud computing involves the access control systems, secure the networking configuration, hardening of the operating system through baselines and compliance.

Configuration of Access Control for Local Access

You must have a plan to address access control to the Cloud-hosting environment.

Physical access to servers has to be limited to users who need access for a specific purpose. Personnel who administer physical hardware should not have other types of administrative access.

Secure KVM

Before we describe how to secure KVM, we should firstly define what KVM is.

According to the "**Red Hat**":

"**Kernel-based Virtual Machine (KVM)** is an open source virtualization technology built into Linux". Specifically, KVM lets you turn **Linux** into a hypervisor that allows a host machine to run various machine; isolated virtual environments called **virtual machines**

(**VMs**) or guests. KVM is part of Linux. If you have any latest version of **Linux**, you have got **KVM**."

The **VM-Series** for KVM allows service providers and organization alike to add next-generation firewall and advanced threat prevention capabilities to their Cloud-based initiatives and Linux-based virtualization. KVM is a popular open-source hypervisor that enables service providers and organizations to deploy and manage the VM-Series across a range of Linux operating systems including **Ubuntu** and **CentOS/RHEL**.

Now, we are starting to describe how to secure KVM.

Access to host must be performed by secure KVM; for additional security, access to KVM devices have to need a checkout process. A secure KVM will prevent data leakage from the server to the connected computer, along with preventing un-secure **emanations**. The **Common Criteria (CC)** provides guidance on different security levels and a list of KVM products that meet those security levels. Multi-factor authentication has to be considered for remote console access. All access should be logged and routine audits are performed.

A secure KVM will meet the following design criteria:

- **Fixed Firmware:** It cannot be re-programmed, preventing attempts to modify the logic of the KVM.
- **Housing Intrusion Detection:** Causes the KVM to become inoperable and the **LEDs** to flash repeatedly if the housing has been opened.
- **Isolated Data Channels:** Located in each KVM port and make it impossible for data to be transferred between connected computers via KVM.
- **Push-button Control:** Need physical access to KVM when switching between connected computers.
- **Tamper warning labels on each side of the KVM:** This provides clear visual evidence if the enclosure has been compromised.
- **Selective USB Access:** Only authorized human interface device USB devices (such as keyboard and mice) to prevent unintentional and insecure data transfer.
- **Safe Buffer Design:** Does not incorporate with a memory buffer, and the keyboard buffer is automatically cleared after data transmission, preventing the transfer of keystrokes or other data when switching between computers.

> **Note:**
>
> **Linux:** A family of free and open-source software operating systems based on the Linux kernel, developed by Linus Torvalds.

> **Virtual Machine (VM):** VM is an emulation of a computer system. VM is based on computer architecture and provides the functionality of a physical computer. Their implementations may involve specialized software, hardware, or a mixture of both.
>
> **VM-Series:** A virtualized form of a factor to the next-generation firewall that can be deployed in a range of public and private Cloud computing environments based on technologies from Amazon Web Services (AWS), Cisco, Citrix, Google, KVM, Microsoft, OpenStack, and VMware.
>
> **Ubuntu:** An open source software operating system that runs from the desktop to the Cloud, to all your internet-connected things.
>
> **CentOS:** Community Enterprise Operating System is a Linux distribution that provides a free, enterprise-class, community-supported computing platform functionally compatible with its upstream source, RHEL.
>
> **RHEL:** Red Hat Enterprise Linux is a Linux distribution developed by Red Hat and targeted towards the commercial market.
>
> **Common Criteria (CC):** An international set of guidelines and specifications developed for evaluating information security products, specifically to ensure they meet an agreed-upon security standard for government deployments.
>
> **LED:** A light-emitting diode is a semiconductor light source that emits light when current flows through it.

Console-based Access Mechanisms

Console based access to virtual machines (VM) is significant. Regardless of the vendor platform, all VM management software provide a "**manage by console**" option. The use of these consoles to access, configure, and manage VMs provide an administrator the opportunity to control almost every component of VMs configuration and usage easily. Therefore, a bad actor or hacker can achieve the same level of access and control by using these consoles if they are not properly secured and managed. The use of access controls for console access is available in every vendor platform and have to be implemented and regularly audited for compliance as a best practice.

Securing Network Configuration

The network layer is significant for the entire system and data center security. Four main technologies are used for its security.

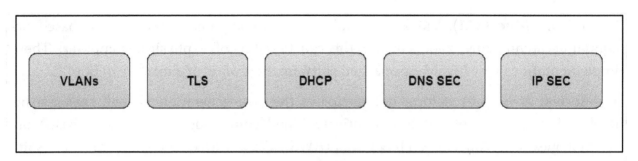

Figure 5-1: Networking Layers

VLANs

The network can be one of the weakest components of any system.

The virtual machine network needs as much protection as the physical network. By using VLANs, you can improve networking security in your environment. In simple terms, a VLAN is a set of workstations within a LAN that can communicate with each other as though they were on a single isolated LAN. It is an IEEE standard networking scheme with specific tagging methods that allow routing of packets to only those ports that are part of the VLAN.

When properly configured, VLANs provide a dependable means to protect a set of machines from accidental or malicious intrusions. VLANs let you segment a physical network so that two machines in the network can transmit packets back and forth unless they are part of the same VLAN.

Besides, VLAN communicates with each other as though they were on a single, isolated LAN because a VLAN does the following:

- Broadcasts packets sent by one of the workstations will reach all the others in the VLAN.
- Broadcasts sent by one of the workstations in the VLAN will not reach any workstations that are not in the VLAN.
- Broadcasts sent by workstations that are not in the VLAN will never reach workstations that are in the VLAN.
- All workstations can communicate with each other without the need to go through a gateway.

Purpose of VLANS

The main reason for splitting a network into LAN is to reduce congestion on a large LAN. Initially, LAN was very flat; all the workstations were connected to a single piece of coaxial cable, or to sets of chained hubs. In a flat LAN, every packet that any device puts onto the wire gets sent to every other device on the LAN. As the number of workstations on the

typical LAN grew, they started to become congested; there were just too many collisions because most of the time when a workstation tried to send a packet it would find that a packet sent by any other device already occupied the wire.

VLANs can help reduce network traffic by forming many broadcast domains, to splitting up a more extensive network into smaller independent segments with some broadcasts being sent to each device on the entire network.

Transport Layer Security (TLS)

Transport Layer Security (TLS) is a cryptographic protocol designed to provide communication security to an entire network. It uses X.509 certificates to authenticate a connection and to replace a symmetric key. This key is used to encrypt any data sent over the connection. The TLS protocol allows server or client applications to communicate across a network in a way designed to ensure confidentiality. TLS has two layers that are defined below.

TLS Handshake Protocol

Allows the client or server to authenticate each other and to communicate an encryption algorithm and cryptographic keys before data is sent or received.

TLS Record Protocol

Provides connection security and makes sure that the connection is reliable and secure. Used to encapsulate higher-level protocols, between them TLS handshake protocol.

Dynamic Host Configuration Protocol (DHCP)

Dynamic Host Configuration Protocol (DHCP) is a client or server protocol that automatically provides an Internet Protocol (IP) host with its IP address and other related configuration information such as the default gateway and subnet mask. RFCs 2131 and 2132 define DHCP as an Internet Engineering Task Force (IETF) standard based on Bootstrap Protocol (BOOTP), a protocol with which DHCP shares various implementation details. DHCP allows hosts to obtain needed TCP/IP configuration information from a DHCP server.

The DHCP server considerably reduces configuration efforts because an administrator does not have to manually assign each computer with IP addresses and other IP-related settings.

DHCP Advantages

DHCP provides the following advantages.

- **Reliable IP Address Configuration:** DHCP reduced configuration errors caused by manual IP address configuration, such as typographical errors, or address

conflicts caused by the assigning of an IP address to one or more computer at the same time.

- **Reduced Network Administration:** DHCP includes the following benefits to reduce network administration:
  - Automated and centralized TCP/IP configuration.
  - The capability to classify TCP/IP configurations from a central location.
  - The capability to assign a complete range of additional TCP/IP configuration values through DHCP options.
  - The skilful handling of IP address changes for clients that must be updated frequently, such as those for portable devices that move to different locations on a wireless network.
  - The forwarding of initial DHCP messages by using a DHCP relay agent, which removes the need for a DHCP server on every subnet.

DNS SEC

Before understanding DNS SEC, you first need to know how the DNS system works.

DNS is used to translate a domain name (like ipspecialist.net) into numeric Internet address like (197.166.1.0). DNS is a hierarchical, distributed database that contains a mapping of DNS domain names to multiple forms of data such as the Internet Protocol (IP) addresses. DNS allows you to use friendly names, such as www.ipspecialist.net, to efficiently address computers and other resources on a TCP/IP-based network.

Now, we move to the DNS SEC.

DNSSEC is a suite of **Internet Engineering Task Force (IETF)** that adds security to the Domain Name System (DNS) protocol by enabling DNS responses to be validated. DNSSEC provides authenticated denial-of-existence, data integrity, and origin authority. With DNSSEC, the DNS protocol is much less susceptible to specific types of attacks, especially DNS spoofing attacks.

If an authoritative DNS server supports it, a DNS zone can be secured with DNSSEC using a process called zone signing. To signing a zone, with DNSSEC adds validation to support a zone without modifying the simple mechanism of a DNS query and response.

Validation of DNS responses occurs via the use of the digital signature that is included with DNS responses. These digital signatures are contained in new, DNSSEC-related resources records that are generated and added to them during the zone signing.

When a DNSSEC-aware forwarding or recursive DNS server receives a query from a DNS client for a DNSSEC-signed zone, it will request that the authoritative DNS server also send DNS records and then attempt to validate the DNS response using these records. A

forwarding or recursive DNS server identifies the zone supports DNSSEC if it has a DNSKEY, also known as a trust anchor, or that zone.

Threats to the DNS Infrastructure

The following are the common ways in which attackers can threaten the DNS infrastructure:

- **Data modification**: An attacker may attempt to spoof valid IP addresses in IP packets that the attacker has created. This gives these packets the appearance of coming from a valid IP address in the network. In a valid IP address, the attacker can gain access to the network and destroy data or perform other attacks.
- **Denial-of-Service attack**: When an attacker attempts to deny the availability of network services by flooding more than one DNS servers in the network with queries.
- **Footprinting**: An attacker obtains the process by which DNS zone data, including DNS domain names, computer names, and Internet Protocol (IP) addresses for sensitive network resources.
- **Redirection**: When an attacker can redirect queries for DNS names to servers that are under the control of the attacker.
- **Spoofing**: When a DNS server accepts and uses inappropriate information from a host that has no rights to give the information. DNS spoofing is malicious cache poisoning where forged data is placed in the cache of the name servers.

IP SEC

IPsec is a transit encryption protocol used for VPN tunnels that can utilize cryptographic algorithms such as AES and 3DES.

IPsec is a framework for a set of protocols used for security at the network layer that is convenient for implementing virtual private networks and for remote user access via private networks.

However, remote users are treated as full members of the network. Nothing is invisible – they have direct access to the underlying infrastructure. Therefore, if they are malicious, they can start digging around and looking for vulnerabilities in seconds.

VPNs provide remote access to their networks. It is potentially the highest risk factor for third-party data breaches because IPsec is readily exploitable by hackers.

IPsec provides two choices of security service:

- **Authentication Header (AH)**: AH provides authentication of the sender of data,

- **Encapsulating Security Payload (ESP)**: ESP provides both authentication of the sender and the encryption of data as well.

OS Hardening via Application of Baseline (e.g., Windows, Linux, VMware)

Each operating system will be hardened to provide only essential ports, protocols, and services to meet organizational needs and have in place for supporting technical controls such as file integrity monitoring, antivirus, and logging as part of their baseline operating, building standard, or template.

Operating systems and virtual machines are deployed using the minimum amount of services and functionality required for them to run. Security assessments and vulnerability scans are run against the internal and external environment; these scans demonstrate whether only the minimum number of ports are open.

Baseline Configuration by Platform

There are numerous differences between Windows, Linux, and VMware configurations.

Windows

Microsoft provides several tools to measure the security baseline of a Windows system.

- The use of a toolset such as the **Windows Server Update Service (WSUS)** makes it possible to perform **patch management** on a Windows host and monitor for compliance with a pre-configured baseline.
- The **Microsoft Deployment Toolkit (MDT)**, either as a stand-alone toolset or integrated into the **System Center Configuration Manager (SCCM)** product, will allow you to create, manage, and deploy more than one Microsoft Windows Server OS baseline images.
- At least one of the **Best Practice Analysers (BPAs)** that Microsoft provides should also be considered.

Linux

The Linux distribution in use will play a large part to help determine when the baseline deployment will appear. The security features of each Linux distribution have to be considered, and the one that best meets the organization's security needs, have to be used. However, you still have to be familiar with the recommended best practices for Linux baseline security.

VMware

VMware vSphere has essential tools that allow the user to build custom baselines for their particular deployments. These tools range from host and storage profiles, which force configuration of an **ESXi** host to mirror a set of preconfigured baseline options, to the **VMware Update Manager (VUM)** tool, which allows for the updating of more than one

ESXi hosts with the latest VMware security patches to allow updates to the virtual machines running on the host. VUM can be used to monitor compliance with a pre-configured baseline.

Note:

Windows Server Update Services (WSUS): WSUS is a computer program developed by Microsoft Corporation that enables administrators to manage the distribution of updates and bug fixes released by Microsoft for computers that are using Microsoft products in an organizational environment. WSUS downloads these updates from the Microsoft Update website and then distributes them to computers on a network. WSUS is an integral component of Windows Server.

Microsoft Deployment Toolkit (MDT): MDT is a computer program that allows network deployment of Microsoft Office and Microsoft Windows.

Microsoft System Centre Configuration Manager (SCCM): Microsoft SCCM is a systems management software product developed by Microsoft for managing large groups of computers running Windows, Linux, and UNIX, etc. Microsoft SCCM is also known as ConfigMgr.

Best Practices Analyzer (BPA): In Windows management, best practices are guidelines that are considered the ideal way to configure a server as defined by experts. BPA is a server management tool that is available in Windows Server 2012 R2, Windows Server 2012, and Windows Server 2008 R2.

ESXi: VMware ESXi is an enterprise-class, type-1 hypervisor developed by VMware for deploying and serving virtual computers. As a type-1 hypervisor, ESXi is not a software application that is installed on an operating system; instead, it includes and integrates essential OS components, such as a kernel.

VMware Update Manager (VUM): VUM is a software for automating patch management.

Availability of Stand-Alone Hosts

As a Cloud Security Professional (CSP), you can be called upon to help the organization in a secure way to host a virtualized model. The organizational needs and requirements will be identified and documented before a decision can be finalized as to which hosting environment(s) are the best to deploy.

Generally, the organization seeks to;

- Create secure, isolated, dedicated hosting of specific Cloud resources; the use of a stand-alone host would be the right choice.

- Make the Cloud resources available to end users, so they appear as if they are independent of any other resources and are **isolated**; either a stand-alone host or a shared host configuration that offers multi-tenant secured hosting capabilities would be appropriate.

The CSP needs to understand the organizational requirements because they will drive the choice of hosting model and the architecture for the Cloud security framework.

Availability of Clustered Hosts (e.g., Distributed Resource Acheduling (DRS), Dynamic Optimization (DO), storage clusters, maintenance mode, high availability)

A cluster host is a host that is configured to control over the role of another host server within a cluster. This method reduces the danger inherent in a single point of failure and makes more efficient use of network resources.

Besides, a cluster host is a host machine that can support numerous guest operating systems on another physical machine. Therefore, when a physical machine goes down for maintenance or reboot, the cluster host has to be configured in a way that would allow it to support all of the original server's guest operating systems. This way is transparent to the end user, and it reduces a possible single point of failure.

Distributed Resource Scheduler (DRS)

DRS is like a load balancing utility that assigns and shifts computing workloads to available hardware resources in a virtualized environment.

DRS can be configured to recommend workload balancing or to move workloads automatically. DRS users can improve resource allocation with affinity rules and anti-affinity rules. The DRS allows administrators to prioritize resources according to application importance.

The Distributed Power Management (DPM) feature of DRS can consolidate workloads in off-peak (at a time when demand is less) hours to reduce energy consumption in the data centre. DRS also helps in scheduled server maintenance by balancing VMs' workloads across other hosts.

Dynamic Optimization (DO)

- Dynamic optimization can be configured on host clusters that support live migration.
- Dynamic optimization can be configured on a host group; to migrate VM within host clusters with a particular aggressiveness and frequency. Aggressiveness

determines the amount of load imbalance that is needed to initiate a migration throughout dynamic optimization.

- Due to nature, VM is migrated every 10 minutes with medium aggressiveness. When configuring aggressiveness and frequency for dynamic optimization, an administrator should consider the resource cost of additional migrations against the advantages of balancing the load between hosts in a host cluster. By default, a host group inherits Dynamic Optimization settings from its parent host group.

- If you set up dynamic optimization on a host group without a cluster, it will not affect the migration process.

- Dynamic optimization can be set up for clusters with more than two nodes. If a host group contains host clusters or stand-alone hosts that do not support live migration, dynamic optimization cannot be performed on those hosts. Any hosts that are in maintenance mode are also excluded from dynamic optimization. Besides, VMM only migrates highly available VMs that use shared storage. If a host cluster contains VMs that are not highly available, those VMs are not migrated throughout Dynamic Optimization.

- On-demand dynamic optimization is also available for specific host clusters by using the Optimize Hosts action in the VMs and Services workspace. It can be performed without configuring dynamic optimization on host groups. After dynamic optimization is requested for a host cluster, VMM lists the VMs that will be migrated for the administrator's approval.

Storage clusters

Clustered storage is the use of more than two storage servers that work jointly to increase capacity, performance, or reliability. Clustering distributes workloads to each server, manages the transfer of workloads among servers, and provides access to all the files from any server regardless of the physical location of the file.

There are two main clustered storage architectures available.

Tightly Coupled

A tightly coupled cluster has a proprietary physical backplane into which controller nodes connect. While this backplane fixes the maximum size of the cluster, it provides a high-performance interconnect among servers for load-balanced performance and maximum scalability as the cluster grows. Additional I/O ports, array controllers, and capacity can connect into the cluster as demand dictates.

Loosely coupled

A loosely coupled cluster provides cost-effective building blocks that can begin small and grow as applications demand. A loose cluster provides performance, I/O, and storage capacity within the same node. Therefore, performance scales with capacity and vice versa. While the clusters can grow quite large in theory, the scalability is limited by the performance of the interconnect and the resultant trade-offs in communication with the cluster controllers.

Maintenance mode

Maintenance mode is utilized when configuring or updating different components of Cloud computing. While in the maintenance mode, customer access is blocked and alteration is disabled, although logging is still enabled.

When you place a host in maintenance mode, you must service it, for instance, to install more memory. A host enters or leaves maintenance mode only as the result of a user request.

VMs that are running on a host entering maintenance mode must be migrated to another host (either manually or automatically by DRS) or shut down. The host is in a state of Entering Maintenance Mode until all running VMs are powered down or migrated to different hosts. You cannot power on VMs or migrate VMs to a host entering maintenance mode.

When no more running VMs are on the host, the host's icon changes to include under maintenance mode and the host(s) Summary panel shows the new state. While in maintenance mode, the host does not allow you to deploy or power on a VM.

High availability

A High Availability (HA) cluster is many hosts that work like a single system and provide continuous updates.

Typically, HA clusters are used for backup, load balancing, and failover purposes. To properly configure an HA cluster, the hosts in the cluster need to have access to the similar shared storage. This permit virtual machines on an existing host to fail over another host without any downtime in the event of a failure.

HA clusters can range from two nodes to the number of nodes, but storage administrator needs to understand the number of virtual machines and hosts they add to an HA cluster because too many can complicate load balancing.

Note:

Affinity Rule: A set of rules that establishes a relationship between more than two VMware virtual machines (VMs) and hosts.

Virtual Machine Manager (VMM): VMM is part of the System Centre suite, used to configure, manage and transform traditional data centers, and to help provide a unified management experience across on-premises, service provider, and the Azure Cloud.

Backplane: A backplane is a group of electrical connectors in parallel with each other; therefore, each pin of each connector is linked to the same relative pin of all the other connectors, forming a computer bus. It is used as a backbone to connect numerous printed circuit boards to make up an entire computer system.

Manage Physical Infrastructure for Cloud Environment

Managing the physical infrastructure for a Cloud environment will cover various essential components, ranging from remote access, OS baselines and patch management, performance and hardware monitoring, backup and recovery, network security, logging, analysis, and overall management of the environment.

Configuring Access Controls for Remote Access (e.g., RDP, Secure Terminal Access)

One of the most increasingly popular remote access techniques which permit **teleworkers** access in internal business applications and data is to allow them to log into virtual desktops. A **Virtual Desktop Infrastructure (VDI)** can be operated on-premises, while Cloud-based VDI has a large number of advantages. Cloud-based remote access through VDI is typically called **Desktop as a Service (DaaS)**, and it takes away the upfront cost, buildout and management complexities from internal IT staff and offloads those duties to a Cloud Services Provider (CSP). A properly tuned DaaS could be the most efficient way to provide internal computing resources to remote workers around the world.

Some other techniques to provide remote access are;

- Remote Desktop Protocol (RDP) permit for desktop access to remote systems
- Access through a secure terminal

If you wish to use more locally deployed, software-based remote access technologies like **IPsec** or **SSL VPN**, the Cloud can still help. Numerous IT departments have discovered that moving their authentication mechanisms out of their private data centers and to Cloud-based remote access allows for easier management and a more efficient approach.

Typically, Hybrid Cloud designs left the authentication component in the private side of the network. However, a number of organizations are more convenient with the security and stability of public Cloud services, they have found that moving the customer

management and authentication to the Cloud allows for a more centralized management experience for both publicly and privately hosted company resources.

Note:

Teleworkers: Telecommuting, also called telework, teleworking, working from home, mobile work, remote work, and flexible workplace, is a work arrangement in which

employees do not commute or travel (such as by bus or car) to a central place of work, such as an office building, warehouse, or store.

Virtual Desktop Infrastructure (VDI): VDI is a set of technologies that allow the corporations to host various desktop OS instances on a centralized server farm in an organizational data center.

Desktop as a Service (DaaS): DaaS is a Cloud computing used to provide a third-party host at the back end of a virtual desktop infrastructure (VDI) deployment.

OS Baseline Compliance Monitoring and Remediation

While establishing an OS baseline compliance monitoring and remediation, it determines who is responsible for the secure configuration of the underlying OS installed in the Cloud environment based on the deployment method and the services that are used.

Regardless of who is responsible, a secure baseline has to be established, all deployments and updates have to be made from a change-controlled and version-controlled master image.

Perform automated and ad hoc vulnerabilities are scanning and monitoring activities on the underlying infrastructure to validate compliance with all baseline's requirements. This will ensure that any regulatory-based compliance issues and risks are discovered and documented. Resolved or remediate any deviation promptly.

Adequately supporting infrastructure and tools have to be in place to allow for the patching and maintenance of proper infrastructure without any impact on the Cloud customer. Typically, patch management and other remediation activities need entry into maintenance mode. Various virtualizations vendors offer OS image baselining features as a part of their platforms.

The particular technology and activities that will be used to create, document, manage and deploy, OS image baselines vary by vendor. Follow the best practice guidance and recommendations provided by the vendor.

Patch Management

According to the **NIST SP 800-40 Revision 3**:

"Patch management is the process for identifying, acquiring, installing, and verifying patches for systems and products. Patches fix security and functionality issues in software and firmware."

From a security standpoint, patches are most often of interest because they are minimizing software flaw vulnerabilities; applying patches to reduce these vulnerabilities adequately minimize the opportunities for exploitation. Patches serve other purposes than just fixing software flaws; they can also add new features to software and firmware, including security capabilities.

New features can also be added through upgrades, which bring software or firmware to a newer version in a much broader change than just applying a patch. Upgrades may also fix security and functionality issues in previous versions of software and firmware. Besides, vendor's typically prevent supporting older versions of their products, which include no longer releasing patches to address new vulnerabilities, thus making older unsupported versions less secure over time. Upgrades are then essential to get such products to a supported version that is patched and that has continuous support for patching newly discovered vulnerabilities.

Numerous challenges complicate patch management. Organizations that do not overcome these challenges would be unable to patch systems efficiently and effectively, leading to compromises that were easily preventable. Organizations can reduce the time they spend dealing with patching and they can use those resources for addressing other security concerns. Numerous organizations have mainly operationalized their patch management, making it more of a core IT function than a part of security. However, it is still essential for all organizations to carefully address patch management in the context of security because patch management is so crucial in achieving and maintaining sound security.

Organizations have to implement the following recommendations to enhance the efficiency and effectiveness of their enterprise patch management technologies.

- Organizations have to deploy enterprise patch management tools using a phased approach.
- Organizations have to minimize the risks associated with enterprise patch management tools through the application of standard security techniques that have to be used when deploying any business-wide application.
- Organizations have to balance their security requirements with their needs for usability and availability

Performance Monitoring

Performance monitoring is essential for the secure and reliable operation in Cloud computing. Data on the performance of the underlying components may provide early indications of hardware failure. Typically, four components are recommended for monitoring in Cloud computing.

Network: Excessive dropped packets

Disk: When a disk is full, it causes a slow read and writes to the disks.

Memory: Excessive memory usage of full utilization of available memory allocation.

CPU: Excessive CPU utilization.

To follow the vendor-specific monitoring recommendation, guidelines, best practice and thresholds for performance are needed. While each vendor will have specific thresholds and ranges for acceptable operation identified by area for their platforms and products, generally, for each of the four subareas identified, a lower value based on measurement over time will indicate enhanced performance.

Hardware Monitoring

In Cloud computing, regardless of how many virtualized infrastructures you deploy, there is always physical infrastructure, simple is that it has to be managed, monitored, and maintained.

Increase your monitoring of the four main components discussed in the previous section to include the physical hosts and infrastructure that the virtualization layer rides on top of. The same monitoring processes apply, as have already been discussed. The only difference to account is the need to add some additional components that are given in the physical lane of these systems, such as CPU temperature and fan speed within the Data center hosting the physical hosts.

Several of the monitoring systems that will be deployed to address virtualized infrastructure can be used to monitor the physical performance aspects of the hosts as well. These systems can also be used to notify on thresholds, established for performance based on numerous methods, whether it is activity-based, task-based, metric-based, or time-based. Each vendor will have its specific procedures and tools to be deployed to monitor their infrastructure according to their requirements and recommendations.

Make sure that, you need to understand the vendor recommendations and best practices pertinent to their environments and they are implemented and followed as needed to make sure of the compliance.

Redundant System Architecture

The redundant system architecture is a standard practice in Cloud computing. It is used to accomplish the following:

- Permit for additional hardware items to be incorporated directly into the system as a real-time online component
- Shares the load of the running system, or in a hot standby mode
- Permit for a controlled failover, to reduce downtime

Work with the vendor(s) that supply the data center infrastructure to completely understand what the available resources are for designing and implementing system resiliency through redundancy.

Monitoring Functions

Several hardware systems provide built-in monitoring functions particular to the hardware itself, separate from any centralized monitoring that the corporation may involve in. Remember that which vendor-specific hardware system monitoring capabilities are already bundled or included in the platforms then they are asked to be responsible for.

The use of any vendor-supplied monitoring capabilities to their complete extent is essential to increase system reliability and performance. Hardware data has to be collected along with the data from any external performance monitoring undertaken.

Monitoring hardware may provide early indications of hardware failure and have to be treated as a requirement to make sure the availability and stability of the entire systems that are being managed.

Few of virtualization platforms provide the capability to disable hardware and migrate live data from the failing hardware if specific thresholds are met.

You must have work with other security professionals in the organization on the networking and administration teams to thoroughly understand and plan for the appropriate use of these types of technology options.

Backup and Restore of Host Configuration

Configuration data for hosts in the Cloud computing have to be a part of a backup plan.

You have to perform the routine test and restore hosts as a part of the disaster recovery plan to validate the proper functioning of the backup system. Although, this process is similar regardless of the vendor equipment that is to be used to supply hosts to the corporation and vendor software/hardware that is to be used to create and manage backups across the organization.

You need to understand the critical configuration information for all of the infrastructure that you manage. Make sure that this information is being backed up continuously in line with the corporation's existing backup policies. Besides, make sure that this information is being integrated into, accounted within the BCP or DRP plans for the organization.

The highest challenge in this domain is understanding the extent of your access to the hosts and configuration management that they are allowed to do as a result. Typically, this way framed concerning two most important capabilities.

- **Control:** The ability to decide who and what is allowed to access a customer data, programs and the ability to perform actions (such as erasing data or disconnecting a network) with high confidence, both that the actions have been taken and that no additional actions were taken that would subvert the customer's intent (e.g., a customer's request to create a data object that should not be subverted by the silent generation of copy).
- **Visibility:** The ability to monitor the status of customer data and programs and how others are accessing customer data and programs.

However, the extent to which customers may require relinquishing control or visibility depends on many factors, including physical possession and the ability to configure protective access boundary mechanism around a customer(s) computing resource. This can be driven by choice of both the service model and deployment model.

Implementation of Network Security Controls (e.g., firewalls, IDS, IPS, honeypots, vulnerability assessments)

The traditional model of defense in depth, which needs a design thought process that seeks to create mutually reinforcing layers of protective systems and policies to manage them, has to be considered as a baseline. Using a defense-in-depth strategy to drive design for the security architecture of Cloud-based systems makes it essential to examine each layer's purpose and to understand the impact of the choices that are to be made as the model is assembled.

Firewalls

A firewall is a network security device or a system security software that monitors the incoming and outgoing network traffic and filters it as per the defined set of rules and conditions either to permit or deny them from entering or leaving the device. Firewalls are joined into a wide assortment of arranged gadgets to channel movement and lower the hazard that malevolent parcels going over the general population web can cause to the security of a private system. Firewalls may likewise be bought as individual programming applications. While the two primary types of firewalls are host-based and network-based

firewalls. A host-based firewall is introduced in the light of individual servers and screens approaching and friendly flags. A network-based firewall can be incorporated with the Cloud's foundation, or it can be a virtual firewall benefit.

Although the above features provide isolation in some sense, the following are the few reasons a dedicated firewall appliance (either in hardware or software) is preferred to be deployed at the gateway of public internet in a production environment:

Risks	Protection by firewall
Access by untrusted entities	Firewalls try to categorize the network into different portions. One portion is considered as a trusted portion of the internal LAN. Public internet and interfaces assigned as outside interfaces are considered as an untrusted portion. Similarly, servers accessed by untrusted entities are placed in a particular segment known as a Demilitarized Zone (DMZ). By allowing only specific access to these servers, like port 90 of the web server, firewall hide the functionality of network device, which makes it difficult for an attacker to understand the physical topology of the network.
Deep Packet Inspection	One of the exciting features of the dedicated firewall is their ability to inspect the traffic more than just IP and port level. By using digital and certificates, Next Generation Firewalls available today can inspect traffic up to layer 7. A firewall can also limit the number of established, as well as half-open TCP/UDP connections to mitigate DDoS attacks.
Access Control	By implementing local AAA or by using ACS/ISE servers, the firewall can permit traffic based on AAA policy.
Antivirus and protection from infected data	By integrating IPS/IDP modules with firewall, malicious data can be detected and filtered at the edge of the network to protect the end-users.

Table 5-2: Firewall Risk Mitigation Features

Types of Firewall

- Packet filtering firewall
- Circuit-Level gateway firewall
- Application-level firewall
- Stateful multilayer inspection firewall
- Transparent firewall

- Next-generation firewall (NGFW)
- Personal firewall

Intrusion Detection System (IDS)/ Intrusion Prevention System (IPS)

IDS analyze and monitor network traffic for signs which specify that the attackers are using a known cyber threat to infiltrate or theft data from your network. IDS systems compare the existing network activity to a known threat database to detect many types of behaviors like malware, port scanners, and security policy violations.

IPS live in a similar domain of the network as a firewall, between the external and the internal network. IPS proactively deny network traffic based on a security profile if that packet represents a known security threat.

The main difference between them is that IDS is a monitoring system, while IPS is a control system.

Typically, IDS and IPS create confusion as both modules are created by multiple vendors and different technologies are used to define the technical concepts are also the same. Sometimes the same technology may be used for detection and prevention of some threat.

Just like other products, some vendors also have developed many solutions for implementing IDS/IPS for the security of the network.

The placement of the sensor within a network differentiates the functionality of IPS over the IDS. When a sensor is placed in line with the network, i.e., the common in/out of specific network segment terminates on a hardware or logical interface of the sensor and goes out from second hardware or logical interface of the sensor, then every single packet will be analyzed and passed through sensor only if it does not contain anything malicious. By dropping the malicious traffic, the trusted network or a segment of it can be protected from known threats and attacks. This is the basic working of the Intrusion Prevention System (IPS). However, the inline installation and inspection of traffic may result in a minor delay. IPS may also become a single point of failure for the whole network. If 'fail-open' mode is used, the good and malicious traffic will be allowed in case of any failure within the IPS sensor. Similarly, if 'fail-close' mode is configured, the whole IP traffic will be dropped in case of sensor's failure.

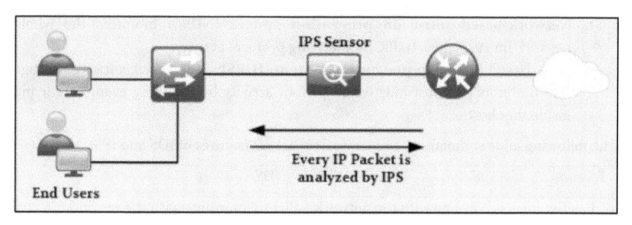

Figure 5-2: In-line Deployment of IPS Sensor

If a sensor is installed in the position as shown below, a copy of every packet will be sent to the sensor to analyze any malicious activity.

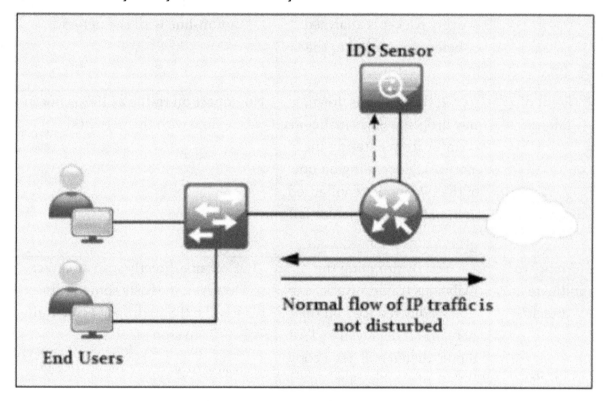

Figure 5-3: Sensor Deployment as IDS

In other means, the sensor, running in promiscuous mode will perform the detection and generate an alert if required. As the normal flow of traffic is not disturbed, no end-to-end delay will be introduced by implementing IDS. The only downside of this configuration is that IDS will not be able to stop malicious packets from entering the network because IDS is not controlling the overall path of traffic.

IDS can be classified into two main types.

- **Network-based intrusion prevention system (NIPS):** monitors the whole network for suspicious traffic by analysing protocol activity.
- **Host-based intrusion prevention system (HIPS):** an installed software package that monitors one host only for suspicious activity by analysing events occurring inside that host.

The following table summarizes and compares various features of IDS and IPS.

Feature	IPS	IDS
Positioning	In-line with the network. Every packet goes through it.	Not in-line with the network. It receives a copy of every packet.
Mode	In-line/Tap	Promiscuous
Delay	Introduces delay because every packet is analyzed before forwarded to the destination.	Does not introduce delay because it is not in-line with the network.
Point of failure?	Yes. If the sensor is down, it may drop as well as malicious traffic from entering the network, depending on one of the two modes configured on it, namely fail-open or fail-close.	No impact on traffic as IDS is not in-line with the network.
Ability to mitigate an attack?	Yes. By dropping the malicious traffic, attacks can be readily reduced on the network. If deployed in TAP mode, then it will get a copy of each packet but cannot mitigate the attack	IDS cannot directly stop an attack. However, it assists some in-line device like IPS to drop specific traffic to stop an attack.
Can do packet manipulation?	Yes. Can modify the IP traffic according to a defined set of rules.	No. As IDS receive mirrored traffic, so it can only perform the inspection.

Table 5-3: IDS/IPS Comparison

<u>Ways to Detect an Intrusion</u>

When a sensor is analysing traffic for something strange, it uses multiple techniques base on the rules defined in the IPS/IDS sensor. Following tools and techniques can be used in this regard:

- Anomaly-based IDS/IPS
- Policy-based IDS/IPS
- Reputation-based IDS/IPS
- Signature-based IDS/IPS

Honeypots

A honeypot is used to detect, deflect, or in a similar manner counteract attempts at unauthorized use of information systems. In general, a honeypot consists of a computer, data, or a network site that appears to be the part of a network but is isolated and monitored which also seems to hold information or a resource of value to attackers. The two types of honeypots are production honeypots and research honeypots.

- **Production Honeypots:** are simple to manage, detects only limited information, and are utilized primarily by organizations.
- **Research Honeypots**: are run to collect information about the motives and tactics of the black hat community targeting diverse networks.

Besides, some risks are associated with deploying honeypots in the organization. You must make sure that they understand the legal and compliance problems that may be associated with the use of a honeypot. Honeypots have to be segmented from the production network to make sure that any potential activity generated by them does not contain the ability to affect any other system.

Vulnerability assessments

A vulnerability assessment is a process of classifying, identifying, and prioritizing vulnerabilities in applications, computer systems, networks infrastructure and providing the corporations to assessing with the awareness, essential knowledge and risk background to understand the threats to its environment and react appropriately.

This process is intended to detect threats and the risks they pose typically involves the use of automated testing tools such as network security scanner, whose outcome are listed in the vulnerability assessment report.

Corporations of any size, or even a single person who faces a large number of attacks, can benefit from some vulnerability assessments but multinational corporations and other

types of corporations that are subjected to continue attacks will benefit most from the vulnerability assessment.

Because security vulnerabilities can allow the attackers to access IT systems and applications, it is essential for the corporations to identify and remediate vulnerabilities before they can be exploited. A comprehensive vulnerability assessment, as well as a management program, can assist corporations to improve the security of their entire networks and IT systems.

<u>Types of Vulnerabilities Assessments</u>

Vulnerability assessment depends on discovering different forms of network and system vulnerabilities that means the assessment process includes using multiple forms of tools, scanners, and methodologies to identify vulnerabilities, threats and risks as well.

Some of the vulnerability assessment scans are:

- Application Scans
- Database scans
- Host-based scans
- Network-based scans
- Wireless network scans

Log Capture and Analysis (e.g., SIEM, Log Management)

Logging the events, securing the logs and making them available for analysis is the most important for any security program and will be the main considerations and focus of the Cloud Security Professional (CSP).

Security Information and Event Management (SIEM)

SIEM is a methodology to security management that join SIM (security information management), and SEM (security event management) functions into the single security management system.

The basic principles of every SIEM system is to aggregate significant data from various sources that can identify deviations from the norm and take appropriate action.

For example:

When a potential issue is detected, a SIEM might log additional information, generate an alert and instruct other security controls to prevent an activity's progress.

Besides, A SIEM system can be set up locally or hosted in an external Cloud-based environment. A SIEM system can support the initial detection of these events.

- A locally hosted SIEM system provides easy access and lesser risk of external disclosure
- An external SIEM system may prevent tampering of data by an attacker

The use of SIEM systems is also beneficial as they map to and support the implementation of the Critical Controls for Effective Cyber-Defense. The Critical Controls for Effective Cyber-Defense (the Controls) are a recommended set of actions for cyber-defense that provide specific and actionable ways to prevent most pervasive attacks. They were developed and are maintained by a consortium of thousands of security professionals from across the public and private regions. An underlying theme of the control is the support for large-scale, and standard-based security automation for the management of cyber-defenses.

Log Management

Log management is the collective processes and policies used to administer and facilitate the analysis, archiving, generation, storage, transmission, and eventual disposal of the maximum number of log data generated within an information system.

In a Cloud-computing environment, a log is automatically produced and time-stamped documentation of significant events that are specified to the system. Virtually all IT systems and software applications generate log files.

Effective log management is most important to both security and compliance. Analyzing, documenting and monitoring system events is an essential component of **security intelligence (SI)**.

> **Note:**
>
> **The CIS Critical Security Controls for Effective Cyber Defense:** The Centre for Internet Security (CIS) Critical Security Controls for Effective Cyber Defense is a publication of best practice guidelines for computer security. The publication was initially developed by the SANS Institute, and the ownership transferred to Centre for Internet Security (CIS).
>
> **Security intelligence (SI):** SI is the significant information used for securing corporations from internal and external threats along with the processes, policies, and tools designed to gather and analyze that information.

Management Plane

In a traditional data center, many operations will typically impact a single client or system, as most data centers reside on physical hardware and are segregated from other systems. There are exceptions to this rule for organization-level services such as DNS, file servers, etc. However, careful coordination and management are most important because various

IT systems and different consumers are directly affected by operational decisions. With large Cloud environments, careful planning and management is essential to operating an IT system.

Scheduling

Cloud computing manages a multiple form of virtualized resources, which makes scheduling a significant component. In the Cloud environment, a customer may utilize a large number of virtualized assets for every task. Eventually, manual scheduling is not a sufficient solution. The primary objective of task scheduling is to slate tasks to reduce time loss and enhance performance.

In general, scheduling is a decision-making process that allows resource sharing among hundreds of activities by determining their execution order on the set of available resources. The emergence of distributed systems brought new challenges on scheduling in computer systems, including grids, clusters, and more recently Clouds.

Orchestration

The orchestration is the automatic configuration, coordination, and management of software and computer systems.

Cloud orchestration is the use of programming technology to manage the interconnections and interactions between workloads on public and private Cloud infrastructure. It connects automated tasks into a cohesive workflow to achieve a goal, with permissions oversight and policy enforcement.

Cloud orchestration is often used to deploy, provision, or start servers; acquire and assign storage capacity; manage networking; develop VMs; and authorize to particular software on Cloud services. This is achieved through three main, interconnected components of Cloud orchestration which are:

- Resource orchestration
- Service
- Workload

An orchestration platform can integrate authorization checks for compliance and security.

Cloud orchestration technology needs to work with heterogeneous systems, potentially servicing a global Cloud deployment in different physical locations and with different Cloud providers. Several hundreds of Cloud orchestrator users can run public Cloud and private deployments.

Several hundreds of tools exist for automation of server configuration and management, including **Terraform, Salt, Puppet,** and **Ansible.**

Maintenance

When considering management-related activities and the need to control and organize them to ensure accuracy and impact, you must think about the impact of change. It is significant to schedule system repair and maintenance, as well as customer notifications, to make sure that they do not disrupt the organization's systems. When scheduling maintenance, the Cloud provider will need to make sure that sufficient resources are available to meet expected demand, and Service Level Agreement (SLA) needs. You have to ensure that proper change-management procedures are implemented and followed for all IT systems and scheduling and notifications are communicated efficiently to all parties that will potentially be affected by the work. Consider using automated system tools that send out messages.

Usually, a host system is placed into **maintenance mode** before beginning any work on it that will need system downtime, rebooting, and any disruption of services. For the host to be placed into maintenance mode, the VMs currently running on it should be powered off or moved to another host. The use of automated solutions such as workflow or tasks to place a host into maintenance mode is supported by all virtualization vendors and is something that you have to have an understanding of.

Regardless of whether the decision to enter maintenance mode is manual or automated, ensure all appropriate security protections and safeguards continue to apply to all hosts while in maintenance mode and to all VMs while they are being moved and managed on alternate hosts as a result of maintenance mode activities being performed on their primary host.

Build Logical Infrastructure for Cloud Environment

While the physical infrastructure of a Cloud environment is taken into an account on precise and specific hardware and other physical assets, the logical infrastructure is much more summarised and is instead focused on the actual organizational requirements of the consumer. It eliminates the specifics of platforms and software, and instead focuses on the aspects that are more relevant to the consumers, such as locations, processes, regulations, and roles.

Secure Configuration of Virtual Hardware Specific Requirements

When configuring virtual hardware, it is important to understand the requirements of the underlying host systems. In various instances, specific configurations and settings will need to be employed on the VMs to compare the capability and requirements of the physical hosts. These requirements will be identified by the virtual host vendor, and they will need to be compared by those building and configuring the images of virtual devices. These

settings enable for the appropriate allocation and management of the CPU and memory resources from the host systems to the VMs running with them.

From the storage perspective, various steps have to be taken for proper security configuration. Immediately after the installation, any default authorizations supplied by the vendor have to be changed immediately. These default authorizations are very useful for the potential attacker and are typically one of the first targets utilized to comprise a system. All needless APIs and interfaces have to be disabled to prevent any potential comprise, along with saving the on system resource overhead. Testing has to be conducted to make sure that storage controllers and the system can manage the normal loads as well as meet the requirements for high availability and redundancy. As with any component of configuration and system, vendor recommendations for best practices guidelines always have to be adapted and consulted to the specific requirements.

Within a Cloud environment there are two main network models, with the proper model that is dependent on the specific requirements and configurations of the Cloud environment. Usually, the networking model has physical switches combined with virtual networks at the hypervisor level. The converged networking model with the storage and data/IP networks into a single virtualized design is intended for use with Cloud environments. Traditionally, networking model can utilize conventional security networking tools, while the converged networking model will utilize entire virtualized tools. Therefore, by default of a traditional networking model and the combination of physical and virtualized system, typically, there can be a disconnection among the two as it relates visibility with the virtualized networks completely. The converged networking models, being designed and optimized for Cloud usage, often maintains good visibility and performance under Cloud operated loads.

Installation of Guest O/S Virtualization Toolsets

Because the virtualized environment can run multiple forms of Operating Systems (OS) within it that's why it is essential to make sure that the proper toolsets are installed and available for it. Each OS vendor will have their virtualization tools and Cloud services sets that always have to be used to make sure optimal compatibility and accurate performance of the OS within the environment. Typically, these can be augmented with a third party and other toolsets, but following the recommended best practices and configuration guidelines provided by the vendor will make sure optimal performance, security, and visibility into the guest OSs.

Run Logical Infrastructure for Cloud Environment

There are numerous considerations for the management and operation of a Cloud infrastructure. A secure network configuration will help in isolating customer's data and assist in preventing or reducing denial-of-service attacks. Various key methods are mostly used to implement network security controls in a Cloud environment, including converged appliances, physical devices, and virtual appliances.

You must be aware with best practices guidelines for secure network design, such as defense in depth, along with the design considerations specific to the network topologies you may be handling, such as a single tenant, and multi-tenant hosting systems as well. Besides, you will have to be aware of the vendor-specific recommendations and needs of the hosting platforms that they can support.

Secure Network Configuration

The section is just a high-level summary of the compatibility and functionality of the technology being described. Please refer to the "**Running a Physical Infrastructure for Cloud Environments**" section of this domain for specific details as required when studying this section.

VLAN's

VLANs allow for the logical isolation of hosts on a network. In a Cloud-computing environment, VLANs can be used to isolate the customer networks, management network, and the storage network. VLANs can also be utilized to separate customer data.

TLS

Transport Layer Security (TLS) allows for the encryption of data in transition among hosts. Deployment of TLS for internal networks will prevent the **sniffing** of traffic by a malicious user. A TLS VPN is one of the significant procedures to allow for remote access to the Cloud environment.

DHCP

DHCP is most important for orchestration and automation within a Cloud-computing environment. Security professionals are well understood of the adage that you should never use DHCP within a server and data centre, instead, have IP addresses configured and set statically. This way has passed mostly, though, in favor of using DHCP with reservation. With DHCP, IP address is not always issued dynamically from a pool. Within a Cloud-computing environment, DHCP is used to centralize the assigning of IP addresses and statically maintain them, node names, hostname, IP, MAC address are set and not changed, they are always assigned to the same virtual machine. This enables for the highest speed

and flexibility with automation and eliminates the requirements for configuration such as network settings at the host level, which are instead centrally administrated and maintained.

DNS

DNS servers have to be locked down and provide the required services and to use Domain Name System Security Extensions (DNSSEC) when it is possible. DNSSEC is a set of DNS extensions that provide authentication, integrity, and **authenticated denial-of-existence** for DNS data. Zone transfers have to be disabled. If an attacker comprises DNS, they may be able to reroute data or hijack.

IPSEC

IPsec VPN is one core procedure to access in the Cloud-computing environment remotely. If an IPsec VPN is utilized, IP whitelisting, will only allow authorized IP addresses, which is considered as a best practice for access. Multi-factor authentication can also be used to improve security.

OS Hardening via Application of a Baseline (e.g., Windows, Linux, VMware)

A baseline is a preconfigured group of settings, to secure, or **harden**; a machine which is a common practice. The baseline has to be configured to enable the minimum services and software to be implemented onto the system that is required to make sure that the system can perform as needed. A baseline configuration has to be established for each Operating System (OS) and the virtualization platform in use. The baseline has to be designed to meet the customer requirement. There are various sources for recommended baselines. By establishing a baseline and continuously monitoring for compliance, the provider can identify any deviations from the baseline.

Capturing a Baseline

The Cloud Security Professional (CSP) should consider the items outlined next as the bare minimum requirements for establishing a functional baseline to use in the enterprise. There may be other procedures as well that would be involved in multiple ways, based on specific policy or regulatory requirements pertinent to a particular organization. There are various sources of guidance on the methodology for building a baseline that the CSP can recommend to if required.

- A fresh installation of the target OS needs to be performed. It may be physical or virtual.
- All essential configuration of the host OS has to be accomplished as per the requirements of the baseline creation.

- All essential security patches have to be downloaded and installed from the proper vendor repository.
- All unnecessary services have to prevent and set to disabled to make sure that they do not run.
- All unnecessary software has to be deleted from the system.
- An image of the OS baseline has to be captured and stored for future deployment. This image has to be placed under change management control where appropriate access controls are applied.
- Complete documentation has to be created, captured, and stored for the baseline being created.
- The baseline OS image also has to be placed under the **Configuration Management (CM) system** and cataloged as a **Configuration Item (CI)**.
- The baseline OS image has to be updated on a documented schedule for security patches and any additional essential configuration updates as required.
- The OS baseline has to be audited to make sure that all essential items have been appropriately configured.

Availability of the Guest OS

A guest OS is a software installed on either a partitioned disk or a Virtual Machine (VM) that describes an operating system which is different from the host operating system.

Main advantages of a Cloud-computing environment are the redundancy. Redundant system hardware can be used to assist in averting system outages due to hardware failure. Generators and backup power supplies can be used to make sure that the hosts contain power, even if the electricity is shut down for a period. Besides, technologies such as high availability and fault tolerance are essential to consider as well. High availability has to be used where the objective is to reduce the effect of system downtime. Fault tolerance has to be used where the objective is to remove the system downtime as a threat to system's availability altogether.

High Availability

In the Cloud-computing environment, different customers will have different availability requirements. These can include components such as automatic migration and live recovery if the underlying host goes down.

Cloud vendors will have their particular toolsets available to provide for **high availability** on their platform. It is essential to understand the vendor's requirement and capability within the high availability domain and to make sure these are documented appropriately as a part of the **BCP or DRP** process within the organization.

Fault Tolerance

Network components, storage arrays, and servers with built-in fault tolerance capabilities have to be utilized. Besides, if there is a fault tolerance solution that a vendor makes available through software deployment that is appropriately scaled for the level of fault tolerance essential by the guest OS, consider it as well.

Note:

Disaster Recovery Plan (DRP): A documented structured approach with instructions for responding to unintended incidents.

Business Continuity Plan (BCP): A document that consists of the essential information an organization needs to continue operating during an unintended event.

Configuration management (CM): A governance and systems engineering process for ensuring consistency between logical and physical assets in an operational environment.

Configuration Item (CI): A component of a system that can be recognized as a self-contained component for purposes of identification and change control.

Manage Logical Infrastructure for Cloud Environment

In the Cloud-computing environment, the logical design has to include measures to limit remote access to only those individuals who has authorized access, provide the capability to monitor the Cloud infrastructure, and allow for the remediation of systems in the Cloud-computing environment, along with the restoring and backup of a guest OS.

Access Control for Remote Access

When support is globally distributed data centers, secure Cloud-computing environments and organizations, have to provide remote access to third party personnel and employees with whom they have contracted. This includes field technicians, help-desk support and IT personnel, etc.

A Cloud Remote Access solution has to be capable of providing secure access wherever is required and **extranet** capabilities for authorized remote users. The service has to utilize TLS/SSL as a secure transport mechanism and require no software clients to be implemented on mobile and remote users' Internet-enabled devices.

The most prominent advantage of the Cloud-computing environment is the reduction of the attack surface; there are no open ports. There are other prominent advantages of a remote access solution that can include:

- Accountability of the one who gains access to the data center remotely with a tamper-proof audit trail.
- Constantly monitoring to view privileged activities as they are happening or as a recorded playback for forensic analysis. Sessions can be remotely terminated or intervened when required for more efficient and secure IT compliance and cybersecurity operations.
- Secure access without exposing the privileged credential to the customer, reducing the risk of keylogging or credential exploitation.
- Secure isolation among the remote user's desktop and the target system they are connecting to so that any potential malware does not spread to the target systems.
- Session control over who can access, enforcement of workflows such as automatic termination when idle, managerial approval, session duration limitation, and ticketing integration.

Remote Desktop Protocol (RDP)

RDP is a secure network communications protocol designed for remote management, along with the remote access to applications, virtual desktops, and an RDP terminal server.

Besides, RDP enables network administrators to analyze and solve those issues which individual subscribers encounter remotely. RDP is offered for many versions of the Windows OS. RDP is also offered in mac OS version and it is offering freeware licensing as well.

Note:

Extranet: A private network that uses Internet technology and the public telecommunication system to securely share part of an organization's information or operations with customers, partners, suppliers, vendors, and other businesses. It's a part of an organization's intranet that is extended to users outside the organizations.

OS Baseline Compliance Monitoring and Remediation

Tools have to be placed to monitor the OS baselines of the system in the Cloud-computing environment. When changes are detected, there has to be a process for root cause determination and remediation.

It is essential to understand the toolsets available for use based on the vendor platform(s) that is to be managed. Both VMware and Microsoft have their own built-in OS baseline compliance monitoring and remediation solution, as has been described earlier in the **"manage physical infrastructure for Cloud environment"** section. Microsoft has WSUS, VMware has host and storage profiles and VUM. There are APIs available for use that user may take into account, depending on a variety of circumstances.

Regardless of product implementation, the primary objective is to make sure that the real-time or near real-time monitoring of OS configuration and baseline compliance is taken into account within the Cloud-computing environment. Besides, the monitoring data must be centrally managed and stored for audit and change-management purposes.

Any changes made under remediation has to be thoroughly documented and submitted to a **change-management process** for approval. Once approved, the changes being implemented must be managed through a **release-** and **deployment-management process** that is tied directly into configuration and **availability management processes** to make sure that all changes are managed through an entire life cycle within the organization.

Note:

Change-Management Process: A process of determining attainability, implementing, planning, requesting, and evaluating of changes to a system. Its primary objective is to support the processing and traceability of changes to an interconnected set of factors.

Release- and Deployment-Management Process: A process that is intended to manage the development, testing, deployment, and support of software releases.

Availability Management Process: Its objective is to define, analyze, plan, measure and improve all components of the availability of IT services.

Patch Management

In a logical infrastructure, Patch management adopts the procedure that is essential to the physical infrastructure in the Cloud-computing environment.

Patch management is a part of systems management that includes acquiring, testing, and installing numerous patches (code changes) to an administered computer system. Patch management tasks involve maintaining existing knowledge of available patches, deciding which patches are suitable for specific systems, make sure that patches are installed appropriately, testing systems after installation, and documenting every associated procedure, such as particular configurations were needed. There are many products available to automate patch management tasks:

- Gibraltar's Everguard
- Patch link Update
- Ringmaster's Automated Patch Management

Besides, Patches are often ineffective, and can often cause more problems than they fix. Patch management can be viewed as a part of change management.

Patch management experts **Mark Allen**, CTO of Gibraltar Software suggests:

"System administrators perform easy steps to reduce problems, such as performing backups and testing patches on non-critical systems before installations."

Performance Monitoring (e.g., Network, Disk, Memory, CPU)

Lori MacVittie, principal analyst at **Rishidot Research LLC**, said that "**Cloud application monitoring tools can be effective, but they sometimes are not as full-featured as longer established performance monitoring solutions.**"

Besides, performance-monitoring tools have evolved. Traditionally, they were designed to inspect numerous autonomous components, such as Network, Disk, Memory, and CPU. The growth of virtualization has blurred the dividing lines among these devices.

Therefore, vendors have developed new tools designed specifically to evaluate the performance of customer-based Cloud computing applications. Some of Cloud performance-monitoring tools are:

- **BMC's End User Experience Management tool:** Monitors use activity at the group level or even individual and distinguishes among broad and targeted slowdowns.
- **Cloudkick Inc**: Gives customers elasticity; as new servers come online, new monitoring functions become available. Cloud admins can customize alerts and send them through SMS or email.
- **LoadStorm**: A real-time Cloud-monitoring tool that provides graphs with performance metrics updated in one-minute intervals. Between the data highlighted are average response time, error rate, and requests per second, throughput in KB per second, peak response time and a number of concurrent users.
- **SevOne's:** Cloud performance monitoring tool identifies changes in performance behaviour through automated baselining through many data centre components. The organization's traffic analysis functions also support differentiated service models.
- **SOASTA's CloudTest:** Software creates complex tests without the need for programming. Tests can be stopped or paused when an issue is arrived and restarted once it has been resolved.

However, each of these Cloud tools come with some warnings. One issue is presenting organizations with a unified view of their network, server and application performance across physical and virtual infrastructures. Performance data should be funneled to a central location while still allowing users to drill down to troubleshoot individual components.

Backup and Restore of Guest OS Configuration

As a Cloud Security Professional (CSP), it is your responsibility to ensure that the proper backup and restoration capabilities for hosts along with the guest OSs running on top of them are set up and maintained within the organization's Cloud-computing infrastructure. The choices available about built-in tools will vary by vendor platform and are supported, but all vendors will offer few forms of built-in toolsets for backup and restoring the host configurations and also the guest OSs. Typically, this is achieved with a combination of profiles, along with cloning or templates, besides some form of a backup solution.

Whether or not the third-party tool is used to provide the backup and restoration capability will have to be decided based on referencing the SLA(s) that the customer has in place as well as the capabilities of the built-in tools that are available. In addition, the need to reference the existing BCP/DRP solutions in place and ensure coordination with the plans and systems is of vital importance.

Some of the tools are available for backup the guest, OS are:

- VMware Consolidated Backup (VCB)
- vSphere

Implementation of Network Security Controls

The implementation of network security controls has been described widely earlier in the section of "**Manage Physical Infrastructure for Cloud Environment.**" You must adopt and implement best practices guidelines about all security controls generally. About network-based controls, the following best practice guidelines have to be considered:

- Access controls
- Defense in depth
- Deployment of virtual security infrastructure specifically designed to secure and monitor virtual networks (i.e., VMware's vCNS or NSX products)
- Firewalls
- Honeypots/honey nets
- IDS/IPS system deployments
- Secure protocol usage (i.e., IPSec and TLS)
- Separation of traffic flows within the host from the guests through the use of separate virtual switches dedicated to specific traffic
- VLANs
- Zoning and masking of storage traffic

Log Capture and Analysis

Log data must be collected and analyzed for the hosts along with OS guest running on top of the hosts. Multiple forms of tools that allow the user to collect and consolidate log data.

Centralization and offsite storage of log data can reduce tempering, provide the proper access control, and monitoring systems are also considered.

It is your responsibility for understanding the requirements of the organization about log capture and analysis, also to make sure that the essential toolsets and solutions are implemented to make sure that information can be managed using best practices guidelines and standards.

Management Plane

You need to develop a particular management plane for the Cloud-computing environment. You are eventually responsible for the security architecture and resiliency of the systems; you design, implement and manage.

Make sure due diligence and due care are excised in the design and implementation of all components of the organization Cloud security architecture.

Besides, you are also responsible for keeping the record of changes in the vendor's offering that could affect the choices being made or considered about management capabilities and approaches for the Cloud.

It is constantly informed about issues and threats that could affect the secure operation and management of Cloud computing infrastructure along with the mitigation techniques and vendors' recommendations about mitigation that may need to be applied or implemented within the Cloud-computing infrastructure.

Note that **due diligence** is the process of systematically researching and verifying the accuracy of a statement. Also, note that **due care** considers as an effort made by an ordinarily prudent or reasonable party to avoid harm to another, considering the circumstances.

Ensure Compliance with Regulations and Controls (e.g., ITIL, ISO/IEC 20000-1)

One of the most essential components of operations is the compliance with regulations and controls. This is achieved through a series of management components that combines to make sure proper documentation, auditing and accountability procedure are being followed. These components make sure, compliance with regulations internal policies

along with the form of a structured operations management program drives process and implements governance of management oversight. Main components of operations are:

Change Management

Change management is an approach used for managing the transition or transformation of an organization's goals, technologies or processes. The primary goal of change management is to implement strategies for effecting change, controlling change and guiding people to follow the change. Such strategies include having a structured procedure for requesting a change, along with the mechanisms for responding to requests and following them up.

Change Management Process

The process of change management needs to take into consideration that how an adjustment or replacement will affect the employees, process, and systems within the organization. There should be a process for:

- Communicating changes
- Documenting change
- Evaluating its effects
- Planning and testing change
- Scheduling and implementing change

Documentation is a crucial component of change management, not only to manage an audit trail but also to ensure compliance with internal and external controls, including regulatory compliance.

The organization developing a change management program from the ground up typically face daunting challenges. Besides, to a thorough understanding of the organization environment, the change management process needs an accurate accounting of the systems, applications, and employees to be affected by a change. Best practice framework can deliver guiding principles and assist managers to align the scope of proposed changes with available digital and non-digital tools.

Change Management Models

Some most common models for managing change include:

- ADKAR
- Bridges' Transition Model
- IT Infrastructure Library (ITIL)
- Kotter's 8-Step Process for Leading Change
- Lewin's Change Management Model

- McKinsey 7S

Change Management Tools

Digital and non-digital change management tools can guide change management officers to analyze, organize, research, and implement changes. Some of the most common change management software applications include:

- ChangeGear Change Manager (SunView Software)
- ChangeScout (Deloitte)
- eChangeManager (Giva)
- Remedy Change Management 9 (BMC Software)

Change Management Certifications

Change management specialists can earn certifications that identify their ability to manage projects, manage people and help an organization through a period of transition or transformation. Popular certifications for change management are issued by:

- Association of Change Management Professionals (ACMP)
- Change Management Institute (CMI)
- Cornell University's SC Johnson College of Business
- Management and Strategy Institute (MSI)
- Prosci

Change Management in Project Management

Change management is an essential component of project management. The project manager needs to inspect change requests and determine the effect a change will have on the project completely. The team or even a person in charge of change control needs to evaluate the effect, a change in one domain of the project can have on another domain, including:

- Communications
- Costs
- Human resources
- Procurement
- Quality
- Risk
- Schedule
- Scope
- Stakeholders

Continuity Management

Continuity Management or Business continuity management (BCM) is a framework used for recognizing an enterprises risk of exposure to internal and external threats.

The objective of BCM is to provide the enterprises with the ability to effectively respond to threats such as data breaches or natural disasters and secure the business interests of the enterprises. BCM includes

- Business recovery's
- Contingency planning
- Crisis management
- Disaster recovery
- Emergency management
- Incident management

According to ISO 22301, a BCM system highlights the importance of:

- Constant improvement based on objective measurements.
- Implementing and operating controls and measures for managing enterprises overall continuity risks.
- Monitoring and reviewing the performance and effectiveness of the BCM system.
- Understanding continuity and preparedness needs, along with the necessity for establishing BCM policy and objectives.

Note that the International Organization of Standardization standard 22301 (ISO 22301) is a proposed standard that specifies security requirements for disaster recovery preparedness and business continuity management systems (BCMS).

Information Security Management

An Information Security Management System (ISMS) is a set of rules, policies, and procedures for systematically managing an organization's sensitive information, IT services, and IT systems. The objective of ISMS is to reduce risk and assure business continuity by pro-actively limiting the effect of a security breach.

An ISMS often addresses employee behavior and process along with the data and technology. It can be focused on the specific type of data, such as customer data, or it can be implemented in a comprehensive way that becomes an integral part of the organization's culture.

ISO 27001 is a specification for creating an ISMS. It does not mandate particular actions, but includes:

- Constant improvement
- Corrective
- Internal audits
- Preventive action
- Suggestions for documentation

Continual Service Improvement Management

Continual Service Improvement (CSI) is a method used to identify and implement opportunities to make IT processes and services enhanced and to measure the effects of these efforts over time.

This central business management concept was adopted into the continual improvement goals of international standard ISO 20000 for IT service management, and more broadly, it supports various IT service management (ITSM) initiatives.

ITSM includes policies, processes, and procedures that an organization uses to design, deploy, operate and maintain a group of IT services. CSI represents a central tenant of ITSM frameworks, such as IT Infrastructure Library (ITIL), that dictate how organizations deliver access to corporate networks, important business applications such as email and other IT services.

The improvements typically enhance customer's experience, boost service quality, lower costs and make processes more effective and efficient. CSI can be applied to all components of the ITIL framework or another life cycle management approach it can also be used to review and assess improvement recommendations for all phases of the life cycle.

Note that ISO 20000 is a global standard that describes the requirements for an information technology service management (ITSM) system.

Incident Management

Incident management is a part of IT Service Management (ITSM) wherein the IT team returns the service to normal as soon as possible after a disruption, in a way that aims to create an adverse effect on the business as possible.

An incident is an unpredicted event that disrupts the normal process of an IT service. A problem is a core issue that could lead to an incident. Problem management consists of the events taken to reduce the occurrence of an incident.

Incident management guides organization(s) to prepare for unexpected hardware, software and security failings, and it minimizes the duration and severity of disruption from these events. Incident management can adopt the ITSM framework, such as the IT infrastructure library (ITIL) or to follow the best practices guidelines.

Incident Management Process

Typically, Incident Management depends on the temporary workaround to assure services are up and running while the team investigates the incident, identifies the main problem, and develops and roll out a permanent fix. Particular workflows and process in incident

management differs, depending on the way each organization works and the issues they are focusing on.

A large number of incident management workflows start with users and IT staff pre-emptively addressing potential incidents such as a network slowdown. IT staff contains the incidents to stop potential issues in another domain of the IT deployment. Then, they search a temporary workaround or implement a fix also does recovery of the system and release the system back into the production environment. IT staff then reviews and logs the incident for future reference.

Documentation allows the IT staff to search previously unseen and repeated incident trends and address them. If a temporary workaround is taken into account, once the disruption to end clients is reduced, the staff can fix an issue for long lasting.

Types of Incidents

Generally, incidents are categorized as:

- **Low Priorities:** Incidents do not interrupt end users, who often complete work despite the issue.
- **Medium Priorities:** Incidents are issues that affect end users, but the disruption is either brief or slight.
- **High Priorities:** Incidents are issues that will affect most end users and reduce the proper functioning of a system.

Besides, Incidents are classed as hardware, software or security; although in a performance, the issue can often result from any combination of these areas.

- Hardware incidents include downed or limited resources, network issues or other system outages.
- Security incidents encompass attempted and active threats intended to compromise or breach data.
- Software incidents include service availability problems or application bugs.

Incident Management Tools

Incident management teams and help desk are heavily depended on a combination of tools to resolve incidents, including monitoring tools to collect operations data, root cause analysis systems, incident management, automation platforms, and other support products.

Some of the incident management tools are:

- PagerDuty
- VictorOps

- xMatters

Problem Management

Problem management is an integral part of IT service management (ITSM) which aims to resolve incidents and issues caused by end-user's errors or IT infrastructure issues and prevents recurrence of such incidents.

Besides, an incident is an event that disrupts normal operation. A problem is an underlying issue that could lead to an incident.

Problem management can either be reactive or proactive. Reactive means solving problem when an error occur while proactive means identifying issues and potential risks before they become problematic.

Release and Deployment Management

Release and deployment management goals are to plan, schedule, and control the movement of releases to test and live environments. The basic objective of release and deployment management is to assure that the integrity of the live environment is protected and that the right components are released.

The objectives and goals of release and deployment management are:

- Define and agree upon deployment plans
- Build and test release packages
- Make sure the integrity of release packages
- Record and track all release packages in the Definitive Media Library (DML)
- Manage stakeholders
- Check delivery of utility and warranty
- The utility is the functionality delivered by a product or service to meet particular requirements; it is what the service does.
- Warranty is the assurance that a product or service will meet agreed-upon requirements (SLA); it is how the service is delivered.
- Manage risks
- Make sure knowledge is transfer

Besides, new software releases have to be done under the configuration management plan. You have to perform the security testing on all new releases before deployment. Release management is especially crucial for SaaS and PaaS providers.

You may not be directly involved for release and deployment management and may be responsible only tangentially in the process. Regardless of who is responsible, it is imperative that the process is tightly joined to change management, incident and problem

management, along with the configuration and availability management and the help/service desk.

Configuration Management

Configuration Management (CM) is a system engineering and governance process for assuring continuity between physical and logical assets in an operational environment. The CM process seeks to identify and track specific Configuration Items (CIs), documenting functional capabilities and interdependencies. Governance role like administrator, technicians or even software developers can use configuration management tools to confirm the effect of a change that one configuration item has on other desired system.

CM is the operational process that is identified in the IT Infrastructure Library (ITIL) service management framework, although an organization does not require to adopt the ITIL framework to perform CM. It is referred to as Service Asset and CM in ITIL.

For a CM system to operate, it requires a variety of mechanism in which to store the information it governs. Initially, this was known as the Configuration Management Database (CMDB); ITIL V3 introduced the concept of a Configuration Management System (CMS) to replace the CMBD.

A CMBD is a database that stores the all-important information with regards to hardware and software components used in the organization. A CMBD provides an organized view of configuration data and a means of inspecting the data from any desired standpoint.

Most service management tools are implemented with a supporting data repository. Without the governance process of CM validating its contents, in general, the repository is an operational database with unverified data, not a CMBD or CMS. Automated configuration audit and verification components entitle a repository to be leveraged as an authorized essential component of the asset. A mutual audit is also possible. Special CM software is available, such as BMC Software's Atrium and Hewlett Packard Enterprise's Universal Configuration Management Database.

A CM process and supporting repository, CMBD or CMS, face the challenge of overlapping and contradicting data from sources across the organization. The CM plan must include a way to merge and reconcile CIs to present a single point of reference or a single source of truth.

CM is also used in software development and deployment, where it is known as Software Configuration Management (SCM) or Unified Configuration Management (UCM).

Software CM tools, such as Chef and Puppet, can be used jointly with the version-control tools for source code management, such as Apache Subversion and Git.

Service Level Management

Service Level Management (SLM) is one of the essential components in the ITIL Service Delivery domain. It is the most important set of processes within the ITIL framework. It processes to provide a framework by which services are defined, service levels needed to support business processes which are agreed upon. Service Level Agreements (SLAs) and Operational Level Agreements (OLAs) are developed to assure the agreements, and costs of services are also developed.

Executing Service Level Management processes permits IT staff to more accurately and cost effectively provision identified levels of service to the business. The processes ensure business and IT understand their roles and responsibilities and empower the business units.

In the end, business units are justifying to senior management the levels of service needed to support business processes, not IT. Moreover, the built-in constant enhancement processes to make sure that when organization's requirements change, supporting IT services change with them.

Availability Management

The availability Management objective is to define, analyze, plan, measure and enhance all components of the availability of IT services. Availability management is responsible for assuring IT infrastructure, process, tools, roles, and many more, are appropriate for the agreed upon availability target.

The system has to be designed to meet the availability requirements listed in the SLAs. A large number of virtualization platform permits for the management of system availability and can act in the event of a system outage (i.e., failover running guest OSes to a different host).

Capacity Management

Capacity management's aim is to ensure that IT resources are right-sized to meet current and future organization needs cost-effectively. It is an essential component of the ITIL framework.

Capacity management is focused on ensuring the organization IT infrastructure and it is sufficiently provisioned to provide the agreed service-level targets more accurately and cost-effectively. Capacity management takes account of the entire resources essential to deliver IT services within the scope of the defined organizations need.

Capacity management is an analytical function. The system capacity needs to be monitored, and thresholds need to be set to prevent systems from reaching an over-capacity situation.

Conduct Risk Assessment to Logical and Physical Infrastructure

Risk is a measure of the extent to which an entity is threatened by a possible situation or event and is often a function of:

- The adverse effect that would arise if any situation or event occurred
- The probability of occurrence

Information security risks arise from the loss of confidentiality, integrity, or availability of information or information systems and reflect the possible adverse effect on the organizational operations, organizational assets, individuals, or other organizations.

Risk Management Process

The risk management process includes:

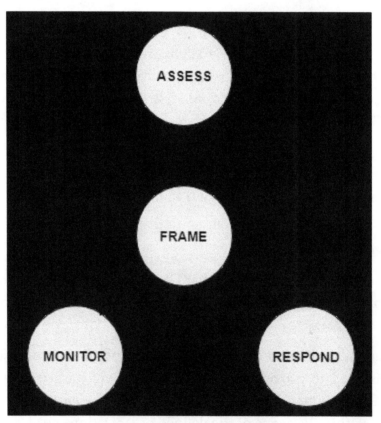

Figure 5-4: Risk Management Process

Framing Risk

Framing risk is the initial phase in the risk management process that addresses how organizations describe the environment in which risk-based decisions are made. It is designed to deliver a risk management procedure intended to address how the organization can access, respond to, and monitor risk. This enables the organizations to coherent the risks that it requires to manage, and also establishes and defines the boundaries for a risk-based decision within the organization.

Risk Assessment

Risk assessment is the process used to identify, estimate, and prioritize information security risks.

According to the NIST Special Publication, 800-39:

"Risk assessment is a key component of the risk management process. The purpose of engaging in risk-assessment is to identify:"

- Threats to organizations such as operations, assets, or individuals or threats directed through organizations against other organizations
- Organizations have the external and internal vulnerabilities
- The harm (i.e., adverse impact) that may occur given the potential for threats exploiting vulnerabilities
- Its high possibility that any harm will occur

Identifying these factors assists to address risks that include the high possibility of harm occurring and the potential degree of harm.

Conducting a Risk Assessment

Assessing risk needs the intense analysis of threats and vulnerability information to determine the extent to which possible situation or event could adversely affect an organization and the likelihood that such possible situations or events will occur.

Organizations have the right of performing a risk assessment in one of the two ways.

- **Qualitative Assessments** often employ a set of methods, principles, or rules for assessing risk based on non-numerical categories or levels such as very low, low, moderate, high, or very high.
- **Quantitative Assessments** often employs a set of methods, principles, or rules for assessing risk based on the use of numbers. This way of assessment efficiently supports cost-benefit analyses of alternative risk responses or system. The following measures and calculations form the basis of quantitative assessments:
  - Single Loss Expectancy (SLE)

- Annualized Rate of Occurrence (ARO)
- Annualized Loss Expectancy (ALO)

Responding to Risk

Risk response provides a consistent, organization-wide response to risk under the organizational risk frame by:

- Building an alternative system for responding to risk
- Evaluating the alternative system
- Determining the proper system consistent with organizational risk tolerance
- Deploying risk responses based on a selected system

Besides, four main components of risk responses are:

Accept Risk

Risk can be accepted. Risk acceptance is the practice of accepting the specific risk, typically based on an organizational decision that may also weight the cost versus the benefits of dealing with the risk in another way.

Avoid Risk

Risk can be avoided. Risk avoidance is the practice of coming up with an alternative so that the risk in question is not realized.

Transfer Risk

Risk can be transferred. Risk transfer is the practice of passing on the risk in question to another entity, such as an insurance company.

Mitigate Risk

Risk can be mitigated. Risk mitigation is the practice of elimination or the significant decreases in the level of the risk presented.

Monitoring Risk

Risk monitoring is a continuous process that tracks and evaluates the levels of risk in an organization. Along with monitoring itself, the discipline tracks evaluate the effectiveness of risk management strategies. The findings that are produced by risk monitoring processes can be used to assist in creating new strategies and updating previous strategies that may have proved to be ineffective.

The objective of risk monitoring is to constantly track the risks that occur and the effectiveness of the responses that are implemented by an organization. Monitoring can help to ascertain whether the suitable policies were adopted, whether new risks can now be identified or whether the old strategies to do with these risks are still valid. Monitoring is most important because a risk is not static.

The Collection, Acquisition, and Preservation of Digital Evidence

According to the **ISO/IEC 27037:2012**:

"It provides guidelines for particular actions in the handling of digital evidence, which are identification, collection, acquisition, and preservation of potential digital evidence that can be of evidential value.

It also guides individuals about everyday situations encountered during the digital evidence handling process and helps organizations in their disciplinary procedures and in facilitating the interchange of potential digital evidence among jurisdictions."

The International Standard Organization (ISO, 2012) mostly deals with the initial process of collecting and storing possible digital evidence and ignore subsequent work with the evidence (e.g., analysis, presentation, and disposal). The individuals who handle digital evidence has to be capable of identifying and managing risks that can arise when utilizing this type of evidence, in order to prevent its debasement and rendering it useless. **Digital Evidence First Responder (DEFR)** have to follow specific general principles to maintain the integrity and reliability of digital evidence. The purpose of these particular procedures needs to include the following:

- Reducing manipulation with digital data or digital devices.
- Documenting all activities and modifications made to the digital evidence, so that an independent professional can form their own opinion about the reliability of submitted evidence.
- Proceeding by the laws of the country.
- DEFR should not act beyond his or her competence.

These primary principles have to lead to the preservation of evidence for investigation objectives. If a change to the evidence cannot be avoided, then all activities that were carried out and the details for them are adequately documented. Some of the components that are involved in handling digital evidences are:

Identification

The identification process involves searching, detecting and documenting digital evidence and digital evidence is represented in both the physical and the logical form. All devices that could contain digital evidence have to be identified throughout this process. DEFR has to carry out a proper investigation of the crime scene to prevent overlooking small, camouflaged devices or material that appears inappropriate at first sight.

Collection

After the identification of devices that may have digital evidence, these devices are eliminated from their current location and moved to the laboratory when they are analyzed and processed as the further step. This process is documented continuously, including packaging and transported to the laboratory. DEFR is essential because it secures the physical material which may be the concern to the digital data that has been collected.

Acquisition

The earlier component of digital evidence consists mainly of producing a copy of evidence and documenting the methods used. If essential, allocated along with the unallocated space, has to be obtained. In general, the original copies generate a similar output of the similar verification function.

Depending on the possible situation, DEFR has to select suitable methods and procedures for acquiring data. In case, this process produces an inevitable change in the created copy, as compared to the original, it is essential to document the data that was changed. If the verification process cannot be carried out, DEFR has to utilize the best possible solution and then justify and vindicate his or her choice of method.

Preservation

In terms of preserving digital evidence, it is essential to secure integrity to make it functional for investigation. DEFR has to be capable of demonstrating the evidence that has not been changed since it is collected and to provide documentation and vindication of all activities that led to its changes.

Practitioners conducting such activities are usually a forensic expert or security professionals. **ISO 27037** guides the following devices:

- Digital storage media used in standard computers like optical and magneto-optical disks, hard drives, floppy disks, data devices with similar functions
- Digital still and video cameras (including CCTV)
- Mobile navigation systems
- Mobile phones, Personal Digital Assistants (PDAs), Personal Electronic Devices (PEDs), memory cards
- Networks based on TCP/IP and other digital protocols
- A standard computer with network connections

Proper Methodologies for Forensic Collection of Data

Digital forensics is the branch of forensic science that focuses on identifying, acquiring, processing, analyzing and reporting on data stored on a computer system, digital device or other storage media.

Each branch of Digital Forensics needs extensive training and experience making it difficult for the forensic examiner to be professional in all domains.

According to the American Academy of Forensic Sciences (AAFS):

"Forensic Science is the application of scientific principles and technological practices to the purposes of justice in the study and resolution of criminal, civil, and regulation issues."

Digital Forensic Process

The digital forensic process is a recognized forensic and scientific process used in digital forensic investigations. This process is mainly used in mobile and computer forensic investigations and contains such components as identification, collection, acquisition, and preservation.

This process is as same as the digital evidence process but some additional points and examples are described here.

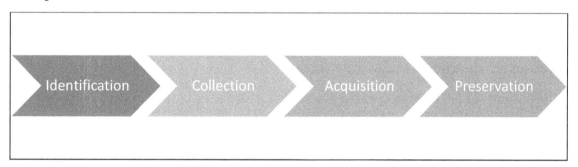

Figure 5-5: Digital Forensic Process

Identification

The forensics process begins with the identification of items that may or may not contain potential digital evidence. Identification is the **"process involving the search for, recognition and documentation of potential digital evidence"** defined by **ISO/IEC 27037:2012.**

Although the identification of potential digital evidence sounds simple in principle, there are subtle complexities.

For example:

Digital evidence has both a physical and virtual representation. Consider a hard drive containing potential digital evidence. The physical location of the evidence is the hard drive, but the evidence itself is the data contained within the drive. Besides, it also may not be at all obvious where potential digital evidence is housed. A server may have some directly attached disks and have an essential component of its storage within a SAN or NAS.

Collection

After possible digital evidence is identified, it needs to be collected:

The collection is the "**Process of gathering items that contain potential digital evidence**" defined by **ISO/IEC 27037:2012.**

Besides, the collection is equivalent to the standard law enforcement practice of seizing items having potential digital evidence under the authority of a legal order and eliminating them to a forensics lab or other facility for processing and analysis.

Acquisition

The acquisition is the "**Process of creating a copy of data within a defined set**" defined by **ISO/IEC 27037:2012**

Besides, an acquisition is mostly used in the private sector due to the organizational requirements to reduce the effect of a continuous investigation. Similar relates to minimizing the effect on other applications, and customers will make acquisition more likely to process in the cloud environment as well.

It has to be noted that the copy created throughout the acquisition process could range from the forensic image of a hard drive to a copy of the contents of a server's memory to the logical contents of a specific user's email box reliant on the purpose and scope of the investigation.

In most cases, the need for the copy is similar: it must be made using an accurate, defensible, well-documented process. Besides, the process needs to include integrity measures to ensure that the copy has not been changed since the acquisition. The multiple forms of potential digital evidence to be copied, and the requirements for the copying process, makes the acquisition a more difficult and challenging process as compared to the Collection.

Preservation

Once potential digital evidence has been collected or acquired, it needs to be preserved. ISO 27037 defines preservation as the "**process to maintain and safeguard the integrity and original condition of the potential digital evidence.**"

The preservation of potential digital evidence is a complex and significant process. Evidence preservation assists to assure admissibility in a court of law. However, digital evidence is very weak and is easily modified or destroyed. Given that the backlog in numerous forensic laboratories ranges from six months to a year (and that delays in the legal system might create further delays). Potential digital evidence may occupy a significant period in storage before it is analyzed or used in a legal proceeding. Storage needs strict access control to secure the items from accidental or deliberate change, along with the proper environmental controls.

Evidence Management

From collection to trail, maintaining evidence is an integral component of the digital forensics. Contain procedures and policies in place for the collection and management of evidence. You may need to gather digital evidence on short notice in some cases. To be aware not to gather data outside the scope of the requesting legal document. Assure legal discovery documents, or order will specify that you and Cloud Service Provider (CSP) be not allowed to disclose any specific activities undertaken in support of the order.

The CSP must also be aware of the issue surrounding the **disclosure** of data collecting activities. Depending on the SLA(s) the customer has in place, the data-collecting activities undertaken to support a forensic examination of a tenant's data which may not have to be disclosed to the tenants or any of the other tenants in a multi-tenant hosting solution.

Manage Communication with Relevant Parties

Communication is always most important and essential aspect among parties with any organization or kind of operation, but especially those parties who have engaged in your business. Cloud services adds an additional layer of complexities and considerations, and is highly recommended in regular communication. For communications to be active and foster optimal relationships, they must be both accurate and concise.

The Five WS and One H

They must clearly identify the "**five WS and the one H**" about communication which is essential, as the ability to do so directly affects the level of success that will be accomplished about aligning the cloud-based solution architecture and needs of the organization. Besides, the ability to successfully drive and coordinate effective governance across the organization is affected by the success or failure of these communication activities.

The "**five WS and the One H**" of communication are:

WS and H	Description
Who	Who is the target of the communication?
What	What is the communication designed to achieve?
When	When is the communication best delivered or most likely to reach its intended target(s)?
Where	Where is the communication pathway best managed from?
Why	Why is the communication being initiated in the initial place?
How	How is the communication being transmitted and how is it being received?

Table 5-4 - WS and H

The ability to make sure concise and clear communication, and, as a result, alignment and successfully achievement of objective, depend on the ability to handle the "**five WS and the one H**" of communication.

It's a CSP responsibility that must drive communication in the organization and through the ecosystem that it supports to make sure the long-term survivability of the organization's architecture that is continuously observed, discussed, and provided for.

Vendors

Communication with vendors is most important and cost-effective. The only way to deploy a better system within your organization is to deploy a system in a cloud because of communication. So, the communication perspective Communication-as-a-Service (CaaS) model is used.

CaaS is an outsourced organization communications solution that can be leased from a particular vendor. Such communications can include Voice over IP (VoIP) services, Instant Messaging (IM), and video conferencing applications using fixed and mobile devices. CaaS has evolved along the same lines as Software as a Service (SaaS).

The CaaS vendor's responsibility is to manage all hardware and software and provide assured Quality of Service (QoS). CaaS enables organizations to deploy communications devices when it is needed. This model removes the significant capital investment and constant overhead for a system whose capability may typically exceed or fall short of current demand.

CaaS provides flexibility, reliability, and expandability. The small, medium, and large-sized organization allows for the addition of devices, modes, or coverage on demand. The network capability and feature set can be continuously changed if essential, so that

functionality keeps pace with demand and resources are not wasted. There is no possibility of the system becoming out-dated and requiring periodic significant upgrades or replacement.

Customers

With a customer's perspective in a cloud-computing environment, cloud-based Customer Relationship Management (CRM) is used. Cloud-based CRM is also known as a Software-as-a-Service (SaaS) or on-demand CRM; data is stored on an external, remote network that personnel can access anytime, anywhere there is an internet connection, typically with a third-party service provider managing deployment and implementation. For instance, **the Cloud's quick**, secure deployment capabilities appeal to organizations with limited technological expertise or resources.

Some organizations may focus on cloud CRM as a cost-effective option. A vendor such as **Salesforce** charge by the user on a subscription basis and provide the option of monthly or yearly payments.

Partners

With a partner's perspective in a cloud-computing environment, cloud-based Partner Relationship Management (PRM) is used. PRM is a mixture of process, software, and approaches, organization use these to business process with partners who sell their products.

PRM system typically includes a partner portal, customer database, and other tools that enable organizations and partners to manage the business leads, revenues, opportunities, and sales metrics. PRM systems track discounting, inventory, operations, and pricing.

In this era, most of the organization rely on partner companies to sell their products on their behalf as a component of a channel approach, rather than using a direct distribution channel.

PRM software has to include:

- Partner portals for vendors to communicate and transfer data with their channel partner;
- Access management features to control who can view the data;
- Collaboration tools for vendors and partner personnel to work jointly and business lead;
- Dashboards with partner performance management tools to measure objectives and monitor results using key performance indicator (KPI);

- Integration with organization tools including calendars, communication channels, content management systems, contract management, expenses, project management, and time management.

Regulators

Initial communication is most important with regulators when developing a cloud environment. As a CSP, you are responsible for assuring that the entire infrastructure is compliant with the regulatory requirements that may apply to the organization.

These requirements will vary significantly based on various factors such as business type, geography, and services offered. However, if some regulatory laws or standards should be implemented or adhered to, you must understand all of the requirements and expectations of compliance to make sure that the organization can prove compliance when asked to do so.

Other Stakeholders

Depending on the application or project, there may be other stakeholders that need to be included in communication processes. It is either specific to the project or specific to regulatory requirements. The CSP must evaluate each set of a possible situation to determine whether there are other appropriate stakeholders, and determine what type of communication is required and its frequency.

Summary

To operate a cloud-computing environment securely, the CSP must be capable of focussing on numerous different issues at the same time. Understanding the physical and logical design components of the cloud environment is the initial step on the path towards operational security and stability. The CSP has to be capable of describing the specifications essential for the physical, logical, and environmental design of the data center along with identifying the essential requirements to build and implement the physical and logical infrastructure of the cloud.

To be able to operate and manage the cloud, the CSP must describe policies and processes that are focused on providing secure access, analysis, availability, maintenance capabilities, and monitoring. The CSP needs to be able to demonstrate the ability to understand, identify, and manage risk within the organization and specifically as it relates to the cloud environment as well. To be able to identify the essential regulations and controls to make sure compliance for the operation and management of cloud infrastructure within the organization along with the understanding and managing the process of conducting a risk assessment of the physical and logical infrastructure are essential as well. The need to

manage the process for collection, acquisition, and preservation of the digital evidence in a forensically sound manner with cloud environments also have to be a focus for the CSP.

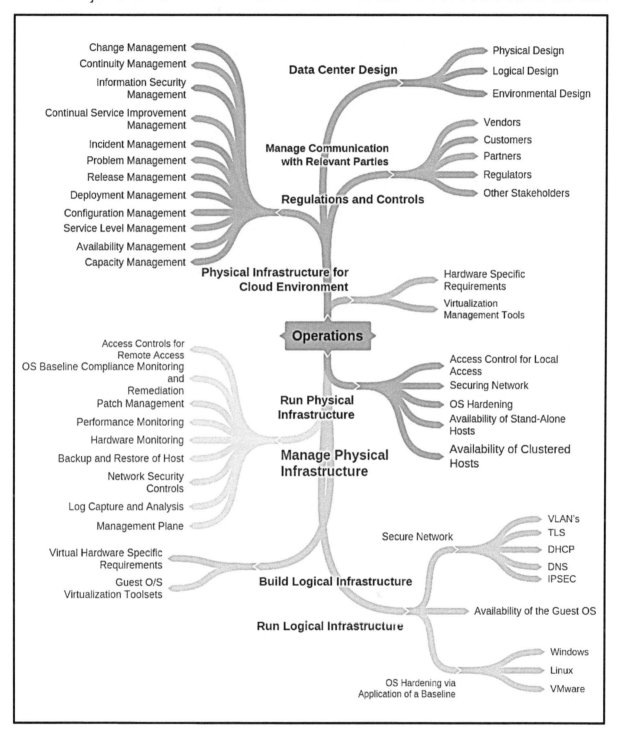

Figure 5-6: Mind map of Operations

Practice Questions

1. Which engineering is a study of HVAC system design?
   a) Mechanical Engineering
   b) Electrical Engineering
   c) Chemical Engineering
   d) Software Engineering

2. Identify the lowest temperature recommended by ASHRAE:
   a) 16°C
   b) 18°C
   c) 20°C
   d) 22°C

3. Identify the highest temperature recommended by ASHRAE:
   a) 23°C
   b) 25°C
   c) 27°C
   d) 29°C

4. Choose the right network controller to build a physical infrastructure:
   a) Traditional networking model
   b) Converged networking model
   c) Both A and B
   d) None of the above

5. Which type of license is offered by **Red Hat Enterprise Linux (RHEL)** for **Kernel-based Virtual Machine (KVM)?**
   a) Floating licensing
   b) Open-source
   c) Proprietary
   d) Source-available

6. Which type of firewall has to be added in the VM series to KVM?
   a) Application-level firewall
   b) Stateful multilayer inspection firewall
   c) Transparent firewalls
   d) Next-generation firewalls (NGFW)

7. Identify the right layer to make up the TLS:
    a) TLS Handshake Protocol
    b) TLS Record Protocol
    c) Both A and B
    d) None of the above

8. Which network technology automatically assign the IP address to the computer?
    a) VLAN
    b) TLS
    c) DHCP
    d) DNS

9. Which networking technology translates the domain name into numeric form?
    a) VLAN
    b) TLS
    c) DHCP
    d) DNS

10. How many clustered storage architectures are available?
    a) Two
    b) Three
    c) Four
    d) Five

11. Which remote access technique is most commonly used in the cloud infrastructure?
    a) Virtual Desktop Infrastructure (VDI)
    b) Remote Desktop Protocol (RDP)
    c) Access through a secure terminal
    d) All of the above

12. How many primary types of a firewall are there?
    a) Two
    b) Three
    c) Four
    d) Five

13. Which primary type of firewall is used in the cloud infrastructure?
    a) Host-based firewall
    b) Network-based firewall

c) Both A and B

d) None of the above

14. Identify the correct vulnerabilities assessment scans:

a) Application Scans

b) Database scans

c) Host-based scans

d) All of the above options

15. Identify the main interconnected components of cloud orchestration:

a) Resource orchestration

b) Service

c) Workload

d) All of the above

16. Identify the right tools to automate server configuration and management:

a) Terraform

b) Salt

c) Puppet

d) Ansible

e) All of the above

17. Identify the right tools to do a cloud performance monitoring:

a) VMware Consolidated Backup (VCB)

b) vSphere

c) None of the above

d) All of the above

18. Which ISO standard defines a BCM system?

a) ISO 22301

b) ISO 27001

c) ISO 20000

d) ISO 27037

19. How many types of incidents are?

a) Low priorities

b) Medium priorities

c) High priorities

d) All of the above

20. Identify the right tools that can perform incident management?
    a) PagerDuty
    b) VictorOps
    c) xMatters
    d) None of the above

Chapter 06: Legal & Compliance

The objective of the Legal and Compliance domain is to provide you an understanding of how to utilize the various legal and regulatory challenges unique to cloud computing. To achieve and maintain compliance, it is important to understand the audit processes utilized within cloud computing, including assurance issues, auditing controls, and the specific reporting attributes.

You will gain knowledge of legal processes and required compliance with regulatory frameworks, which includes investigative methods for crime analysis and evidence-gathering techniques. Organization risk considerations and the impact of outsourcing for design and hosting are explored as well.

Legal Requirements and Unique Risks within the Cloud Environment

As the global nature of cloud computing technology continues to evolve, it essentially simplifies and enables the convenience which was once thought impossible, meeting the internal regulatory laws and legislation is has become a challenge of all the time.

Ensuring adherence, compliance, or conformity with these can be very difficult within traditional "on-premise" environments, or even on the third party/hosted environments-add cloud computing and the complexity increases significantly.

Constantly, when dealing with legal, compliance and regulatory issues, the first step must be to consult with relevant teams or professionals specialized in those domains. As a security professional, your objective should be to establish a baseline understanding of the fluid and ever-changing legal and regulatory landscape with which you may need to interact.

International Legislation Conflicts

Cloud computing provides excellent opportunities for user related to access, automatic updates, cost saving, ease of use, scalable resourcing and so on. From a legal point of view, the reality can be different because cloud computing introduces multiple legal challenges which the security practitioners, architects, professionals etc. need to be aware of. A primary objective is created by the existence of conflicting legal requirements coupled with the inability to apply local laws to a global technology offering. This can result in uncertainty and a lack of clarity on the full scope of risks when operating globally.

In recent years, the amplified use of technology and the rise in the number of businesses operating globally have resulted in the number of trans-border disputes increasing

dramatically. In particular, these included intellectual property, copyright law, and violation of patents. More recently, there have been breaches of legislative requirements, data protection, and other privacy-related components.

Examples

Some examples of recent areas of concern include the following.

According to ZDNet: *"In June 2011, Cloudfare, a web hosting, and Services Company became enmeshed in the middle of a multi-jurisdictional battle over the hacking activities of LulzSec. On June 15, 2011, LulzSec attacked the United States Central Intelligence Agency's (CIA) websites and took them offline. LulzSec contracted to use Cloudflare for hosting services before launching the attacks, but it also used seven hosting companies in Canada, the U.S., and Europe. The ensuing hunt to find and take down LulzSec, involving various intelligence agencies and governments, as well as black and white hat hackers from around the world, caused Cloudfare and other hosting companies to become the targets of Distributed Denial of Service (DDoS) attacks that required the spreading of traffic across 14 data centers globally to successfully thwart."*

Another example

According to the United State District Court: *"In a proceeding in 2014 before the U.S. Court, Microsoft was ordered to turn over an email belonging to a user of its hosted mail service. That email belonged to a user outside the U.S. The email itself was located on a server in a data center in Ireland—outside the U.S., which should be out of the reach of U.S. authorities and subject to the requirements of the EU privacy laws. Microsoft challenged the order and lost."*

Appraisal of Legal Risks Specific to Cloud Computing

Cloud computing adds complexities concerning legal issues. With a traditional data center, the organization will own and control the systems, environment, and resources, along with the data that is housed within them. Even in environments where hosting and support services are contracted out to a third party, the organization offering contract will still hold control over their data and system and usually will be physically segregated within a data center from a network perspective as well as in cages on the data center floor. This makes the legal requirements very clear to the parties for the following types of issues that might arise.

The following issues also contain legislative items that may affect cloud environments:

State law

This law usually refers to the law of each U.S. state (50 states in total, each treated separately), with their state constitutions, state governments, and state courts.

Copyright/Piracy laws

Copyright infringement can be performed for financial or non-financial gain. It usually happens when copyright material is violated upon, made accessible to or shared with others by a party which is not the legal owner of the information.

Intellectual Property Rights

This can describe creations of the mind such as logos, literature, symbols, words, other artistic creations, and literary works. Copyright protection, patents, and trademarks all exist to protect a company's or a person's intellectual entitlements. Intellectual property rights give the individual who created an idea, an exclusive right to their idea for a defined period.

Enforceable Governmental Request

An enforceable governmental request is a request or order that is capable of being performed based on the government's order.

Privacy law

This law can be described as the right of an individual to determine when, how, and to what extent he/she would release personal information. Also, privacy law usually includes language indicating that personal information needs to be destroyed when its retention is no longer required.

Criminal law

Criminal law is a body of rules and statutes that define conduct that is prohibited by the government and is enforced to protect the safety and well-being of the public. Along with defining prohibited conduct, criminal law also defines the punishment when the law is broken. Crimes are categorized based on their seriousness with the categories carrying maximum punishments.

Tort law

This is a body of rights, obligations, and remedies that assures protection for persons suffering harm because of the illegal acts of others. These laws set out that the individual liable for the costs or consequences of the illegal act is the individual who committed the act as opposed to the individual who suffered the consequences. Tort actions are not dependent on an agreement between the parties to a lawsuit.

The Doctrine of the Proper law

Where a conflict of laws occurs, this determines in which jurisdiction the dispute will be resolved, based upon contractual language professing an express selection or a clear intention through a **choice-of-law clause**. If there is not an express selection stipulated, then implied selection might be used to infer the intention and meaning of the parties from the nature of the contract and the circumstances involved.

Conflict of laws

This law relates to a difference between the laws. In the United States (US), the existence of various states with legal rules often at variance makes the subject of conflict of laws especially urgent. The conflict of laws is the basis for deciding which laws are most appropriate in a situation where there are conflicting laws in different states. The conflicting legal rules may come from U.S. federal law, the laws of U.S. states, or the laws of other countries.

Legal Controls

Depending on whether an organization is employing a community, hybrid, or public Cloud, there are some issues that the organization has to understand. The extra dynamic is the presence of a third party: The **Cloud service provider (CSP)**: so, the organization needs to understand how laws and regulations apply to the Cloud. In other words, it becomes essential to understand how laws apply to the different parties involved and how compliance will ultimately be addressed.

Regardless of which models you are using, you must consider the legal issues that apply to how you collect, store, process, and, finally, destroy data. There are likely to be important national and international laws that you, together with your legal functions, need to consider ensuring you are in legal compliance. There can be various compliance requirements such as Safe Harbor, HIPAA, PCI, Sarbanes-Oxley Act (SOX), and GLBA and other technology and information privacy laws and regulations. Failure to comply may mean heavy punishments and liability issues.

These laws and regulations usually specify responsibility and accountability for the protection of information.

Safe Harbor

This program was developed by the U.S Department of Commerce and the Commission to address the Commission's determination that the United States (US) does not have in place of a regulatory framework that provides adequate protection for personal data transferred from the **European Economic Area (EEA)**. Specific industries such as telecommunication carriers, banks, and insurance companies may not be eligible for this program.

HIPAA

The Health Insurance Portability and Accountability Act (HIPAA) is a United States Act used to set out the requirements of the Department of Health and Human Services to adopt national standards for electronic healthcare transactions and national identifiers for employers, health plans, and provider. Protected health information can be stored through Cloud computing under HIPAA. This act was published in 1996.

PCI

According to the Payment Card Industry (PCI), organization: *"The Payment Card Industry is a Security Standards Council and is a global forum for the continuing development, improvement, dissemination, storage, and implementation of security standards for account data protection."*

Sarbanes-Oxley Act (SOX)

The Sarbanes-Oxley Act of 2002 is U.S. legislation enacted to protect shareholders and the public from accounting errors and fraudulent practices in the organization. **Securities and Exchange Commission (SEC)** administered the SOX act, and sets goals for compliance and publishes rules on requirements. SOX is not a set of business practices and does not specify how business ought to store records; rather, it defines the records that are to be stored and for how long.

GLBA

The Gramm-Leach-Bliley Act (GLBA) is a federal law enacted in the US to control the directions that financial institutions manage the private information of individuals. It is a Financial Modernization Act of 1999.

eDiscovery (e.g., ISO/IEC 27050, CSA Guidance)

eDiscovercy (also known as Electronic discovery) is a procedure by which parties involved in litigation, collect, review, and exchange information in electronic formats to use it as evidence.

There are various different electronic formats - or **electronically stored information (ESI)**, as it is recognized in the e-discovery world - that may be sought in e-discovery, ranging from conventional data sources, such as primary email and Microsoft documents, to more modern ones, like instant messaging, social media, and smartphone applications, to more arcane ones like files from a company-specific database.

ISO/IEC 27050

According to the ISO/IEC 27050 standard:

"It aims to put in place internationally-recognized standard procedures and practices for the stages in a process commonly referred to as "e-discovery." The stages of the e-discovery process are generally believed to include the analysis, collection, identification, preservation, processing, review, and production of electronically stored information."

CSA Guidance

According to the Cloud Security Alliance (CSA), *"eDiscovery is the process by which an opposing party obtains private documents for use in litigation and to cover a wide range of potential documents. In particular, discovery need not be limited to documents known at the outset to be admissible as evidence in court; instead, discovery will apply to all documents reasonably calculated to lead to admissible evidence and the evidence that is both relevant and probative."*

EDiscovery Challenges

The challenges associated with e-discovery include the vast volumes of electronic information in the possession or control of number of organization, the ease with which electronic documents are duplicated, transferred and dispersed. The dynamic and changeable nature of electronic information, difficulties with regard to disposal of electronic information when desirable, and the fast pace of technological change which can render obsolete the hardware and/or software required to review electronically stored information.

Possession, Custody, and Control

In most jurisdiction systems in the United States, a party's obligation to produce valuable information is limited to documents and data within its possession, custody or control. Hosting relevant data through a third party, such as a Cloud provider, generally does not obviate a party's obligation to produce information. Nonetheless, not all data hosted by a Cloud provider may be in the control of a client (e.g., disaster recovery systems or specific metadata created and maintained by the Cloud provider to operate its environment). Distinguishing the data that is and is not available to the client may be in the interest of both the client and the provider at the outset of a relationship. The responsibilities of the Cloud service provider as Cloud data supervisor about the production of information in response to legal process is an issue left to each jurisdiction to sort out.

Forensics Requirements

When incidents happen, it could be necessary to perform forensic investigations related to that incident. Depending on the Cloud model that you are deploying, it could not be easy to collect the required information to perform active forensic investigations.

"Cloud computing forensic science is the application of scientific principles, technological practices, and derived and proven methods to reconstruct past cloud computing events through identification, collection, preservation, examination, interpretation, and reporting of digital evidence."

Performing a forensic network analysis on Cloud is not as easy as performing the same investigation compare to the on-premises or traditional environment. This is because you could not have access to the information that you require and, therefore, need to ask the Cloud service provider to provide the information.

Communication in this scenario is essential because of all members that are involved in the incident that work together to collect the most important information related to the incident. In some cases, the Cloud customer could not be able to obtain and review security incident logs because they are in possession of the service provider. The service provider could be under no obligation to provide this information or could be unable to do so without violating the confidentiality of the other tenants sharing the Cloud infrastructure.

ISO has provided a suite of standards specifically related to digital forensics, which includes:

- **ISO/IEC 27037:2012:** Guide for collecting, identifying, and preserving electronic evidence
- **ISO/IEC 27041:2015:** Guide for incident investigations
- **ISO/IEC 27042: 2015**: Guide for digital evidence analysis
- **ISO/IEC 27043:2015:** Incident investigation principles and processes
- **ISO/IEC 27050-1:2016:** Overview and principles for eDiscovery.

The objective of such standards is to promote best practices for the acquisition and investigation of digital evidence. While some security professionals favor specific methods, processes, and controls, **ISO 27050-1** looks to introduce and make certain standardization of approaches globally.

Privacy Issues, Including Jurisdictional Variation

Privacy issues can vary significantly between different jurisdictions. This variation can relate to the types of records and information protected along with the required controls and notifications that apply.

Difference between Contractual and Regulated PII

NIST, in Special Publication (SP) 800-122, defines **Personally Identifiable Information (PII)** as any information about an individual maintained by an agency, including:

- Any information that can be used to distinguish or trace an individual's identity, such as date, name, Social Security Number, and place of birth, mother's maiden name, or biometric records
- Any other information that is linked or linkable to an individual, such as educational, financial, medical, and employment information.

There are two types of PII associated with cloud and non-cloud environments.

Contractual PII

Where an entity or organization processes, transmits or stores PII, as part of its services or business, this information is required to be sufficiently protected in line with relevant local states, national, regional, federal, or other laws. Outsourcing of services, roles, or functions the relevant contract has to list the proper rules and requirements from the organizations which "own" the data and applicable law to which the providers must adhere.

Besides, the contractual components related to PII have to list requirements and appropriate levels of confidentiality, as well as security provisions or requirements necessary. As part of the contract, the provider will be bound by confidentiality, privacy, and information security requirements established by the entity or organization to which it provides services. The contractor could be required to document adherence or compliance with the contract at set intervals and in line with an audit and governance requirements from its customer(s).

Failure to meet or satisfy contractual requirements may lead to penalties (financial or service compensated) through the termination of the contract at the discretion of the organization to which services are provided.

Contractual Components

From a contractual, regulated, and PII perspective, the following components have to be reviewed and fully understood by the CSP contract (along with other most essential components within a Service Level Agreement (SLA)):

- Appropriate/required data security controls
- Audit or right to audit subcontractors
- Location of data
- Removal or deletion of data
- Return of data or restitution of data

- Scope of processing
- Use of sub-contractor

Regulated PII

While many of the previously listed elements could be required for contractual PII, they are in no small extent required and form an essential foundation for the regulation of PII. The key focus and transparent criteria to which the regulated PII should adhere are required under law and statutory requirements, as opposed to the contractual criteria that could be based on best practice or organizational security policies.

A key **differentiator** from a regulated perspective is the "must haves" to satisfy regulatory requirements (such as HIPAA and GLBA) of which failed to do so can result in sizable and crucial financial penalties, through to restrictions around processes, storing, and providing of services.

Regulations are put in place to reduce exposure and to protect entities and individuals from some risks ultimately. They also force and require responsibilities and actions to be taken by providers and processers alike.

The reasons for regulations include (but are not limited to)

- Apply adequate protections
- Create a repeatable and measurable approach to regulated data and systems
- Continue to align with statutory bodies and fulfill professional conduct requirements
- Make sure appropriate mechanisms and controls are implemented
- Establish a standard level of controls and processes
- Protect users
- Provide transparency among customers, partners, and related industries
- Reduce the likelihood of malformed or fractured practices
- Take and make sure due to care

Country-Specific Legislation Related to PII / Data Privacy

Many countries have laws that protect and regulate PII and data privacy; there can be significant variance among numerous jurisdictions as to what is required or allowed. The following is not a comprehensive or complete list of all countries and regulations; rather, it is a sampling of the essential jurisdictions and their respective regulations.

United States (US)

The US has many laws that cover numerous specific aspects of data privacy; there is no particular federal law governing data protection. Interestingly, the term "privacy" is not

mentioned in the US Constitution; however, privacy is recognized differently in specific states and under different circumstances. The **California** and **Montana** constitutions both recognize privacy as an "**inalienable right**" and "**essential to the well-being of a free society.**"

There are few restrictions on the transfer of personal data out of the US, making it relatively easy for organizations to engage CSP located outside of the US. The **Federal Trade Commission (FTC)** and other standard U.S. regulators do, however, hold that the applicable U.S. laws and regulations apply to the data after it leaves its jurisdiction, and the U.S. regulated organization remain liable for the following:

- Data exported out of the US
- Processing of data overseas by sub-contractors
- Sub-contractors using the same protection for the regulated data when it leaves the country.

Most importantly, the **Safe Harbor Program** deals with the international transfer of data. However, it is essential to understand about **Health Insurance Portability and Accountability Act (HIPAA)**, the **Gramm-Leach-Bliley Act (GLBA)**, the **Stored Communications Act (SCA)** and the **Sarbanes-Oxley Act (SOX)**, as they each have an impact on how the U.S handles privacy and data.

Safe Harbor Program, HIPAA, GLBA, and SOX are defined in the legal control section. However, the **Stored Communications Act** is defined in this section.

Stored Communications Act (SCA)

The SCA was enacted in the US in 1986 as part of the **Electronic Communications Privacy Act (ECPA)**. It provides privacy protections for specific electronic communication and computing services from unauthorized access or interception.

European Union (EU)

From an EU standpoint, different levels of data protection in different jurisdictions has resulted in the prohibition of EU data controllers transferring personal data outside of their country to **non-EEA jurisdictions** that do not have a sufficient level of protection.

Therefore, organizations outsourcing to Cloud must have total certainty as to where in the Cloud the data can be stored, or they must agree with the Cloud provider as to the specific jurisdictions in which the data can be processed. This can be very difficult to do, as various Cloud providers process data across many jurisdictions through **federated louds**. This may include **non-EEA countries** where a different, and maybe lower standard of data protection may apply.

Also, this challenge is exacerbated by the fact that it is typically challenging to know precisely where in the network a piece of data is being processed at any given time when there is a network of Cloud servers and data is stored on different servers in different jurisdictions.

This set of conditions raise specific issues and possible concerns relating to standards of data protection and the ability to adhere to obligations under data protection legislation.

<u>Directive 95/46 EC</u>

This directive focuses on the protection of individuals about the processing of personal data and the free movement of such data; it captures the human right to privacy, as referenced in the **European Convention on Human Rights (ECHR)**.

<u>EU General Data Protection Regulation</u>

In 2012, the European Commission proposed a major reform in the EU legal framework on the protection of personal data. The new proposals will strengthen individual rights and tackle the challenges of globalization and new technologies.

The objective is to make sure that individuals have complete ownership and control over their data, and the EU is operating under same data privacy laws and regulations uniformly.

<u>The United Kingdom and Ireland</u>

There is a common standard of protection at the EU level concerning transferring personal data from Ireland and the UK to an EEA country. Challenges arise when data is being transferred from either country to a jurisdiction outside of the EEA. Companies must meet special conditions to make sure that the countries can in question provide a sufficient level of data protection.

Note:

Inalienable Rights: Freedom that each in the US has, which cannot be transferred to another person or surrendered except by the individual having those rights.

Federal Trade Commission (FTC): FTC is a US federal regulatory agency designed to monitor and prevent anticompetitive, deceptive or unfair business practices.

European Union (EU): EU is an economic and political union of 28 countries. It operates an internal (or single) market that allows free movement of goods, capital, services, and people between member states.

European Economic Area (EEA): EEA includes European Union countries and also Iceland, Liechtenstein, and Norway. It allows them to be part of the EU's single market.

EU countries are Austria, Bulgaria, Belgium, Croatia, Republic of Cyprus, Czech Republic, Denmark, Estonia, France, Finland, Greece, Germany, Hungary, Ireland, Italy, Latvia, Lithuania, Luxembourg, Malta, Netherlands, Poland, Portugal, Romania, Slovakia, Slovenia, Spain, Sweden and the UK.

Electronic Communications Privacy Act (ECPA): ECPA is a US federal statute that prohibits a third party from intercepting or disclosing communications without authorization.

European Convention on Human Rights (ECHR): ECHR protects the human rights of people in countries that belong to the Council of Europe.

Federated Clouds: A federated Cloud is the deployment and management of various internal and external cloud computing services to match business needs. A federation is the union of several smaller parts that perform a common action. Federated Cloud is also known as cloud federation.

Difference between Confidentiality, Integrity, Availability, and Privacy

The three main aspects of security are **confidentiality, integrity, and availability**. As more services and data have moved online, especially with the expansion of mobile computing and apps that utilize sensitive information, **privacy** has become a crucial fourth aspect. All four aspects of security work together closely.

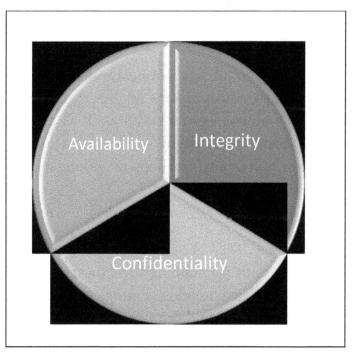

Figure 6-1: Main Components of Security

Confidentiality

Confidentiality is a set of rules that limit access to information. Confidentiality is roughly equivalent to privacy. Security measures are undertaken to make sure confidentiality is designed to prevent sensitive information from reaching the malicious user while ensuring that the right user can get it: Access must be restricted only to the authorized to view the data in question. It is common, as well, for data to be categorized according to the amount and type of damage that could be done should fall into unintended hands. Relatively stringent measures can then be implemented according to those categories.

Sometimes safeguarding data confidentiality may involve specialized training for that privy to such documents. Such training would typically include security risks that could threaten this information. Training can help familiarize authorized people with risk factors and how to secure data against them. Additional aspects of training include strong passwords and password-related best practices and information about **social engineering methods**, to prevent them from bending **data-handling** rules with good intentions and potentially disastrous results.

Integrity

Integrity is the assurance that the information is accurate and trustworthy. Integrity contains maintaining the accuracy, consistency, and reliability of data over its entire life cycle. Data should not be changed in transit, and steps should be taken to make sure that unauthorized people can not transform data (e.g., in a breach of confidentiality). These security measures contain file permissions and user access controls.

Version Control may be used to prevent erroneous changes or accidental deletion by authorized users. Similarly, some means must be in place to detect any changes in data that might occur because of non-human-caused events such as **an Electromagnetic Pulse (EMP)** or server crash. Some data might include checksums, even cryptographic checksums, for verification of integrity. Backups or redundancies must be available to restore the affected data to its correct state.

Availability

Availability is a guarantee of reliable access to the information to authorized people. Availability is ensured by rigorously maintaining all hardware, performing hardware repairs immediately when needed and maintaining a properly functioning operating system environment that is free of software conflicts. It is also essential to keep current with all necessary system upgrades. Providing sufficient communication bandwidth and preventing the occurrence of bottlenecks are equally important. Redundancy, failover, **RAID** even high-availability clusters can mitigate serious consequences when hardware

issues start to occur. Fast and adaptive disaster recovery is important for the worst-case scenarios; that capacity is dependent on the existence of a comprehensive **Disaster Recovery Plan (DRP)**. Protections against data loss or interruptions in connections must include unpredictable events such as fire and natural disasters. To prevent data loss from such occurrences, a backup copy may be stored in a geographically isolated location, perhaps even in a waterproof safe, fireproof. Extra security equipment such as proxy servers and firewalls can guard against downtime and unreachable data due to malicious actions such as network intrusions and **dDenial-of-Service (DoS)** attacks.

> **Note:**
>
> **Redundant Array of Independent Disks (RAID)**: RAID is a way of storing the same data in different places on various hard disks to secure data in the case of a drive failure.
>
> **Disaster Recovery Plan (DRP)**: DPR is a documented, structured approach with instructions for responding to unplanned incidents.
>
> **Denial-of-Service (DoS) attack**: DoS attack is a security event that happens when an attacker prevents legitimate users from accessing specific computer systems, devices, services or other IT resources.

Privacy

Data privacy, also known as information privacy, is the part of information technology that deals with the ability of an organization or individual, has to determine what data in a computer system can be shared with third parties.

In the US, legislation concerning data privacy has been enacted in a sectorial manner, which means that each law or compliance regulation has been created in response to the needs of a particular industry or some part of the population.

Examples:

Children's Online Privacy Protection Act (COPPA): This act gives parents control over what information websites can collect from their kids.

Video Privacy Protection Act: This act prevents unauthorized disclosure of an individual's Personally Identifiable Information (PII) stemming from their rental or purchase of audio-visual material.

Security	Privacy
Security refers to protection against unauthorized access.	Privacy defines the ability to protect personally identifiable information (PII).
Security protects all types of data and information including the ones that are stored electronically.	Privacy means protecting sensitive information related to individuals and organizations.
Security can be achieved without privacy.	Privacy cannot be achieved without security
Security program focuses on all sorts of information assets that an organization collects.	Privacy program focuses on personal information such as names, addresses, social security numbers, login credentials, financial accounts information, etc.
It implements security protocols to provide confidentiality, integrity, and availability of information assets.	It refers to protection of privacy rights concerning the processing of personal data.

Table 6-1: Differences between Security and Privacy

Note:

Social engineering: An attack vector relies heavily on human interaction and typically involves manipulating user into breaking standard security procedures and best practices to gain access to networks, systems, or physical locations, or for financial gain.

Data handling: It is the process of ensuring that data is stored, archived or disposed of safely and securely.

Version Control: A system that records changes to a file or set of files over time so that you can recall specific versions later.

Electromagnetic Pulse (EMP): EMP is an intense burst of electromagnetic (EM) energy caused by an abrupt, rapid acceleration of charged particles, usually electrons.

Audit Process, Methodologies, and Required Adaptations for a Cloud Environment

This section defines the process, methods, and required adaptions necessary for an audit within a cloud environment. Before we define this topic, we first need to define an Audit Process.

> "Audit is an assurance function that some method, standard, or practice is followed. Depending on the type of audit, the auditor systematically examines the evidence for compliance with established criteria."

Internal and External Audit Controls

As the organization moves to the transaction service to the cloud environment, there is a need for continuous assurances from both cloud customers and providers that controls are set up or in the process of being identified.

An organization's internal audit acts as a **third line of defense** after the business or IT functions and risk management functions through

- Independent verification of the cloud program's effectiveness
- Assuring the risk management functions of the organization regarding cloud risk exposure.

The internal audit function can also play a "trusted" advisor and proactively be involved by working with IT and business in identifying and addressing the risk associated with various cloud services and deployment model. In this capacity, the organization is actively taking a risk-based approach on its journey with the cloud. The internal audit function can engage with stakeholders, review the current risk framework with a **clouded lens**, assist with risk mitigation strategies, and perform some cloud audits such as

- The organization's current cloud governance program
- Data classification governance
- Shadow IT

Cloud providers have to include an internal audit in their discussion about new services and deployment models to obtain feedback in the planned design of cloud controls their customers will need, as well as mitigate the risk. The internal audit function will still need to consider how to maintain independence from the overall process; ultimately, it will need actually to perform the audit on these controls.

The internal audit function will also continue to perform audits in the traditional environment, which are directly relied on the output of the organization's risk assessment process.

Cloud customers will want not only to engage in their discussion with cloud providers security professionals but also consider meeting with the organization's internal audit group.

Another potential source of independent verification on internal controls will be the audit performed by external auditors. An external auditor's scope varies significantly from an internal audit, whereas the external audit usually forces on the internal control over financial reporting. Therefore, the scope of services is usually limited to the IT and business environment that support the financial health of an organization and in most cases does not provide specific assurance on cloud risks other than the vendor risk considerations on the financial health of the cloud provider.

Note:

The Third Line of Defense: In the financial services industry, people are used to the third lines of defense for the majority of the risk functions. Generally, the first line of defense for management of risk is the business, the second line of defense is a control function, and the third line of defense is an internal audit.

Cloudless: It is the first service-provider agnostic visibility platform, capable of providing access to packet data in Amazon Web Services (AWS), Microsoft Azure, IBM Bluemix, Google Cloud Platform, Alibaba Cloud, CenturyLink cloud and more; the platform also supports Window and Linux environments

---

Impact of Requirements Programs by the Use of Cloud

Cloud providers and customers are essential to understanding how cloud services will impact the audit requirements set forth by their organization. By default, the cloud, auditors need to understand how they audit and obtain evidence to support their audit.

The CSP needs to understand that traditional auditing methods may not apply to cloud environments.

Because the organization will not have such level of control or access over the physical environment; joined with the reality of geographic distribution of cloud environments, this makes being on site virtually impossible.

Assurance Challenges of Virtualization and Cloud

When you are using virtualization as an essential component in the cloud, it is important to get assess and then get assurances relating to the security of virtual instances.

The task, however, is not a simple one, particularly from an auditing perspective and least of all using **non-invasive systems** that audit the **hypervisor** and associated components.

How can the CSP attest to the security relating to virtualization (sometimes spread across hundreds of devices), in the absence of testing and verification?

Given the evolving technology landscape, the rate at which updates, version upgrades, additional components, and associated system changes are implemented presents the ultimate moving target for the CSP.

Presently, much of the focus is on the continuing confidentiality and integrity of the VM (virtual machine) and its associated hypervisors (conscious that the availability will typically be covered extensively under the SLA). The thought process is that if the availability of the VM is affected, this fact will be captured as part of the general SLA (where confidentiality and integrity may not be explicitly covered under virtualization).

Within the SLAs, items such as

- Mean Time Between Failures (MTBF)
- Mean Time To Repair (MTTR)
- Mean Time To Recovery

All these items may be called out; however, a failure to delve much more in-depth, or specifically focus on VMs or the hypervisor itself, is an issue.

To obtain assurance and perform proper auditing on the VM or hypervisor, the CSP must

- Understand the virtualization management architecture
- Verify system is up-to-date and hardened according to the best practice standards

> **Note:**
>
> **Hypervisor**: Also known as a virtual machine (VM) monitor, is a process that creates and runs VMs. A hypervisor allows one host computer to support several guest VMs by virtually sharing its resources, like memory and processing.
>
> **Mean Time Between Failures (MTBF)**: MTBF is a measure of how reliable a hardware product or component is. For most components, the measure is typically in thousands or even tens of thousands of hours between failures.
>
> **Mean Time To Repair (MTTR)**: MTTR is the average time required to fix a failed device or component and return it to production status.
>
> **Mean Time To Recovery (MTTR)**: MTTR is the average time that a device will take to recover from any failure.

Types of Audit Reports

There are many different audit reports that have been standardized throughout the industry. While they differ in approach and audience, but they have similar design and serve for similar purposes.

SAS

The Statement on Auditing Standards (SAS) Number 70, which is commonly known as SAS 70, is a standard published by the **American Institute of Certified Public Accounts (AICPA)** and is intended to guide auditors when analyzing service organizations individually. Typically, it is also known as a "service auditor's examination."

There are two types of reports under SAS-70.

- **Type 1**: Reports are focused on an evaluation by the auditor as to the service organization's declarations, and to the security controls they have put in place.
- **Type 2**: Audit, the same information, and evaluation are included, but additional evaluations and opinions on behalf of the auditor are added as to the effectiveness in actually meeting the control objectives on behalf of the service organization.

SSAE

The Statements on Standards for Attestation Engagements (SSAE) 16 replaced the SAS 70 as of 2011 and is the standard that most in the United States now use. Rather than focusing on specific control sets, the SSAE 16 is focused on auditing methods. It is also known as the **Service Organization Control (SOC)** report.

There are three types of reports under SSAE 16.

- **SOC 1**: Reports effectively are the direct replacement for the SAS 70 reports and are explicitly focused on financial reporting controls. SOC 1 has two subtypes. Type 1 reports and Type 2 reports.

- **SOC2**: Reporting is a model that incorporates "principles." With the last update to SOC 2 in 2014, five principles were established. Under the guidelines, the security principle must be included with any of the following four to form a complete report: Availability, Confidentiality, Processing Integrity and Privacy.

- **SOC3:** Reports are designed to be for general use. Also, reports will not contain sensitive or proprietary information that a service organization would not want open or available to release and review. SOC 3 reports are similar to the SOC 2 reports.

ISAE

The International Standard on Assurance Engagements (ISAE) 3402 reports was issued by International Auditing and Assurance Standard Board (IAASB). This report was very similar by default and structure to the SOC Type 2 reports. ISAE report is used internationally, but SOC reports used in the US. ISAE reports were developed to provide an international assurance standard for allowing public accountants to issue a report for use by their auditors or organizations as well. ISAE reports have two subtypes.

Type 1: They have aligned with SOC type 2 reports, in that they are based on a snapshot of a single point in time.

Type 2: They are also aligned with SOC Type 2 reports in scope and intents, and typically, they are done for six months to show the management and use of control over the period.

Restrictions of Audit Scope Statements (e.g., SAS 70)

Parameters must be set and enforced to focus an audit's efforts on relevancy and auditability. These parameters are commonly known as audit scope restrictions.

Besides, Audit scope restrictions are used to make sure that the operational impact of the audit is limited, effectively lowering any risk to production environments and high-priority or essential components required for the delivery of services.

Finally, scope restrictions typically specify operational components, as well as the asset restriction, which includes acceptable times and period (e.g., time of day) and acceptable and non-accepted testing methods (e.g., no destructive testing). These limit the impact on a production system.

Gap Analysis

Gap analysis benchmarks and identifies relevant "gaps" against specified standards or frameworks.

Typically, personnel or resources which are not engaged or functioning within the area of scope perform gap analysis. The use of independent or impartial resources is best served to make sure there are no favoritisms or conflicts. You do not want existing relationships to dilute or in any way impact the findings (positively or negatively).

Auditor performed the gap analysis or subject matter expert against a number of listed requirements, which could range from a complete assessment or a random sample of controls (subset), resulting in a report highlighting the findings, including risks, recommendations, and conformity, or compliance against the specified assessment (**ISO 27001:2013**, **ISO 19011:2011**, etc.)

The objective of a gap analysis is to identify and report on any gap or risks that may impact the availability, confidentiality, or integrity of critical information assets. The value of such an assessment is typically determined based on **what we did not know** or for an independent resource to communicate to relevant management or senior personnel such risks, as opposed to internal resources saying **we need or have to be doing it**.

Audit Plan

The audit plan ensures the appropriate focus and emphasis on components that are most important to Cloud computing includes four phases:

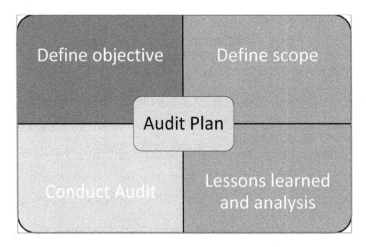

Figure 6-2: Audit Plan

Define Objective

These important objectives have to interpret the goals and outputs from the audit:

- Define audit outputs and format
- Define frequency and audit focus
- Define the number of auditors and subject matter experts required
- Document and define audit objectives
- Ensure alignment with audit or risk management processes and the process is internal.

Define Scope

There are many considerations that defines the audit scope, but some of them are defined here.

- Define cloud services to be audited (IaaS, PaaS, SaaS)
- Define key components of services (storage, utilization, processing)

- Define geographical locations permitted or required
- Define locations for an audit to be undertaken
- Ensure the primary objective and boundaries to which the audit will operate.

Conduct Audit

When conducting an audit, keep the following issues in consideration.

- Proper Staff
- Sufficient tools
- Schedule
- Supervision of audit
- Reassessment

Lessons learned and analysis

Once the audit is completed, management and system staff will analyze the process and findings to determine what lessons have been learned and how continuous improvement process can be applied. There are some points to focus and analysis after an audit:

- Ensure that approach and scope are most important
- Ensure that audit criteria, and scope is accurate
- Ensure that reporting details are sufficient to enable precise, concise, and appropriate business decisions to be made
- Determine opportunities for reporting improvement or enhancement
- Ensure that the accurate skillsets are available and utilized to deliver accurate results and to report

Standards Requirements

Industry group or regulatory bodies have established the standards or to set common configurations, expectations, operational requirements and definitions. There are two primary standards to follow the industry.

ISO/IEC 27018

ISO/IEC 27018 is the first international standard of privacy controls in Cloud computing. ISO 27018 was published on July 30, 2014, by the International Organization for Standardization (ISO) as a new component of the ISO 27001 standard. ISO/IEC 27018 addresses the privacy aspects of Cloud computing for consumers.

Cloud service providers (CSPs) who adopt ISO/IEC 27018 should be aware of the following five fundamental principles:

Consent: Personal data that the CSPs receive may not be used for advertising and marketing unless the customer has expressly consented to allow its use.

Control: Customer will have and maintain explicit control over how their information is to be used by the CSPs.

Communication: Clear records about any incident and their response to it have to be kept by the CSPs and customers have to be notified.

Transparency: CSPs must inform the customers about items such as where their data resides. The CSP also needs to disclose to customers the use of any sub-contractors that will be used to process PII.

Independent and Yearly Audit: To remain compliant, the CSP must subject itself to yearly third-party reviews. This will allow the customers to rely upon the findings to support their own regulatory obligations.

GAPP

Generally Accepted Privacy Principles (GAPP) is the American Institute of Certified Public Accountants (AICPA) standard describes many details to the privacy principles.

According to GAPP, the primary privacy principle groups are the following:

- The entity defines documents, communicates and assigns accountability for its privacy policies and procedures.
- The entity collects personal information only for the purposes identified in the notice.
- The entity discloses personal information to third parties only for the purposes identified in the notice and with the implicit or explicit consent of the individual.
- The entity describes the choices available to the individual and obtains implicit or explicit consent concerning the collection, use, and disclosure of personal information.
- The entity limits the use of personal information to the purposes identified in the notice and for which the individual has provided implicit or explicit consent.
- The entity maintains accurate, complete, and relevant personal information for the purposes identified in the notice.
- The entity monitors compliance with its privacy policies and procedures and has procedures to address privacy-related inquiries, complaints, and disputes.
- The entity provides notice about its privacy policies and procedures and identifies the purposes for which personal information is collected, used, retained, and disclosed.
- The entity provides individuals with access to their personal information for review and update.

- The entity protects personal information against unauthorized access (both physical and logical).

Internal Information Security Management System (ISMS)

An ISMS is a set of policies and procedures used for systematically managing an organization's sensitive data. The objective of an ISMS is to mitigate the risk and make sure business continuity by pro-actively limiting the impact of a security breach.

An ISMS typically addressed employee behavior and processes along with data and technology. It can be targeted towards a specific type of data, such as customer data, or it can be applied in a proper way that becomes part of the organization's culture.

ISO27001 is a specification for creating an ISMS. It does not mandate specific actions but contains suggestions for documentation, internal audits, continual improvement, and corrective and preventive action.

Note that **ISO 27001** (officially known as **ISO/IEC 27001:2005**) is a specification for ISMS. An ISMS is a framework of policies and procedures that includes all legal, physical and technical controls involved in an organization's information risk management processes.

Internal Information Security Controls System

According to the **ISO 27001: 2013**:

"Established guidelines and general principles for initiating, implementing, maintaining, and improving information security management with an organization."

The controls are mapped to address requirements identified through a formal risk assessment.

The following domain makes up the ISO 27001:2013, the most commonly used global standard for ISMS implementation.

- A.5 Security Policy Management
- A.6 Corporate Security Management
- A.7 Personnel Security Management
- A.8 Organizational Asset Management
- A.9 Information Access Management
- A.10 Cryptography Policy Management
- A.11 Physical Security Management
- A.12 Operational Security Management
- A.13 Network Security Management
- A.14 System Security Management

- A.15 Supplier Relationship Management
- A.16 Security Incident Management
- A.17 Security Continuity Management
- A.18 Security Compliance Management

Policies

Policies can be document and articulate in a formal manner the desired or required systems and operations standard for any IT system or organization. They are crucial for implementing an effective data security strategy. Typically, they act as the connectors that hold many parts of the data security together across both technical and non-technical elements. The failure to implement and utilizes policies in a cloud-based computing or a non-cloud based computing would likely become in different part or isolation of activities, efficiently operating as standalone and leading to multiple duplication and limited standardization.

From an organization's perspective, policies are nothing new. Policies have long been providing guiding decisions and principles to make sure that actions and decisions achieve the desired and logical outcome.

From a cloud computing environment, the use of policies, while essential, can go a long way determining the security posture of cloud services, as well as standardizing practices.

There are many types of policies, but few of them are defined below:

Organizational Policies

These policies form the basis of functional policies that can decrease the likelihood of

- Financial loss
- Irretrievable loss of data
- Misuse or abuse of systems and resources
- Reputational damage
- Regulatory and legal consequences

Functional Policies

Organizations that have a well-ingrained and operational ISM use the following functional policies to be regulated properly.

- Acceptable usage policy
- Data classification policy
- Data backup policy
- Disaster recovery policy
- E-mail use policy

- Employee background checks or screening policy
- Human resources security policy
- Information security policy
- Internet use policy
- Incident response or incident management policy
- Information technology policy
- Legal compliance policy or guidelines
- Network security policy
- Password policy
- Remote access policy
- Software security policy
- Segregation of duties policy
- Third-party access policy
- Virus and spam policy

Identification and Involvement of Relevant Stakeholders

A stakeholder is a group, individual or organization who/which may affect, be affected by or perceive itself to be affected by a decision, activity, or result of a project.

Identify Stakeholder is a process of identifying stakeholders regularly throughout the project life cycle and documenting relevant information regarding their interests, independencies, influence, and potential impact on project success.

Also, to reach your target group and achieve your project's goals, you might need to involve external organizations and people. This may include stakeholders in some of the following roles:

- stakeholders that can support your project by providing resources and competencies (e.g., partners, funding bodies, related projects)
- stakeholders influencing your target group and their possibilities to save energy (e.g., service providers, municipal authorities)
- stakeholders who are influenced by your project and may support or oppose it (e.g., family members, neighbors, co-workers).

The goal of stakeholder involvement is to make sure that interactions necessary to the process are accomplished, while not allowing excessive numbers of affected groups and individuals to impede process execution.

- Identify stakeholders relevant to this process and their appropriate involvement.
- Share these identifications with project planners or other planners as appropriate.
- Involve relevant stakeholders as planned.

Specialized Compliance Requirements for Highly Regulated Industries

Organizations operating within highly regulated industries need to be familiar with any specific industry regulatory requirements (e.g., HIPAA for healthcare, PCI for finance, and FedRAMP for the U.S. government). While risk management in a cloud computing environment is a mutual provider or customer activity, accountability entirely remains with the customer. Organizations must consider existing requirements, their existing level of compliance, and any geographic - or jurisdiction - specific restrictions that will make leveraging accurate cloud scale difficult.

Impact of Distributed IT Model

Distributed IT or distributed information systems are becoming increasingly common in conjunction with amplified by the adoption of cloud computing services. The globalization of companies, along with collaboration and outsourcing, continue to allow organizations and users to avail themselves to distributed services.

The drives for adopting such services are many (e.g., increasing enterprise productivity, reducing IS development cost) and the impact in organizations regarding visibility and control over a distributed or effectively dispersed model can be wide-ranging.

The Cloud Service Provider (CSP) needs to review and address the following components to make sure that the distributed IT model does not negatively affect the factors.

Communications/Clear Understanding

Traditional IT deployment and operations typically allow a clear line of sight or understanding of the personnel, their roles, functions, and core areas of focus, either allowing for far more access to individuals, on a name basis or based on their roles. Communications allow for collaboration, information sharing, and the availability of relevant details and information when necessary. This can be from operations, engineering, controls, or development.

Distributed IT models challenge and fundamentally redefine the roles, functions, and ability for direct interactions, such as emails, phone calls, or messengers.

Coordination/Management of Activities

Project management is an essential component, ensuring the smooth and successful delivery of technology projects, deployments, and solutions delivery. Enter the complexity or benefit of distributed and outsourced IT models. There are some benefits when outsourced models are involved in the delivery of services and solutions; mainly when it is their business to ensure such services and solutions are delivered to clients, and even more

so when large-scale services and solutions are available for customers (e.g., Salesforce, Google, and Microsoft).

Governance of Processes/Activities

Effective governance allows for serenity and a level of confidence to be established in an organization. This is even more true with distributed IT and the use of IT services or solutions across dispersed organizational boundaries from a variety of users.

Implications of Cloud to Enterprise Risk Management

The cloud computing signifies a fundamental shift in the way technology is offered. The shift is towards the consumerization of Information Technology (IT) services and convenience.

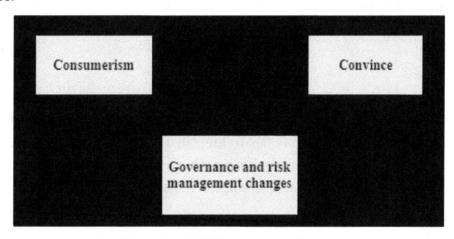

Figure 6-3: Risk Management Changes

Access Providers Risk Management

It is essential for both the cloud customer and the cloud provider, to be focused on risk. The way in which common risk management activities, processes, behaviors, and related procedures are performed may require significant revisions and redesign. After all, the way services are delivered changes delivery mechanisms, locations, and providers - all of which result in governance and risk-management changes.

These changes must be identified at the scoping and strategy phases, through to continuing and recurring tasks. Addressing these risks requires that cloud customer's and the cloud provider policies and procedures to be aligned as closely as possible because risk management needs to be a shared activity to be implemented successfully.

Difference between Data Owner/Controller vs. Data Custodian/Processor

Treating information as an asset needs multiples roles and distinctions to be clearly defined and identified. The following are vital roles associated with data management:

Data Subject: An individual who is the subject of personal data.

Data Controller: A person who (either alone or jointly with other persons) determines the purposes for which and the way in which any personal data is processed.

Data Processor: Concerning personal data is any person (other than an employee of the data controller) who processes the data on behalf of the data controller.

Data Stewards: Commonly responsible for data content, context, and associated business rules.

Data Custodians: Responsible for the safe custody, storage of the data, and transport and implementation of business rules.

Data Owners: Hold the legal rights and complete control over a single piece or set of data elements. Data owners possess the ability to define distribution and associated policies as well.

For example:

Risk Profile

The risk profile is determined by an organization's willingness to take risks, along with the threats to which it is itself exposed. It has to identify the level of risk to be accepted, how risks are taken, and how risk-based decision-making is performed. Also, the risk profile should allow for potential costs and disruptions have to more than one risks being exploited.

It is vitally important that an organization completely engages in a risk-based assessment and review against Cloud computing services, service providers, and the overall impacts on the organization have to utilize Cloud-based services.

Risk Appetite

Fast decision making can lead to significant advantages for the organization, but when assessing and measuring relevant risks in cloud service offerings, its best to have a systematic, measurable, and pragmatic approach to cloud risk management. Undertaking these steps, effectively allow the business to balance the risks off-set any excessive risk components, all while satisfying listed requirements and objectives for security and growth.

Many developing and emerging organizations will more likely to take significant risks when utilizing cloud-computing services so they can be first to the market.

Risk Mitigation

When taking on risk management and associated activities, the approach and desired result always have to reduce and mitigate risks. Mitigation of risks will decrease the exposure to a risk or the likelihood of it occurring. When applying risk mitigation to a cloud

environment or cloud-based assessments, these are most often obtained by implementing additional controls, policies, processes, procedures, or utilizing improved technical security features. Additional access control, vulnerability management, or selecting a particular cloud provider are some of the various examples of risk mitigation or risk reduction.

Different Risk Frameworks

The challenge that having several risk frameworks poses is the significant effort and investment required to perform such risk reviews, along with the time and associated reporting. The risk frameworks include

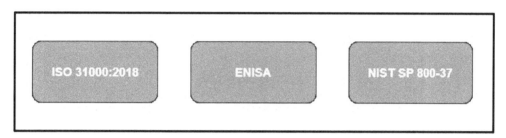

Figure 6-4: Risk Framework

ISO 31000:2018

Technical Committee ISO/TC 262 prepared this standard. This second edition cancels and replaces the first edition (**ISO 31000:2009**) which has been technically revised.

As ISO 31000:2018 is a guidance standard and is not intended for certification purposes; implementing it does not address specific or legal requirements related to risk assessments, risk reviews, and overall risk management. However, implementation and use of the ISO 31000:2009 standard will set out a risk-management framework and process that can assist in addressing organizational requirements and, most importantly, provide a structured and measurable risk-management approach to assist with the identification of cloud-related risks.

ISO 31000:2018 sets out terms and definitions, principles, a framework, and a process for managing risk. Like other ISO standards, it provides many critical principles as a guiding set of rules to enable security professionals and organizations to manage risks. Some of them are listed below:

According to the ISO31000:2018:

- "This standard is for use by people who create and protect value in organizations by managing risks, making decisions, setting and achieving objectives and improving performance.

- Organizations of all types and sizes face external and internal factors and influences that make it uncertain whether they will achieve their objectives.
- Managing risk is iterative and assists organizations in setting strategy, achieving objectives and making informed decisions.
- Managing risk is part of governance and leadership and is fundamental to how the organization is managed at all levels. It contributes to the improvement of management systems.
- Managing risk is part of all activities associated with an organization and includes interaction with stakeholders.
- Managing risk considers the external and internal context of the organization, including human behavior and cultural factors."

ENISA

European Network and Information Security Agency (ENISA).

ENISA produced "**Cloud Computing: Benefits, Risks, and Recommendations for Information Security**," which can be utilized as an effective foundation for risk management. ENISA identifies 35 types of risks for organizations to consider, coupled with "Top 8" security risks based on likelihood and impact. This framework is not globally accepted like ISO Standards.

- Compliance risk
- Data protection
- Isolation failure
- Insecure or incomplete data deletion
- Loss of governance
- Lock-in
- Management interface failure
- Malicious insider

NIST SP 800-37

According to the National Institute of Standards and Technology (NIST) Special Publication (SP) 800-37:

"This publication focused on risk components and the proper analysis of such risks. While NIST serves as an international reference for many of the world's leading entities, it continues to be strongly adopted by the U.S. government and related agency sectors".

Metrics for Risk Management

Risk has to communicate in a way which is concise and simple to understand. It can also be essential to communicate risk information outside the organization. To be successful in this, the organization must agree to a set of risk management metrics.

Using a risk scorecard is recommended. The impact and probability of each risk are assessed separately, and then the outcomes are joined to give an indication of exposure using a five-level scale in each of these quantities:

- Minimal
- Low
- Moderate
- High
- Maximum

This enables a clear and simple graphical representation of project risks.

Likelihood	Minimal	Low	Moderate	High	Critical
	1	2	3	4	5
A (almost certain)	H	H	E	E	E
B (likely)	M	H	H	E	E
C (possible)	L	M	H	E	E
D (unlikely)	L	L	M	H	E
E (rare)	L	L	M	H	H

Table 6-2: Risk Scorecard

> **Note:**
>
> **E = Extreme Risk**: Immediate action required to mitigate the risk or decide if not to proceed.
>
> **H = High Risk**: Action must be taken to compensate the risk.
>
> **M= Moderate Risk**: Action must be taken to monitor the risk.
>
> **L = Low Risk**: Routine acceptance of the risk

Assessment of Risk Environment

To sufficiently evaluate risk in cloud computing, various levels must be accessed. The specific service, vendor or ecosystem is the first component, involves the same analysis to be hosting in a traditional data center, with the addition of cloud-specific aspects added

into the mix. The cloud provider also needs to be evaluated for risk, based on their record of accomplishment, focus, stability, financial health, and future direction.

Outsourcing and Cloud Contract Design

It is essential that things like proper governance be involved in contract design and management of outsourcing. An exhaustive understanding of contracts and contract management is essential and in large organizations is typically managed by a separate department. It is the cloud security professional's responsibility to make sure that these contract managers understand the details of what they are managing so that the organization does not experience undue risk. .

Business Requirements

Before entering into a contract with a cloud supplier, your organization has to evaluate its particular needs and requirements that will form the basis and foundation of the organizational cloud strategy. To develop a cloud strategy, the primary organizational assets will need to be agreed upon and assessed for adequacy or suitability for a cloud environment.

Service Level Agreement (SLA)

Every cloud service provider is subject to local laws and regulation based on its physical location, making it imperative that he/she complies with numerous standards like **HIPAA, GLBA, ISO27001:2005, PCI-DSS, SAS70,** etc. While compliance with these standards provide a level of assurance, regulatory standards may not meet the business requirements of customers might be spread across different geographies and might not be subject to the same laws and regulations.

Users are advised to discuss and review the SLAs with their chief legal officers before the execution of any cloud provider's agreement. The number of standard vendor SLAs will not indemnify or assume liability if a breach occurs.

SLAs must be written by customers to make sure policy compliance and satisfy auditing and regulatory obligations in the domain listed below:

- Backup management
- Communications and networks
- Deployment and availability of required and necessary skills, resource, etc., to assure the quality of the service.
- Systems and applications monitoring
- Information security incident handling
- User management

- Protection against malicious software's
- Vulnerability management and security audit
- Mobile computing and teleworking
- Proper operating procedure to protect data from unauthorized disclosure, modification, removal, and destruction.

SLA Components

While SLAs tend to vary significantly depending on the provider, more often than not they are structured in favor of the provider to expose them to the least amount of risk ultimately.

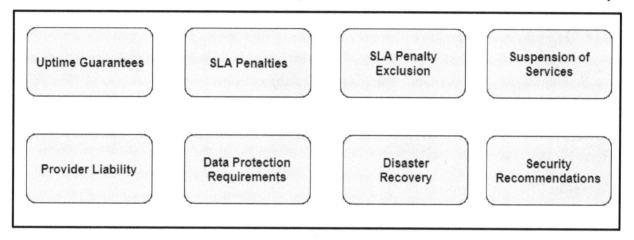

Figure 6-5: SLA Components

Vendor Management

Once an organization decides to move its network and data in a cloud environment, the process of choosing a cloud provider needs to done with care and exhaustive evaluation. cloud computing is still an emerging technology on IT landscape, as such, many companies are scrambling to offer cloud solutions and to become a part of the explosive growth in the IT industry. While the level of competition is indeed beneficial to any customer, it also means that various new organizations are emerging that do not have long-established reputations or track records of performance to evaluate. It is significant to make sure that any vendor being considered is stable and reputable to host critical business system and sensitive data with it. The last thing any organization would want is to give critical business systems to a cloud provider that is not a mature enough to manage the growth and operational demands, or too small a start-up that might not be around when the contract has run its course. Although some organizations are providing cloud services and have extensive track records in IT industry, the start-up trying to gain a share of the explosion in cloud services may offer very low-pricing or added options in an attempt to establish a strong presence in the industry based on the majority of customers using their services.

Selection

There are various factors that must be determined before choosing a cloud provider. The following is a list of essential factors an organization needs to consider in the selection process.

- What is the reputation of the cloud provider?
- How does the organization handle their cloud services?
- Does the organization conform / is it certified against relevant security and professional standards/frameworks? What certifications do an organization have?
- Where are the facilities located for the cloud provider?
- How does the company manage the security incidents?
- Does the cloud provider build their platform on standards and flexibility, or do they focus a lot more on proprietary configurations?

Apart from the number of operational and technological questions with the selection, certifications play a significant role; especially as regulatory compliance becomes increasingly essential and public.

Common Criteria Framework

The Common Criteria (CC) framework (ISO/IEC 15408-1:2009) is an international ISO standard to provide guidelines and specification for evaluating information security products, with the view for ensuring they meet an agreed-upon security standard for governments entities and agencies.

The objective of CC has ensured customers that the products they are buying have been evaluated and that a vendor-neutral third party has verified the vendor's claims.

CC looks at certifying a product only and does not include business or administrative processes. While it views these as beneficial, we are all too aware of the dangers of relying only on technology for robust and effective security.

Contract Management (e.g., right to audit, metrics, definitions, termination, litigation, assurance, compliance, access to Cloud/data)

The most critical business activity amplified by the significant outsourcing of roles and responsibilities, contract management needs governance to be relevant and useful. Contract management involves meeting ongoing requirement, monitoring contract performance, adhering to contract terms and handling any outages, incidents, violation, or variations to contractual obligations. The role of the cloud management and cloud governance should not be underestimated or overlooked.

Remember that the contract is the only proper format that will be reviewed and assessed as part of a dispute between the cloud service provider and the cloud customer.

The primary considerations and components of the contract are as follows:

Right to Audit

Right to audit has to allow for the organization owning the data to audit or engage the services of an independent party to ensure if the contractor or sub-contractor is satisfying contractual and regulatory requirements.

Metrics

The contract has to clearly define what criterias are to be measured as far as system's performance and availability is concerned, and the agreement between the cloud provider and cloud customer as to how the criteria will be measured, collected, quantified, and processed.

Definitions

The contract has to include agreed-upon definitions of any terms and technologies. However, it may seem obvious to people in the industry what many terms mean; having them in the contract formalizes the definitions and makes sure that everyone has the same understanding.

Termination

Termination should the need arise; the contract should clearly define the terms under which a party can terminate the contract, and what conditions are needed as part of doing so. This will often include specific processes for formal notice of non-performance, remedy steps and timelines that can be taken, along with potential penalties and termination costs, depending on the reasons for and timing of such action.

Litigation

Sometimes, the cloud customer could be the subject of legal action, which would likely also impact the cloud provider and need their involvement. The contract will document the responsibilities for both parties in such a situation, along with the required response times and potential liabilities.

Access to Cloud or Data

How both users and the cloud customer will get access to systems and data is a key contract and SLA component. This includes multifactor authentication requirements, along with supported identity providers and systems. From the cloud customer's perspective, this

defines what level of administrative or privileged access they are granted, depending on which cloud model is used and the services offered by its concerned cloud provider.

Execute Vendor Management

For managing outsourced and cloud services, the SLA is essential in documenting the responsibilities and expectations of all vendors and customers involved. The SLA orders requirements for uptime, support, response time, incident management, and virtually all operational aspects of the contract. The SLA also clears appropriate penalties for non-compliance and the impact they will have on the entire contract and satisfactory performance of it.

Supply-chain Management (e.g., ISO/IEC 27036)

With the nature of modern applications built on a myriad of different components and services, the supply chain of any application or system is emerging to a scale far outside a single organization. This complexity makes the security of an entire system increasingly tricky, as a breach of any components of the supply chain can affect all other components or the overall application or the system itself.

There are many complexities and risks in supply chain management:

- Financial instability of provider
- Single points of failure
- Data Breaches
- Malware infestations
- Data loss

To resolve these complexities and risks in supply chain management, follow the **ISO/IEC 27036** standard because the international standard provides guidelines and solution to the overall system and application.

According to the **ISO/IEC 27036**:

"**ISO/IEC 27036** is a standard for providing guidance on the evaluation and treatment of information risks involved in the acquisition of goods and services from suppliers. The implied context is business-to-business relationships, rather than retailing, and information-related products."

ISO/IEC 27036 is a various form of standards.

As an information security standard, the products most obviously covered by the standards include:

- IT outsourcing and cloud computing services;
- There are many professional services, e.g., security guards, cleaners, delivery services (couriers), equipment maintenance or servicing, consulting and specialist advisory services, knowledge management, research and development, manufacturing, logistics, source code escrow and healthcare;
- Provision of ICT hardware, software, and services including telecommunications and Internet services;
- On-demand products and services where the acquirer specifies the requirements and typically has an active role in the product design.

Also, Information security guidance to the vendors and customers of cloud services.

Responding to risks specific to the provision of cloud services that can have an information security impact on organizations using these services.

Summary

When taking into account the issues that the legal and compliance domain raises, the CSP must be able to focus on various different issues constantly. These issues include understanding how to recognize the numerous legal requirements and unique risks related with the cloud environment about legislation, legal risks, controls, and forensic requirements. Besides, the CSP must able to describe the potential personal and data privacy issues specific to personal identifiable information (PII) with the cloud environment. There is a need for concise and clear definition of the process, the methods, and the required adaptions necessary to execute an audit in a cloud environment. The CSP also needs to be able to understand the implications of cloud to organization risk management. The CSP should be able to assist the organization to accomplish the levels of understanding required to address risks via a proper audit process. They must address supply chain management and contract design for outsourced in a cloud environment is important as well.

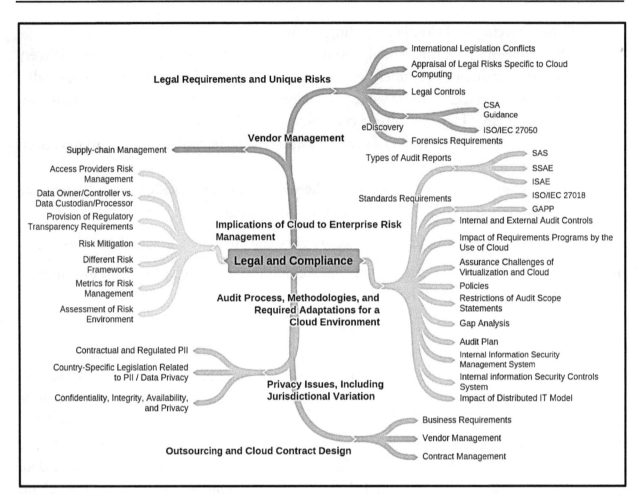

Figure 6-6: Mind map of Legal and Compliance

Practice Questions

1. Which organization developed the Safe Harbor program?
   a) ISO
   b) U.S Department of Commerce
   c) IEC
   d) None of the above

2. When was the Health Insurance Portability and Accountability Act (HIPAA) published?
   a) 1994
   b) 1995
   c) 1996
   d) 1997

3. Which organization has administered the Sarbanes-Oxley Act?
   a) U.S Department of Commerce
   b) ISO
   c) Security and Exchange Commission (SEC)
   d) None of the above

4. Which act is a Financial Modernization Act?
   a) HIPAA
   b) SEC
   c) GLBA
   d) None of the above

5. Which ISO standard provides guidance for incident investigation?
   a) ISO/IEC 27037:2012
   b) ISO/IEC 27041:2015
   c) ISO/IEC 27042: 2015
   d) ISO/IEC 27050-1:2016

6. Which ISO standard provides a principle of eDiscovery?
   a) ISO/IEC 27037:2012
   b) ISO/IEC 27041:2015
   c) ISO/IEC 27042: 2015
   d) ISO/IEC 27050-1:2016

7. Which program or act deals with the international transfer of data?
   a) Safe Harbor Program
   b) HIPAA
   c) GLBA
   d) SCA

8. When was the Stored Communications Act (SCA) published?
   a) 1986
   b) 1987
   c) 1988
   d) 1989

9. How many types of PII associated with Cloud and non-Cloud environments?
   a) Two types
   b) Three types
   c) Four types
   d) Five types

10. How many types of audit reports are used in Cloud computing?
    a) Two types
    b) Three types
    c) Four types
    d) Five types

11. Which organization published the Statement on Auditing Standards (SAS)?
    a) U.S Department of Commerce
    b) Security and Exchange Commission (SEC)
    c) American Institute of Certified Public Accounts (AICPA)
    d) None of the above

12. Which audit report is also known as a service auditor's examination?
    a) SAS
    b) SSAE
    c) ISAE
    d) None of the above

13. Which audit report is also known as a Service Organization Control (SOC)?

a) SAS

b) SSAE

c) ISAE

d) None of the above

14. Which organization is published the International Standard on Assurance Engagements (ISAE) report?

a) International Auditing and Assurance Standard Board (IAASB).

b) Security and Exchange Commission (SEC)

c) American Institute of Certified Public Accounts (AICPA)

d) None of the above

15. How many phases are there in audit plan?

a) One

b) Two

c) Three

d) Four

16. Which organization owns the Generally Accepted Privacy Principles (GAPP)?

a) International Auditing and Assurance Standard Board (IAASB).

b) Security and Exchange Commission (SEC)

c) American Institute of Certified Public Accountants (AICPA)

d) None of the above

17. How many types of risks are identified in the ENISA?

a) 34

b) 35

c) 36

d) 37

18. Common Criteria (CC) framework follows this standard:

a) ISO/IEC 15408-1:2009

b) ISO/IEC 27042: 2015

c) ISO/IEC 27050-1:2016

d) None of the above

19. Identify the appropriate steps of security under the privacy issues?

a) Confidentiality, Integrity, Availability

b) Confidentiality, Integrity, Availability, and Privacy

c) Confidentiality, Integrity, Availability, and Credibility

d) None of the above

20. Identify the correct types of SLA components?

a) Uptime Guarantees, Suspension of Service, Provider Liability, Data Protection Requirements, Disaster Recovery, Security recommendation

b) Uptime Guarantees, Integrity, Provider Liability, Data Protection Requirements, Disaster Recovery, Security recommendation

c) Uptime Guarantees, Suspension of Service, Availability, Data Protection Requirements, Disaster Recovery, Security recommendation

d) None of the above

Answers:

| Chapter 1: Architectural Concepts & Design Requirements |

1. **a, b, c**

Explanation: Cloud computing is a new operational model and set of technologies for managing shared pools of computing resources. Cloud computing is the practice of using a network of remote servers hosted on the internet to store, manage and process data rather than using a local server or personal computer. It is the on-demand delivery of computing resources through a Cloud services platform with pay-as-you-go pricing.

2. **e**

Explanation: The advantage of Cloud computing is go global in minutes, increased speed and agility, stop spending money on running and maintaining data centers, benefits from massive economies of scale.

3. **b**

Explanation: Integrity: Ensuring that information is not subject to unauthorized modification.

4. **b**

Explanation: A Cloud Service Provider (CSP) offers cloud-based platform, application, infrastructure, or storage services. The CSP will possess the data centre, owns and deals with the resources (hardware or software), employs the staff, monitors service provision and security, and gives administrative assistance to the customer.

5. **a, b, c**

Explanation: Key Cloud computing characteristics are on-demand self-service, broad network access, rapid elasticity and scalability, multi-tenancy, resource pooling, and measured service.

6.**b**

Explanation: Broad network access: Capabilities are accessible over the network and available through standard devices including laptops and mobile devices.

7.**b**

Explanation: Cloud service customer can arrangement computing capabilities, as required, naturally or with little cooperation or earlier correspondence with the Cloud service.

8.a

Explanation: Virtualization is making virtual image of something such as server, storage, operating system.

9. d

Explanation: The advantage of virtualization technology is as

- A big step towards new technology making life easier and better.
- It helped to make Cloud computing more efficient and eco-friendly
- It is one of the cost-saving, hardware-reducing and energy-saving technique.
- Isolation
- Resource sharing
- Aggregation of resources
- Dynamical resources

10.a, b, c

Explanation: SaaS, PaaS, NaaS, IaaS are the Cloud service model

11. c

Explanation: Cloud networking introduces another path to deploy, operate, and manage distributed enterprise networks.

12. d

Explanation: There are some advantages of Cloud data base as

- No software licensing
- On-demand Oracle and MS SQL server solution
- No hardware provisioning
- Portal-based self-service database solution
- Cost effective estimated 20% to 75% lower cost.

13. c

Explanation: A cloud database is a database that typically runs on cloud computing platform, access to is gives as a service.

14.a

Explanation: The acronym of DSaaS is Data Storage as a service.

15.b

Explanation: PaaS (Platform as a Service) provides a platform allowing customers to develop, run, and manage applications without the complexity of building and maintaining the infrastructure.

16. **b**

Explanation: DSaaS enables user to pay for the measure of data storage he/she is utilizing.

17. **c**

Explanation: The advantage of Cloud encryption is as:

Encrypted data is only readable for authorized parties with access to the decryption keys. Encrypting data guarantees that if that data falls into the wrong hand, it is useless as long as its keys stay secure.

Cloud encryption is critical for industries that need to meet regulatory compliance requirements

18. **b**

Explanation: Data in-motion is data effectively moving from one location to another such as across the internet or through a private network.

19. **d**

Explanation: There are different types of sanitization for each type of media as clearing, disposal, purging, destroying, shredding.

20. **c**

Explanation: Hypervisor-based virtualization technology is the best choice of implementing methods to achieve a secure Cloud environment.

Chapter 2: Cloud Data Security

1. **d**

Explanation: IaaS uses the following storage types:

- Volume storage
- Object storage

2. **a, c**

Explanation: It is essential to be aware of the relevant data security technologies you may need to deploy or work with to ensure the confidentiality, integrity, and availability of data in the Cloud.

Potential controls and solutions can include

- Encryption
- DLP
- File and database access monitor
- Obfuscation, anonymization, tokenization, and masking

3. **d**

Explanation: For database encryption, you should understand the following options:

- File-level encryption
- Transparent encryption
- Application-level encryption

4. **b**

Explanation: Where national or community laws or regulations determine the purposes and means of processing, the controller or the specific criteria for his nomination may be designated by national or community law.

The customer determines the ultimate purpose of the processing and decides on the outsourcing or the delegation of all or part of the concerned activities to external organizations. Therefore, the customer acts as a controller. In this role, the customer is responsible and subject to all the legal duties that are addressed in the Privacy and Data Protection (P&DP) laws applicable to the controller's role. The customer may task the service provider with choosing the methods and the technical or organizational measures to be used to achieve the purposes of the controller.

5. **a**

Explanation: The following points show key capabilities common to IRM solutions:

Persistent Protection: Make sure that documents, messages, and attachments are protected at rest, in transit, and even after they are distributed to recipients

Dynamic Policy Control: Allows content owners to define and change user permissions (view, forward, copy, or print) and recall or expire content even after distribution

Automatic Expiration: Provides the ability to automatically revoke access to documents, e-mails, and attachments at any point, thus allowing information security policies to be enforced wherever content is distributed or stored

Continuous Audit Trail: Provides confirmation that content was delivered and viewed and offers proof of compliance with your organization's information security policies

Support for existing Authentication Security Infrastructure: Reduces administrator involvement and speeds deployment by leveraging user and group information that exists in directories and authentication systems

6. **b**

Explanation: Since the other options are not entirely applicable to Cloud computing, the only reasonable method remaining is encrypting the data. The process of encrypting the data to dispose of it is known as crypto-shredding or digital shredding.

TO using an encryption method to rewrite the data in an encrypted format to make it unreadable without the encryption key.

7. **b**

Explanation: To determine the necessary controls to be deployed, you must first understand

- Function(s) of the data
- Location(s) of the data
- Actor(s) upon the data

Once you understand and document these three items, you can design the appropriate controls and apply them to the system to safeguard data and control access to it. These controls can be of a preventative, detective (monitoring), or corrective nature.

8. **b**

Explanation: PaaS utilizes the following data storage types:

- Structured
- Unstructured

9. **c**

Explanation: Data loss prevention tool implementations usually conform to the following topologies:

Data in Motion (DIM): Referred to as network-based or gateway DLP. In this topology, the monitoring engine is deployed **near the organizational gateway** to monitor outgoing protocols such as HTTP/HTTPS/SMTP and FTP.

Data at Rest (DAR): Referred to as storage-based. In this topology, the DLP engine is installed where the data is at rest, usually one or more storage sub-systems and file and application servers.

Data in Use (DIU): Referred to as client- or endpoint-based, the DLP application is installed on a user's workstations and endpoint devices.

10. **a**

Explanation: Data discovery tools differ by technique and data matching abilities. Three basic analysis methods are employed:

- Metadata
- Labels
- Content analysis

11. **b**

Explanation: The **Cloud Security Alliance Cloud Controls Matrix (CCM)** is an essential and up-to-date security controls framework that is addressed to the Cloud community and stakeholders. A fundamental richness of the CCM is its ability to provide mapping/cross relationships with the main industry-accepted security standards, regulations, and controls frameworks such as the ISO 27001/27002, ISACA's COBIT, and PCI-DSS.

12. **d**

Explanation: A data retention policy is an organization's established protocol for retaining information for operational or regulatory compliance needs. A good data retention policy should define

- Retention periods
- Data formats
- Data security
- Data retrieval procedures for the enterprise

13. **c**

Explanation: To support continuous operations, the following principles must be adopted as part of the security operation policies:

1. Audit logging

The continuous operation of audit logging is comprised of three important processes:

2. Detecting new events:
3. Adding new rules:
4. Reducing false positives:
- Contract/authority maintenance
- Secure disposal
- Incident response legal preparation

14. **c**

Explanation: In a Cloud environment, the container is not a storage type. Both the object and volume storage types are used within Infrastructure as a Service (IaaS), and the structured storage type is used as part of a Platform as a Service(PaaS) offering.

15. **a**

Explanation: Billing records would most likely be available in a Software as a Service (SaaS) environment if required or allowed by the contract. The other options like network capture, management plane logs, and operating system logs would all be solely accessible and used by the Cloud provider in a SaaS environment, as none of the systems that generate those logs falls under the responsibility or access allowed to the Cloud customer.

16. **b**

Explanation: On the user's device is the right choice of data-in-use monitoring. Integrated with the database server would provide coverage for data at rest, while on the network boundary would provide coverage for data in transit. On the application server is also not applicable as the actual use and viewing of data would occur through the client, as well as being outside the immediate security enclave of the application.

17. **a**

Explanation: Monitoring is not a feature of a SIEM solution. The solutions work by aggregating data, which can then be used for alerting on conditions, but not used in the sense of system monitoring. Dashboards are also a common feature of SIEM solutions to present reporting and alerting outputs to management or users.

18. **b**

Explanation: HIPAA governs the protection of healthcare-related data.

19. **c**

Explanation: Chain of custody is not part of an IRM solution, as it is central to eDiscovery and other legal mechanisms. With an IRM solution and the protection of data assets, the concepts of expiration, policy control, and the auditing of acceptable and authorized users are all key components.

20. **d**

Explanation: None of the environments gives responsibility for physical security to the Cloud customer. In all Cloud hosting environments, the Cloud provider has sole responsibility for the physical infrastructure and the security of it.

Chapter 3: Cloud Platform & Infrastructure Security

1. **d**

Explanation: The components of Cloud infrastructure are physical environment, compute, network and communication, virtualization, storage, and management plane.

2. **a**

Explanation: Cloud data centers are designed to support protect security and availability of customer data.

3. **c**

Explanation: network and communications is another imperative of Cloud infrastructure because it provides the best way for customers and users to access their applications, systems, and software tools.

4. **c**

Explanation: Software-Defined Networking is the acronym of SDN.

5. **a**

Explanation: There are two types of hypervisors

- Type 1 hypervisor
- Type 2 hypervisor

6. **d**

Explanation: There are various counter-measures that can be executed in the Cloud infrastructure includes Access management, Identity and access reporting, Centralized directory, Role-based access control, User access certifications, and Separation of duties.

7. **b**

Explanation: Data in use in protected through secure API calls and web services by means of the use of encryption, dedicated network pathways, or digital signatures.

8. **d**

Explanation: Below are the relevant Virtualization system protection consideration Protecting the management plane

- Isolation of the management network from other networks
- Proper network design as well as properly operating components, such as, firewalls.
- Use of trust zones

9. **b**

Explanation: Identity and access management innovation can be utilized to capture, record, initiate, and manage user identities and their access permissions.

10. **a**

Explanation: Authentication is the process for confirming the identity of the user.

11. **b**

Explanation: Federated Identity enables a user to access an application in one domain, such as software as a Service (SaaS) application, using the authentication that occurred in another domain, such as corporate Identity Management (IdM) system.

12. **a**

Explanation: Recovery Service Level is the acronym of RSL.

13. **b**

Explanation: RPO is the amount of data that a company would require to maintain and recover in order to function at a level suitable to management.

14. **b**

Explanation: RTO is the period of time within which applications, systems, or functions must be recovered in the event of a disaster to the point where management's objectives for BC/DR are happened.

15. **C**

Explanation: The capacity for an enterprise to follow what applications users are accessing (and when) is a concern from both a security and regulatory viewpoint.

Chapter 4: Cloud Application Security

1. **A**

Explanation: Use the SOAP envelope and then HTTP (SMTP/FTP) to transfer the data.

2. **b**

Explanation: SOAP provides a web services feature.

3. **a**

Explanation: Static Application Security Testing (SAST) is considered a white-box test, where the application test performs an analysis of the application byte code, source code, and binaries without executing the application code.

4. **b**

Explanation: Dynamic Application Security Testing (DAST) is considered a black-box test, where the tool should find specific execution paths in the application being analysed.

5. **b**

Explanation: DAST is used against applications in their running state.

6. **a**

Explanation: The most common software vulnerabilities are found in the Open Web Application Security Project (OWASP) Top 10. There are OWASP 10 entries for 2017 are

- Injection attack
- Broken Authentication
- Sensitive Data Exposure
- XML External Entities (XXE)
- Broken access control
- Security Misconfiguration
- Cross-site scripting (XSS)
- Insecure Deserialization
- Using Components with Known Vulnerabilities
- Insufficient Logging and Monitor

7. **a**

Explanation: There are two types of federations.

- Web-of-trust model
- Third party identifier

8. **c**

Explanation: The SDLC process is a set of stages or phases that drive a software development project from conception and requirement gathering through requirement, designing, development, testing, and maintenance.

9. **b**

Explanation: STRIDE has following parts

- Spoofing
- Tampering
- Repudiation
- Information
- Disclosure
- Elevation

10. **a**

Explanation: DAM can be network-based (NDAM) or agent-based (ADAM).

11. **d**

> **Explanation:** A WAF is a protocol layer 7 in the OSI model. Layer 7 is the application layer in the OSI Model.
>
> 12. **d**
>
> **Explanation:** An API gateway is a device that filters API traffic; it can be installed as a proxy or as a specific part of your application's stack before data is processed.

Chapter 5: Operations

1. **a**

Explanation: HVAC system design is a study of mechanical engineering, based on the principles of thermodynamics, fluid mechanics and heat transfer.

2. **b**

Explanation: The American Society of Heating, Refrigeration, and Air Conditioning Engineers (ASHRAE) recommended that the lowest temperature is 18°C.

3. **c**

Explanation: The American Society of Heating, Refrigeration, and Air Conditioning Engineers (ASHRAE) recommended that the highest temperature is 27°C.

4. **c**

Explanation: The two networking models that have to be considered are traditional and converged.

5. **b**

Explanation: Kernel-based Virtual Machine (KVM) is an open source virtualization technology built into Linux.

6. **d**

Explanation: The VM-Series for KVM allows service providers and organization similar to add next-generation firewall and advanced threat prevention capabilities to their cloud-based initiatives and Linux-based virtualization.

7. **c**

Explanation: There are two layers which made the TLS. TLS Handshake Protocol and TLS Record Protocol.

8. **c**

Explanation: Dynamic Host Configuration Protocol (DHCP) is a client or server protocol that automatically provides an Internet Protocol (IP) host with its IP address and other related configuration information such as the default gateway and subnet mask.

9. **d**

Explanation: DNS is used to translate a domain name (like ipspecialist.net) into numeric Internet address like (197.166.1.0). DNS is a hierarchical, distributed database that contains a mapping of DNS domain names to multiple forms of data such as the Internet Protocol (IP) addresses.

10. **a**

Explanation: There are two main clustered storage architectures available. Tightly coupled and Loosely Coupled.

11. **d**

Explanation: Most increasingly popular remote access techniques to permit teleworkers access to internal business applications and data is to allow them to log into virtual desktops. These are

- Virtual Desktop Infrastructure (VDI)
- Remote Desktop Protocol (RDP) permit for desktop access to remote systems
- Access through a secure terminal

12. **a**

Explanation: The two primary types of firewalls are host-based and network-based firewalls.

13. **b**

Explanation: A host-based firewall is introduced in the light of individual servers and screens approaching and friendly flags, while network-based firewall can be incorporated with the Cloud's foundation, or it can be a virtual firewall benefit.

14. **d**

Explanation: Cloud orchestration is often used to deploy, provision, or start servers; acquire and assign storage capacity; manage networking; develop VMs; and authorize to particular software on Cloud services. This is achieved through three main, interconnected components of Cloud orchestration which are:

- Resource orchestration
- Service
- Workload

15. **e**

Explanation: Several hundreds of tools exist for automation of server configuration and management, including Terra**form, Salt, Puppet, and Ansible.**

16. **c**

Explanation: Vendors have developed new tools designed specifically to evaluate the performance of customer-based Cloud computing applications. Some of Cloud performance-monitoring tools are:

- BMC's End User Experience Management tool

- Cloudkick Inc
- LoadStorm
- SevOne's
- SOASTA's CloudTest

17. **a**

Explanation: According to ISO 22301, a BCM system highlights the importance of:

- Constant improvement based on objective measurements.
- Implementing and operating controls and measures for managing enterprises overall continuity risks.
- Monitoring and reviewing the performance and effectiveness of the BCM system.
- Understanding continuity and preparedness needs, along with the necessity for establishing BCM policy and objectives.

18. **d**

Explanation: Generally, incidents are categorized as:

- Low priorities
- Medium priorities
- High priorities

19. **d**

Explanation: Some of the incident management tools are:

- PagerDuty
- VictorOps
- XMatters

Chapter 6: Legal and Compliance

1. **b**

Explanation: The U.S Department of Commerce developed safe Harbor program.

2. **c**

Explanation: The Health Insurance Portability and Accountability Act (HIPAA) was published in 1996.

3. **c**

Explanation: The Securities and Exchange Commission (SEC) administers the Sarbanes-Oxley Act.

4. **c**

Explanation: The Gramm-Leach-Bliley Act (GLBA) is a federal law enacted in the US to control the ways that financial institutions deal with the private information of individuals. It is a Financial Modernization Act of 1999.

5. **b**

Explanation: ISO/IEC 27041:2015: Guide for incident investigations

6. **d**

Explanation: ISO/IEC 27050-1:2016 provide a principle for eDiscovery.

7. **a**

Explanation: Safe Harbor Program deals with the international transfer of data.

8. **a**

Explanation: Stored Communications Act (SCA) was enacted in 1986 in the USA.

9. **a**

Explanation: There are two types of PII associated with cloud and non-cloud environments.

Contractual PII and Regulated PII.

10. **b**

Explanation: There are three types of audit reports.

SAS, SSAE, ISAE

11. **c**

Explanation: The Statement on Auditing Standards (SAS) Number 70, which is commonly known as SAS 70, is a standard published by the American Institute of Certified Public Accounts (AICPA).

12. **a**

Explanation: The Statement on Auditing Standards (SAS) Number 70, which is commonly known as SAS 70, is a standard published by the American Institute of Certified Public Accounts (AICPA). Typically, it is also known as a "service auditor's examination."

13. **b**

Explanation: The Statements on Standards for Attestation Engagements (SSAE) 16 replaced the SAS 70 as of 2011 and is the standard that most in the United States now use. It is also known as the Service Organization Control (SOC) report.

14. **a**

Explanation: International Auditing and Assurance Standard Board (IAASB) issued the International Standard on Assurance Engagements (ISAE) 3402 reports.

15. **d**

Explanation: There are four phases of the audit plan.

- Conduct audit

- Define objective
- Define scope
- Lesson Learned and analysis

16. c

Explanation: Generally, Accepted Privacy Principles (GAPP) is the American Institute of Certified Public Accountants (AICPA) standard describing detailed to the privacy principles.

17. b

Explanation: European Network and Information Security Agency (ENISA) identifies 35 types of risks for organizations to consider, coupled with a "Top 8" security risks based on likelihood and impact.

18. a

Explanation: The Common Criteria (CC) framework (ISO/IEC 15408-1:2009) is an international ISO standard to provide guidelines and specification for evaluating information security products.

19. a

Explanation: The three main aspects of security are confidentiality, integrity, and availability. As more services and data have moved online, especially with the explosion of mobile computing and apps that utilize sensitive information, privacy has become a crucial fourth aspect.

20. a

Explanation: These are correct components of SLA

- Data Protection Requirements
- Disaster Recovery
- Provider Liability
- Security recommendation
- SLA Penalties
- SLA Penalty Exclusions
- Suspension of Service
- Uptime Guarantees

Acronyms:

- 3DES — Triple Advanced Encryption Standard
- AAA — Authentication, Authorization, And Accounting
- AAFS — American Academy of Forensic Sciences
- ACL — Access Control List
- ACMP — Association of Change Management Professionals
- ACS — Access Control Server
- ADAM — Agent-based Database Activity Monitoring
- AES — Advanced Encryption Standard
- AICPA — American Institute of Certified Public Accounts
- ALO — Annualized Loss Expectancy
- ANSI — American National Standards Institute
- AONT-RS — All-or-Nothing Transform with Reed-Solomon
- APEC — Asia-Pacific Economic Cooperation
- API — Application Programming Interface
- ARO — Annualized Rate of Occurrence
- ASHRAE — American Society of Heating, Refrigeration, and Air Conditioning Engineers
- ASP — Active Server Pages
- AWS — Amazon Web Services
- BCM — Business Continuity Management
- BCMS — Business Continuity Management Systems
- BCP — Business Continuity Plan
- BCP — Business Continuity Plan
- BI — Business Intelligence
- BICSI — Building Industry Consulting Service International Inc.
- BIOS — Basic Input Output System
- BOOTP — Bootstrap Protocol
- BOSS — Business Operation Support Services
- BPAs — Best Practice Analyzers
- CaaS — Communication-as-a-Service
- CC — Common Criteria
- CCM — Cloud Controls Matrix
- CDN — Content Delivery Network
- CentOS — Community Enterprise Operating System

- CI   Configuration Item
- CIP   Critical Infrastructure Protection
- CIS   Center for Internet Security
- CISO   Chief Information Security Officer
- CM   Configuration Management
- CMDB   Configuration Management Database
- CMI   Change Management Institute
- CMMS   Cloud-based Maintenance Management Systems
- CMS   Configuration Management System
- COBIT   Control Objectives for Information and Related Technologies
- COBOL   Common Business-Oriented Language
- COPPA   Children's Online Privacy Protection Act
- CPR   Cloud Provider Responsibility
- CPU   Central Processing Unit
- CRM   Customer Relationship Management
- CSA   Cloud Security Alliance
- CSM   Cloud Security Models
- CSO   Chief Security Officer
- CSP   Cloud Service Provider
- CSP   Cloud Security Professional
- CSRF   Cross-Site Request Forgery
- CTO   Chief Technology Officer
- DaaS   Desktop as a Service
- DAM   Database Activity Monitoring
- DAR   Data at Rest
- DAST   Dynamic Application Security Testing
- DB   Database
- DBMS   Database Management System
- DDoS   Distributed Denial of Service
- DEFR   Digital Evidence First Responder
- DHCP   Dynamic Hosting Control Protocol
- DIM   Data in Motion
- DIU   Data in Use
- DLP   Data Loss Prevention
- DML   Definitive Media Library
- DMZ   Demilitarized Zone
- DNS   Domain Name System
- DNSSEC   Domain Name System Security

- DO   Dynamic Optimization
- DoS   Denial of Service
- DPM   Distributed Power Management
- DR   Disaster Recovery
- DRM   Digital Rights Management
- DRP   Disaster Recovery Planning
- DRS   Distributed Resource Scheduling
- DSaaS   Data Storage as a Service
- ECHR   European Convention on Human Rights
- ECPA   Electronic Communications Privacy Act
- EDRM   Enterprise Digital Right Management
- EEA   European Economic Area
- EMP   Electro Magnetic Pulse
- ENISA   European Network and Information Security Agency
- ER   Enterprise Responsibility
- ESI   Electronically Stored Information
- EU   European Union
- FERPA   Family Educational Rights and Privacy
- FIPS   Federal Information Processing Standard
- FTC   Federal Trade Commission
- FTP   File Transfer Protocol
- GAPP   Generally Accepted Privacy Principles
- GB   GigaBit
- GCE   Google Compute Engine
- GLBA   Gramm-Leach-Bliley Act
- GRC   Governance, Risk, and Compliance
- HA   High Availability
- HIPAA   Health Insurance Portability and Accountability Act
- HIPS   Host-based intrusion prevention system
- HSM   Hardware Security Module
- HTML   Hypertext Markup Language
- HTTP   Hypertext Transfer Protocol
- HTTPS   Hypertext Transfer Protocol
- HVAC   Heating, ventilation, and air conditioning
- HVAC&R   Heating, Ventilation, Air Conditioning and Refrigeration
- IaaS   Infrastructure as a Service
- IAASB   International Auditing and Assurance Standard Board
- IAM   Identity and Access Management

- IAQ   Indoor air quality
- IDA   International Development Association
- IDCA   International Data Center Authority
- IdM   Identity Management
- IDS   Intrusion Detection System
- IEC   International Electrotechnical Commission
- IEEE   Institute of Electrical and Electronics Engineers
- IETF   Internet Engineering Task Force
- ILM   Information Life cycle Management
- IM   Instant Messaging
- IoT   Internet of Things
- IP   Internet Protocol
- IPS   Intrusion Prevention System
- IPSec   Internet Protocol Security
- IPSEC   Internet Protocol Security
- IRM   Information Rights Management
- ISACA   Information Systems Audit and Control Association
- ISAE   International Standard on Assurance Engagements
- ISAM   Indexed Sequential Access Method
- ISE   Cisco Identity Services Engine
- ISMS   Information Security Management System
- ISO   International Standard Organization
- IT   Information Technology
- ITOS   Information Technology Operation & Support
- ITSM   Information Technology Service Management
- J2EE   Java Platform, Enterprise Edition
- JSON   JavaScript Object Notation
- JSP   Java Server Pages
- KMIP   Key Management Interoperability Protocol
- KMS   Key Management System
- KPI   Key Performance Indicator
- KVM   Kernel-based Virtual Machine
- LAN   Local Area Network
- LDAP   Lightweight Directory Access Protocol
- LED   Light-Emitting Diode
- LUN   Logical Unit Number
- MDT   Microsoft Deployment Toolkit
- MFA   Multi-Factor Authentication

▪	MSI	Management and Strategy Institute
▪	MTBF	Mean Time between Failures
▪	MTTR	Mean Time To Repair
▪	MVPC	Multi-Vendor Pathway Connectivity
▪	NaaS	Network as a Service
▪	NDAM	Network-based Database Activity Monitoring
▪	NERC	North American Electric Reliability Corporation
▪	NFPA	National Fire Protection Association
▪	NGFW	Next-generation firewalls
▪	NIC	Network Interface Card
▪	NIPS	Network-based intrusion prevention system
▪	NIST	National Institute of Standards and Technology
▪	OLAs	Operational Level Agreements
▪	ORM	Object-relational Mapping
▪	OS	Operating System
▪	OWASP	Open Web Application Security Project
▪	P&DP	Privacy and Data Protection
▪	PaaS	Platform as a Service
▪	PCI DSS	Payment Card Industry Data Security Standard
▪	PDAs	Personal Digital Assistants
▪	PDU	Power Distribution Units
▪	PEDs	Personal Electronic Devices
▪	PHP	Hypertext Preprocessor
▪	PII	Personally Identifiable Information
▪	PKI/PKO	Public Key Infrastructure/Operations
▪	PRM	Partner Relationship Management
▪	QoS	Quality of Service
▪	RAID	Redundant Array of Independent Disks
▪	RBAC	Role-Based Access Control
▪	RDM	Raw Device Mapping
▪	RDP	Remote Desktop Protocol
▪	REST	Representational State Transfer
▪	RFP	Request for proposal
▪	RHEL	Red Hat Enterprise Linux
▪	RPO	Recovery Point Objective
▪	RSL	Recovery Service Level
▪	RSO	Reduced sign-on
▪	RTO	Recovery Time Objective

- RTO   Recovery Time Objective
- SaaS   Software as a Service
- SAML   Security Assertion Markup Language
- SAN   Storage Area Network
- SAS   Statement on Auditing Standards (SAS)
- SAST   Static Application Security Testing
- SCA   Stored Communications Act
- SCCM   System Center Configuration Manager
- SCM   Software Configuration Management
- SDLC   Software Development Life cycle
- SDN   Software-Defined Networking
- SEC   Securities and Exchange Commission
- SEM   Security Event Management
- SI   Security Intelligence
- SIEM   Security Information and Event Management
- SIM   Security Information Management
- SLA   Service Level Agreement
- SLE   Single Loss Expectancy
- SLM   Service Level Management
- SMTP   Simple Mail Transfer Protocol
- SOA   Service-oriented architecture
- SOAP   Simple Object Access Protocol
- SOX   Sarbanes-Oxley Act
- SP   Special Publication
- SQL   Structured Query Language
- SR   Shared Responsibility
- SSAE   Statements on Standards for Attestation Engagements (SSAE)
- SSL   Secure Socket Layer
- SSMS   Secret Sharing Made Short
- SSO   Single sign-on
- STRIDE   Spoofing, Tampering, Repudiation, Information, Disclosure, and Elevation
- TCP   Transport Control Protocol
- TLS   Transport Layer Security
- TPM   Trusted Platform Module
- UCM   Unified Configuration Management
- UDP   User Datagram Protocol
- UN   European Union

- USB   Universal Serial Bus
- VCB   VMware Consolidated Backup
- VDI   Virtual Desktop Infrastructure
- VLAN   Virtual Local Area Network
- VM   Virtual Machine
- VMM   Virtual Machine Monitor
- VMM   Virtual Machine Manager
- VoIP   Voice over IP
- VPN   Virtual Private Network
- VPS   Virtual Private Storage
- VUM   VMware Update Manager
- WAF   Web Application Firewall
- WORM   Write Once Read Many
- WS   Web Services
- WSDL   Web Services Description Language
- WSUS   Windows Server Update Service
- XML   Extensible Markup Language
- XSS   Cross-Site Scripting
- XXE   XML External Entities

References:

Architectural Concepts & Design Requirements

- https://www.omicsonline.org/open-access/virtualization-in-cloud-computing-2165-7866-1000136.pdf
- https://www.researchgate.net/publication/234166321_Cloud_Computing-Storage_as_Service
- https://www.snia.org/sites/default/files/Hibbard_Best-Practices-for-Cloud-Security-and-Privacy_V2_Final_0.pdf
- https://downloads.cloudsecurityalliance.org/assets/research/security-guidance/security-guidance-v4-FINAL.pdf
- http://moriel.smarterthanthat.com/tips/java/java-user-input-validation/
- https://aerohive-www-cdn.aerohive.com/wp-content/uploads/Aerohive_Whitepaper_Cloud_Networking.pdf
- http://www.centurylink.com/asset/business/enterprise/brochure/cloud-database.pdf
- https://www.cio.com/article/2424886/cloud-computing/cloud-computing-definitions-and-solutions.html
- https://www.slideshare.net/biswajitcet13/cloud-computing-73291168
- http://shodhganga.inflibnet.ac.in/bitstream/10603/160088/8/08_chapter%202.pdf
- https://www.omg.org/cloud/deliverables/CSCC-Interoperability-and-Portability-for-Cloud-Computing-A-Guide.pdf
- http://www.di.fc.ul.pt/~nuno/PAPERS/security3.pdf
- https://www.sumologic.com/blog/cloud/cloud-computing-security-data-resiliency/
- https://searchmicroservices.techtarget.com/definition/cloud-service-governance
- https://digitalguardian.com/blog/what-cloud-encryption
- https://digitalguardian.com/blog/data-protection-data-in-transit-vs-data-at-rest
- https://www.ma.rhul.ac.uk/static/techrep/2014/RHUL-MA-2014-9.pdf
- https://www.stratoscale.com/blog/networking/security-cloud-networking-fw-acls/
- https://www.getkisi.com/blog/move-access-control-cloud-9-benefits-cloud-access-control-systems
- https://www.researchgate.net/publication/273950406_Security_Aspects_of_Virtualization_in_Cloud_Computing
- https://ws680.nist.gov/publication/get_pdf.cfm?pub_id=50819
- https://www.hack2secure.com/blogs/owasp-top-10-cloud-security-risk

- https://www.researchgate.net/publication/312166397_Data_recovery_and_business _continuity_in_Cloud_computing_A_Review_of_the_Research_Literature
- https://www.researchgate.net/publication/322321070_Cost_benefit_analysis_of_clo ud_computing_in_education
- https://core.ac.uk/download/pdf/55330412.pdf

Cloud Data Security

- https://learning.oreilly.com/library/view/the-official-isc2/9781119207498/c02.xhtml
- https://learning.oreilly.com/library/view/ccsp-certified-cloud/9781259835452/ch03.html#ch03
- https://learning.oreilly.com/library/view/the-official-isc2/9781119207498/c02.xhtml
- https://en.wikipedia.org/wiki/FIPS_140-2
- https://learning.oreilly.com/library/view/ccsp-isc2-certified/9781119277415/c04.xhtml
- https://learning.oreilly.com/library/view/ccsp-certified-cloud/9781259835452/ch03.html#ch03
- https://learning.oreilly.com/library/view/the-official-isc2/9781119207498/c02.xhtml
- https://downloads.cloudsecurityalliance.org/assets/research/security-guidance/security-guidance-v4-FINAL.pdf
- https://research.cloudsecurityalliance.org/tci/index.php/explore/
- https://cloudsecurityalliance.org/working-groups/Cloud-controls-matrix/#_overview
- https://quizlet.com/299810273/ccsk-domain-01-cloud-computing-concepts-and-architectures-flash-cards/
- https://www.iso.org/standard/43757.html
- https://downloads.cloudsecurityalliance.org/initiatives/collaborate/safecode/SAFE Code-CSA-cloud-White-Paper.pdf
- https://learning.oreilly.com/library/view/the-official-isc2/9781119207498/c02.xhtml
- https://learning.oreilly.com/library/view/ccsp-certified-cloud/9781259835452/ch03.html#ch03
- https://learning.oreilly.com/library/view/the-official-isc2/9781119207498/c02.xhtml
- https://en.wikipedia.org/wiki/FIPS_140-2

- https://learning.oreilly.com/library/view/ccsp-isc2-certified/9781119277415/c04.xhtml
- https://learning.oreilly.com/library/view/ccsp-certified-cloud/9781259835452/cho3.html#cho3
- https://downloads.cloudsecurityalliance.org/assets/research/security-guidance/security-guidance-v4-FINAL.pdf
- https://research.cloudsecurityalliance.org/tci/index.php/explore/
- https://cloudsecurityalliance.org/working-groups/cloud-controls-matrix/#_overview
- https://quizlet.com/299810273/ccsk-domain-01-cloud-computing-concepts-and-architectures-flash-cards/
- https://learning.oreilly.com/library/view/the-official-isc2/9781119207498/c02.xhtml
- https://learning.oreilly.com/library/view/ccsp-certified-cloud/9781259835452/cho3.html#cho3
- https://learning.oreilly.com/library/view/the-official-isc2/9781119207498/c02.xhtml
- https://en.wikipedia.org/wiki/FIPS_140-2
- https://learning.oreilly.com/library/view/ccsp-isc2-certified/9781119277415/c04.xhtml
- https://learning.oreilly.com/library/view/ccsp-certified-cloud/9781259835452/cho3.html#cho3
- https://learning.oreilly.com/library/view/the-official-isc2/9781119207498/c02.xhtml
- https://downloads.cloudsecurityalliance.org/assets/research/security-guidance/security-guidance-v4-FINAL.pdf
- https://research.cloudsecurityalliance.org/tci/index.php/explore/
- https://cloudsecurityalliance.org/working-groups/cloud-controls-matrix/#_overview
- https://quizlet.com/299810273/ccsk-domain-01-cloud-computing-concepts-and-architectures-flash-cards/
- https://www.iso.org/standard/43757.html
- https://cloudsecurityalliance.org/wp-uploads/2011/09/Domain-5.docx
- https://www.bmc.com/blogs/saas-vs-paas-vs-iaas-whats-the-difference-and-how-to-choose/
- https://learning.oreilly.com/library/view/ccsp-certified-cloud/9781259835452/cho3.html#cho3

- https://downloads.cloudsecurityalliance.org/initiatives/collaborate/safecode/SAFECode-CSA-cloud-White-Paper.pdf
- https://cromwell-intl.com/cybersecurity/isc2-ccsp/standards-and-regulations.html
- https://learning.oreilly.com/library/view/ccsp-certified-cloud/9781259835452/ch03.html#ch03

Cloud Platform & Infrastructure Security

- https://downloads.cloudsecurityalliance.org/assets/research/security-guidance/csaguide.v3.0.pdf
- https://downloads.cloudsecurityalliance.org/assets/research/security-guidance/security-guidance-v4-FINAL.pdf
- https://learning.oreilly.com/library/view/ccsp-certified-cloud/9781259835452/ch04.html
- https://www.vmware.com/topics/glossary/content/cloud-computing-infrastructure
- https://downloads.cloudsecurityalliance.org/assets/research/security-guidance/security-guidance-v4-FINAL.pdf
- https://www.pingidentity.com/en/resources/client-library/articles/authentication-authorization-audit-logging-account-management.html

Cloud Application Security

- https://learning.oreilly.com/library/view/ccsp-certified-cloud/9781259835452/ch05.html#ch05
- https://dzone.com/articles/what-is-insecure-deserialization
- https://www.symantec.com/content/dam/symantec/docs/other-resources/web-application-firewall-owasp-top-10-2017-coverage-en.pdf
- https://www.owasp.org/index.php/Category:OWASP_Top_Ten_Project
- https://learning.oreilly.com/library/view/ccsp-certified-cloud/9781259835452/ch05.html#ch05
- https://www.apriorit.com/dev-blog/548-cloud-based-testing
- https://learning.oreilly.com/library/view/ccsp-certified-cloud/9781259835452/ch05.html#ch05
- https://learning.oreilly.com/library/view/ccsp-isc2-certified/9781119277415/c07.xhtml

- https://www.uacg.bg/filebank/acadstaff/userfiles/publ_bg_397_SDP_activities_and_steps.pdf
- https://learning.oreilly.com/library/view/ccsp-certified-cloud/9781259835452/ch05.html#ch05
- https://learning.oreilly.com/library/view/ccsp-certified-cloud/9781259835452/ch05.html#ch05
- http://www.softwaretestingandistqb.com/what-is-a-business-requirement/
- https://www.owasp.org/index.php/SQL_Injection
- https://www.owasp.org/index.php/Buffer_Overflow
- https://www.whizlabs.com/blog/cloud-security-risks/
- https://www.whizlabs.com/blog/cloud-security-for-beginners/
- https://www.sei.cmu.edu/research-capabilities/all-work/display.cfm?customel_datapageid_4050=21232
- https://www.whizlabs.com/blog/cloud-security-for-beginners/
- https://www.safaribooksonline.com/library/view/ccsp-certified-cloud/9781259835452/ch05.html#ch05
- https://study.com/academy/lesson/stride-threat-model-example-overview.html
- https://dzone.com/articles/is-the-stride-approach-still-relevant-for-threat-m
- https://www.safaribooksonline.com/library/view/ccsp-certified-cloud/9781259835452/ch05.html#ch05
- https://www.cloudflare.com/learning/ddos/glossary/web-application-firewall-waf/
- https://www.techopedia.com/definition/30937/database-activity-monitoring-dam
- https://en.wikipedia.org/wiki/XML_firewall
- https://www.ibm.com/support/knowledgecenter/en/SS9H2Y_7.5.0/com.ibm.dp.doc/xmlfw_introduction.html
- https://www.nginx.com/learn/api-gateway/
- https://www.computer.org/csdl/mags/pc/2010/04/mpc2010040013.pdf
- https://hackernoon.com/federated-identities-a-developers-primer-655a160d66cb
- https://en.wikipedia.org/wiki/Federated_identity#cite_note-2

Operations

- https://en.wikipedia.org/wiki/Dike_(geology)
- https://en.wikipedia.org/wiki/Request_for_proposal
- https://www.idc-a.org/
- https://en.wikipedia.org/wiki/HVAC
- https://en.wikipedia.org/wiki/Thermal_comfort

- https://en.wikipedia.org/wiki/Indoor_air_quality
- https://en.wikipedia.org/wiki/Mechanical_engineering
- https://en.wikipedia.org/wiki/Thermodynamics
- https://en.wikipedia.org/wiki/Fluid_mechanics
- https://en.wikipedia.org/wiki/Heat_transfer
- https://en.wikipedia.org/wiki/ASHRAE
- https://trustedcomputinggroup.org/resource/trusted-platform-module-tpm-summary/
- https://searchservervirtualization.techtarget.com/tip/Using-VMware-Distributed-Power-Management
- http://techgenix.com/windows-server-nic-teaming/
- https://www.redhat.com/en/topics/virtualization/what-is-KVM#
- https://downloads.cloudsecurityalliance.org/assets/research/collaborative/Security-Considerations-for-Private-vs-Public-Clouds.pdf
- https://en.wikipedia.org/wiki/Linux
- https://en.wikipedia.org/wiki/Virtual_machine
- https://www.paloaltonetworks.com/products/secure-the-cloud/vm-series
- https://www.ubuntu.com/
- https://en.wikipedia.org/wiki/CentOS
- https://en.wikipedia.org/wiki/Red_Hat_Enterprise_Linux
- https://whatis.techtarget.com/definition/Common-Criteria-CC-for-Information-Technology-Security-Evaluation
- https://en.wikipedia.org/wiki/Light-emitting_diode
- http://ijettjournal.org/2015/volume-25/number-4/IJETT-V25P232.pdf
- https://docs.microsoft.com/en-us/windows-server/networking/technologies/dhcp/dhcp-top
- https://www.techopedia.com/definition/31693/dynamic-host-configuration-protocol-server-dhcp-server
- https://docs.microsoft.com/en-us/windows-server/networking/technologies/dhcp/dhcp-top
- https://blog.cloudsecurityalliance.org/2016/03/31/four-security-solutions-not-stopping-third-party-data-breaches/
- https://downloads.cloudsecurityalliance.org/initiatives/secaas/SecaaS_Cat_10_Network_Security_Implementation_Guidance.pdf
- https://cloudsecurityalliance.org/wp-content/uploads/2012/08/Encryption-SecaaS-Peer-Review-cat8.docx

- https://downloads.cloudsecurityalliance.org/star/self-assessment/Hyland-Hyland-Cloud-CCM-3.0.1-2017-10-02.pdf
- https://www.techopedia.com/definition/27485/cluster-host
- https://searchvmware.techtarget.com/definition/Storage-Distributed-Resource-Scheduler-DRS
- https://docs.microsoft.com/en-us/system-center/vmm/vm-optimization?view=sc-vmm-1807
- https://whatis.techtarget.com/definition/clustered-storage
- https://pubs.vmware.com/vsphere-50/index.jsp?topic=%2Fcom.vmware.vsphere.solutions.doc_50%2FGUID-68DE940C-C2DC-47D3-B660-D3BA5A8B5A75.html
- https://searchdisasterrecovery.techtarget.com/definition/high-availability-cluster-HA-cluster
- https://docs.microsoft.com/en-us/system-center/vmm/overview?view=sc-vmm-1807
- https://en.wikipedia.org/wiki/Backplane
- https://searchnetworking.techtarget.com/tip/Cloud-based-remote-access-Scenarios-for-success
- https://en.wikipedia.org/wiki/Telecommuting
- https://downloads.cloudsecurityalliance.org/assets/research/sdp/sdp_for_iaas.pdf
- https://searchvirtualdesktop.techtarget.com/definition/desktop-as-a-service-DaaS
- https://nvlpubs.nist.gov/nistpubs/SpecialPublications/NIST.SP.800-40r3.pdf
- https://www.varonis.com/blog/ids-vs-ips/
- https://en.wikipedia.org/wiki/Intrusion_detection_system
- https://en.wikipedia.org/wiki/Honeypot_(computing)
- https://searchsecurity.techtarget.com/definition/vulnerability-assessment-vulnerability-analysis
- https://searchsecurity.techtarget.com/definition/security-information-and-event-management-SIEM
- https://searchitoperations.techtarget.com/definition/log-management
- https://en.wikipedia.org/wiki/The_CIS_Critical_Security_Controls_for_Effective_Cyber_Defense
- https://whatis.techtarget.com/definition/security-intelligence-SI
- https://www.sciencedirect.com/science/article/pii/S0167739X17321519
- https://www.sciencedirect.com/science/article/pii/S1574013718301187
- https://en.wikipedia.org/wiki/Orchestration_(computing)
- https://searchitoperations.techtarget.com/definition/cloud-orchestrator

- https://searchservervirtualization.techtarget.com/definition/guest-OS
- https://searchdisasterrecovery.techtarget.com/definition/disaster-recovery-plan
- https://searchdisasterrecovery.techtarget.com/definition/business-continuity-action-plan
- https://searchitoperations.techtarget.com/definition/configuration-management-CM
- https://www.techopedia.com/definition/4436/configuration-item-ci
- https://searchenterprisedesktop.techtarget.com/definition/Remote-Desktop-Protocol-RDP
- https://searchnetworking.techtarget.com/definition/extranet
- https://en.wikipedia.org/wiki/Change_management_(engineering)
- https://searchitchannel.techtarget.com/definition/release-management
- https://wiki.en.it-processmaps.com/index.php/Availability_Management
- https://searchenterprisedesktop.techtarget.com/definition/patch-management
- https://searchcloudcomputing.techtarget.com/tip/Cloud-performance-monitoring-tools-have-evolved-but-are-still-lacking
- https://searchcio.techtarget.com/definition/change-management
- https://searchcio.techtarget.com/definition/business-continuity-management-BCM
- https://searchdisasterrecovery.techtarget.com/definition/ISO-22301-International-Organization-of-Standardization-standard-22301
- https://whatis.techtarget.com/definition/information-security-management-system-ISMS
- https://searchitoperations.techtarget.com/definition/continual-service-improvement
- https://searchcio.techtarget.com/definition/ISO-20000
- https://searchitoperations.techtarget.com/definition/IT-incident-management
- https://searchwindowsserver.techtarget.com/definition/problem-management
- https://wiki.en.it-processmaps.com/index.php/Release_and_Deployment_Management
- https://searchitoperations.techtarget.com/definition/configuration-management-CM
- https://searchdatacenter.techtarget.com/definition/configuration-management-database
- https://www.helpsystems.com/solutions/it-operations-management-automation/service-delivery-itil-version-2/service-level-management
- https://en.wikipedia.org/wiki/Capacity_management

- https://www.skillmaker.edu.au/risk-monitoring/
- https://www.iso.org/standard/44381.html
- https://www.researchgate.net/publication/283226153_Standard_ISO_270372012_and_Collection_of_Digital_Evidence_Experience_in_the_Czech_Republic
- https://rm.coe.int/16806b3058
- https://en.wikipedia.org/wiki/Digital_forensic_process
- https://downloads.cloudsecurityalliance.org/initiatives/imf/Mapping-the-Forensic-Standard-ISO-IEC-27037-to-Cloud-Computing.pdf
- https://whatis.techtarget.com/definition/Communications-as-a-Service-CaaS
- https://searchcrm.techtarget.com/definition/CRM
- https://searchsalesforce.techtarget.com/definition/partner-relationship-management-PRM

Legal & Compliance

- https://www.zdnet.com/article/cloudflare-how-we-got-caught-in-lulzsec-cia-crossfire/
- https://assets.documentcloud.org/documents/1149373/in-re-matter-of-warrant.pdf
- https://www.pcisecuritystandards.org/
- https://www.exterro.com/basics-of-e-discovery/
- https://www.lexology.com/library/detail.aspx?g=ff831b36-35a7-49a5-8e9e-6773a7bf455c
- http://www.businessdictionary.com/definition/inalienable-rights.html
- https://searchcompliance.techtarget.com/definition/FTC-Federal-Trade-Commission
- https://www.gov.uk/eu-eea
- https://searchcompliance.techtarget.com/definition/Electronic-Communications-Privacy-Act-ECPA
- https://www.equalityhumanrights.com/en/what-european-convention-human-rights
- https://whatis.techtarget.com/definition/federated-cloud-cloud-federation
- https://learning.oreilly.com/library/view/ccsp-certified-cloud/9781259835452/ch07.html#ch07
- https://whatis.techtarget.com/definition/Confidentiality-integrity-and-availability-CIA#
- https://searchcio.techtarget.com/definition/data-privacy-information-privacy
- http://www.differencebetween.net/technology/internet/difference-between-security-and-privacy/

- https://learning.oreilly.com/library/view/auditing-cloud-computing/9781118116043/chapter02.html
- https://www.cio.com/article/3217751/data-management/three-lines-of-defense-for-data-management.html
- https://www.ixiacom.com/products/cloudlens-public
- https://www.vmware.com/topics/glossary/content/hypervisor
- https://whatis.techtarget.com/definition/MTBF-mean-time-between-failures
- https://searchstorage.techtarget.com/definition/mean-time-to-repair-MTTR
- https://en.wikipedia.org/wiki/Mean_time_to_recovery
- https://whatis.techtarget.com/definition/information-security-management-system-ISMS
- https://whatis.techtarget.com/definition/ISO-27001
- https://www.iso.org/obp/ui/#iso:std:iso-iec:27001:ed-2:v1:en
- https://pmstudycircle.com/2012/06/identify-stakeholders-project-management/
- http://mechanisms.energychange.info/step/5
- http://chrguibert.free.fr/cmmi12/cmmi-dev/text/7938cba-6059.php
- https://searchcloudsecurity.techtarget.com/tip/How-do-SLAs-factor-into-cloud-risk-management
- https://www.iso.org/obp/ui/#iso:std:iso:31000:ed-2:v1:en
- https://www.iso.org/obp/ui/#iso:std:iso:31000:ed-1:v1:en
- https://downloads.cloudsecurityalliance.org/initiatives/secaas/SecaaS_Cat_2_DLP_Implementation_Guidance.pdf
- http://www.iso27001security.com/html/27036.html

About Our Products

Other Network and Security related products from IPSpecialist LTD are:

	CEHv10 2nd Edition Technology Workbook
	CCNA Security 2nd Edition Technology Workbook
	Certified BlockChain Expert (CBEv2) Technology Workbook
	CCNA-CyberOps SECFND Technology Workbook
	CompTIA Network + Technology Workbook
	CompTIA Securitty + 2nd Edition Technology Workbook
	Certified Information System Security Professional (CISSP) Technology Workbook
	CCNA Routing and Switching Technology Workbook
	CCDA Technology Workbook
	CCDP Technology Workbook
	CCNP Routing and Switching - Route Technology Workbook
	CCNP Routing and Switching - Switch Technology Workbook
	CCNP Routing and Switching - Troubleshoot Technology Workbook
	CCNP Security - SENSS Technology Workbook
	CCNP Security - SITCS Technology Workbook
	CCNP Security - SIMOS Technology Workbook
	CCNP Security - SITCS Technology Workbook

Upcoming products from IPSpecialist LTD are:

	CEHv10 3rd Edition Technology Workbook
	CompTIA A+ 220-1001 Technology Workbook
	CompTIA A+ 220-1002 Technology Workbook
	CompTIA Cloud Essential Technology Workbook
	CompTIA Pentest+ Technology Workbook

Note from the Author:

Reviews are gold to authors! If you have enjoyed this book and helped you along certification, would you consider rating it and reviewing it?

Link to Product Page: